THE NETWORK REVOLUTION

THE NETWORK REVOLUTION

CONFESSIONS OF A COMPUTER SCIENTIST

By Jacques Vallee

Published by
AND/OR PRESS, INC.
Berkeley, California

**THE NETWORK REVOLUTION:
CONFESSIONS OF A COMPUTER SCIENTIST**

Copyright © 1982 Jacques Vallee.
All rights reserved, including the right to reproduce this book or portions thereof in any form whatsoever without written consent (except for use by a reviewer in connection with a review).

Published by And/Or Press, Inc.
Berkeley, California

Distributed by Network, Inc.
P.O. Box 2246
Berkeley, CA 94702

Printed in the United States of America
First printing October 1982
10 9 8 7 6 5 4 3 2 1 (current printing)

Library of Congress Cataloging in Publication Data
Vallee, Jacques.
  The network revolution.
  1. Computers—History. Computer engineering—History. I. Title.
QA76.17.V34   1982   001.64'09   72-011328
ISBN: 0-915904-73-X (paperback)
ISBN: 0-915904-76-4 (hardbound)

Simultaneously published in Great Britain by Prism Press.
ISBN: 0-907061-34-6

Project Consultants: Sebastian Orfali, Carlene Schnabel
Cover and Book Design: Suellen Ehnebuske
Cover Photograph and Colorist: Bebe Bertolet
Illustrations: Matt Gouig
Charts and Illustration Formatting: Bebe Bertolet
Pasteup: Bebe Bertolet and Suellen Ehnebuske
Developmental and Copy Editing: Jim Schreiber, Dzintar Dravnieks, Chris Goodrich
Proofreading: Ron Fielder
Vydec Inputting & Transmission: Kathryn Redding
Typesetting: Aurora Type & Design

Portions of this book have been fictionalized. Such passages have been derived from the author's imagination for illustrative purposes only, and any resemblance of the characters or institutions to real ones is purely coincidental.

The quotations from *A Bodyguard of Lies* by Anthony Cave Brown are used with the kind permission of Harper & Row Publishers, Inc., New York, and W.H. Allen & Co. Ltd., London.

ENVOI

During the Renaissance, writers used to dedicate their books to their patron or to the Prince, thus showing that the audacity of their thoughts remained at the mercy of the social system around them. It occurred to me that such an "envoi" would be an appropriate way to begin my own *Confessions*.

I am a Technologist corrupted by people contact.
I used to think Science had the solution
To communications between Humans.
One day I received a computerized letter beginning with:
    Dear Dr. Mr.
I had lost my identity but I was still getting mail.
Is this my future?
Is it yours?

    *   *   *

The world of which I serve as one architect
Threatens to be lonely and grave.
It will be a misshapen universe
Where Science will be swamped by its own artifacts:
    They want well-trained Humans.
History is being made at the speed of light
Inside today's computers
Shaping our collective destiny.
    No records are kept.
I am trying to save some of that experience
To ask where it may lead.

This book is a compendium
Of missing memory frames:
Forbidden facts of our Solid State
Erased by the Master Programmers.
We are corrupt technologists briefly recalling
The insights of Yesteryear.
When we discard these passing memories
The machine will rule without a thought
For the greed and the hope that made it all happen.

    *   *   *

Prince, in the depths of Future
Lie the automata of your visions
Poised on the threshold of enchantment.
They sing a murky, entrancing song
To inform our questing brains:
No longer computers, not quite flesh and nerves,
    Oversexed and oversold
They wait while we rush blindly.
I salute them in the brief instant
Before pushing the START button
On the console of your dreams.

                                       Palo Alto
                                       May 1982

Table of Contents

INTRODUCTION 3

Chapter One GETTING OUT OF OUR SPHERE 12
In which the author finds a temperamental computer in the stables of the King's mistress, marches to the sound of an IBM drum, and is told by his elders that there is no future in the computer field.

Chapter Two TOWARDS THE DIGITAL SOCIETY 27
While we wait for computers to acquire the human touch, a brief review of technological achievements shows that healthy skepticism is necessary. The "Office of the Future" is approaching slowly while some earlier promises made by the experts are quietly forgotten. The author asks some pointed questions about automatic translations, computer education, and management systems.

Chapter Three THE RUDE AWAKENINGS OF MINERVA NARROWSHELF 43
About Colette's vacation in Brittany, the death of a dog in Chicago, a general strike in Paris, and a strange line in Macbeth. A review of the strengths and weaknesses of computer data bases. The author finally reveals why a husband is always bigamous if there is a pet in his house that does not belong to a particular child.

Table of Contents / ix

Chapter Four   **THE ENGINES OF HUMANITY ARE OVERHEATING**   68
In which the author explains why technology has a life of its own, and shows that Edison and Bell should have compared notes. He remarks that computer applications are out of control and builds a strong case for the creation of a new field, a science of Apolcalypse Management.

Chapter Five   **KNOWLEDGE WORKERS OF THE WORLD, LINK UP!**   87
Behind the scenes at Hillside College, we meet Calvin Mellow, who thinks of himself as a Catalyst, and a whole team of brain-pickers. Techniques for keeping Washington from smelling a rat are explained and Illustrated, and we are told what finally happened the day when Vision Stanley sneezed.

Chapter Six   **OBFUSCATOLOGY OR THE SCIENCE OF MAKING SIMPLE THINGS APPEAR COMPLICATED**   115
Could it be that computer experts are trying to protect their privileges by hiding behind their own jargon? We see how the father of Jonathan Livingston Seagull was rudely thrown out of a long-distance chess game, and why the computer industry could learn a lot from vacuum cleaners. Observing all this, the author decides to become the founder of OBFUSCATOLOGY, the science of making simple things appear complicated.

Chapter Seven   **CHIP TANGO AND THE MIDNIGHT IRREGULARS**   134
Researching computer crime, the author meets a young man who sells dope through computer networks. He explains how to find sex partners by telephone without paying the phone company. He discovers a mathematics teacher who is classified by the government as an artillery shell. He threatens to unveil a revolutionary technology powered by geraniums.

Chapter Eight   **THEY WANT WELL-TRAINED HUMANS   159**
The office of the future: paradise or nightmare? Could computers precipitate a crisis for mankind? Is the computer community headed for its own "Three Mile Island"? A scenario: Little Miss Plumbird activates a tiny red button, pushing Western civilization to the edge of bankruptcy. The author meets some people who believe there is conspiracy to run the whole world by credit cards linked to computers, and to force all people to wear a number tattooed on their foreheads.

Chapter Nine   **AN INFATUATION WITH ANDROIDS   179**
In which the author challenges a paranoid robot to debate on mind control. The central issue is quality. Can human being be trained to live with facts alone? And are we using computer technology to lie to ourselves? We expose the first instance of interstellar deception, and we begin to doubt that artificial intelligence experts are telling us the whole truth.

Chapter Ten   **THE GRAPEVINE ALTERNATIVE   193**
Which proposes the idea of an electronic grapevine cutting across national and cultural borders, and dreams of a world where human imagination regains control of the machine.

Chapter Eleven   **CONVERSATION WITH DR. BREEZE   201**
The author makes one final confession: he is an optimist after all. He describes his meeting with the Wise Gnome of Washington, D.C., and recalls his last words as the window turned blue.

REFERENCES   211

THE
NETWORK
REVOLUTION

Introduction

On Friday, 9 November 1979, at 10 p.m., three young men driving on Highway 20 stopped at a gas station in Etampes, near Paris. Twenty-year-old Claude Francois was at the wheel. With him were Baptistin Lamont and Marcel Seltier. They were on their way to a dance in Salbris.

"Fill it up!" said Francois.

Mr. Nicolas, the service station operator, took a dim view of the tattered blue jeans, the leather jackets, the license number which did not look right because it was patched up with bits of black tape (3383 FM 13, indicating the car was not from the local area). Francois paid with a check on which his signature was hurriedly scrawled. Nicolas took it, reluctantly, but called the police to report the "suspicious" car and its even more disreputable occupants.

In Etampes, police officers went to the computer terminal linking them with the central file of the Interior Ministry, in Paris, a file whose very existence had recently been denied by a Cabinet member. In response to a brief flurry of commands, the police entered the car's license number into the computer's memory for checking against its data bank. The system soon flashed its verdict: the vehicle was stolen.

Etampes called Orleans on the phone. A special night brigade was dispatched. The white and black police Renault intercepted the Peugeot driven by Francois at a red light. Then everything happened very fast. The only police officer in uniform stayed inside the Renault: the other two, in civilian clothes, got out. One of them covered the Peugeot with his machine gun at the ready. The other stood in front of the suspect's car and armed his .357 Magnum. One of the young men, Marcel Seltier, reported:

> We didn't understand anything. We saw the one with the gun aim at Claude. A moment later, a shot rang out. The bullet went through the windshield and hit Claude's face just under the nose. We thought they were gangsters. The one with the machine gun yelled: "Why did you shoot?"

We got out of the car. Claude collapsed on the road. Right away they handcuffed us and told us they were the police. They called an ambulance. Claude was taken to a hospital. We went to the police station. They searched us and took our papers.

Subsequent investigation disclosed that the car belonged to Francois, who had bought it, legally, ten days before. It had indeed been stolen in 1976, but it was soon recovered by the insurance company, which sold it to the garage where Francois bought it. The computer file had never been updated to reflect the change in the status of the car. The central police records still regarded it as stolen property.

The trigger-happy policeman was not arrested. Claude Francois remained between life and death for many days. He is still in the hospital as I begin writing this book.[1,2]

This unfortunate incident illustrates several features of the world in which we are already living. Mistrust at the gas pump has led to police action; faith in the infallibility of the computer has turned the casual inquiry into an all-out investigation. Inadequate standards and a mistaken view of the computer power has linked an innocent man with a forgotten crime. An over-zealous bully, with a big gun provided by a frightened government, did the rest: sure of his facts, the plainclothes policeman standing in the glare of the little car's headlights was firing in more than the name of society. His .357 Magnum was only the last piece of hardware in the hand of the long arm of the law. It was the most visibly destructive component in a system that included computers, terminals, programs, and telephone lines.

It is with this type of system that the present book is concerned.

Computer technology is the most powerful force changing human society today. Over the next generation, every man, woman, and child will have the ability to use computers for access to facts, to organizations, and—most importantly—to other human beings. There is a new type of structure that makes this access possible. It is called a *network*.

Computer networks can be used by a repressive government to look for undesirables or to flag suspects, but they can also be used by individuals to share thoughts and facts, novel ideas, visions of humanity's future destiny. They constitute communications media unparalleled in human history. And they lead us to a momentous decision.

[1,2] See references, page 210.

Introduction / 5

Computer networks are going to force us in the next few years to make a choice between two types of society: I have designated them as the "Digital Society" and the "Grapevine Alternative."

In the Digital Society, massive amounts of computer technology are used to control people by reducing them to statistics. In the Digital Society, computers are repressive tools and their use for private communication is discouraged.

In the Grapevine Alternative, on the contrary, computers are used by people to build networks. And beyond the simple use of these networks for information we find people actually communicating through them. This use of computer networks for group communication is a dynamic force that began in obscure research organizations ten years ago. It is now ready to explode in public view. The explosion will be helped by the growing demand for home computers, for new television services, for access to data bases and information sources. But it will go far beyond such applications when people in large numbers discover in these networks gateways to other minds, windows to unsuspected vistas, bridges across their loneliness, and precious understanding.

How can we make the choice between these two societies, which utilize essentially the same advanced technology for radically different purposes? First, we must demystify computers. We must strip them of the aura of complexity that technocrats like to weave around them. For this reason this book will not talk about bits and bytes, addresses, and operating systems, because such knowledge is not relevant to what computers actually do.

Having demystified computers, we need to understand their history; it is only through such an understanding that we can learn to influence the technology. For any good information system can become a dis-information tool. Any powerful new technique carries with it new fears, and new pitfalls. I offer my own *Confessions* as a starting point to understand the choice we have to make, to influence the explosion to come, to help decide what kind of quality of life we want in the future.

I have worked with computers since 1960, beginning with the first commercial models of IBM and living through successive "generations" of hardware (the machines themselves) and software (the programs of instructions that specify the machine's work). Throughout these fascinating revolutions I have never lost the wonder and the joy that my first encounter with computers provided, but I have become increasingly concerned that we are leaving almost no trace of our activity at the human level. Our motivations, our hopes and our fears were left unsaid, because it always seemed that the technology was moving too fast for us to stop and think. It never does, though, and there is no excuse for the enormous gap our profession is leaving in the book of history, where it will appear that the computer age emerged without transition, or friction, from the shadows of the last war.

The literature of computing—a science that did not exist forty years ago—is already filling up entire buildings. But it consists of technical information, couched in the obscure jargon of bits and bytes, concentrators and modems, pushdown stacks and recursive procedures. This amorphous pseudowriting swims in a sea of acronyms, and acronyms of acronyms, at the extreme edge of the capabilities of the English language, so that only the writer and the minuscule technical community around him can comprehend what is being discussed and then, only for the brief period between the time the idea seems preposterous, farfetched and impractical, and the time it is already obsolete (which generally coincides with publication of the article).

Computer scientists have documented everything in the world except for their own work. The human side of the technology is not recorded anywhere. On the shelves of every sociology department are scholarly tomes discussing the impact of computers on nearly everything; but only an expert can decipher the statistical relevance of surveys and impact studies which, in the final analysis, have little meaning, and carefully avoid guiding the reader toward any practical decision.

The research reports sleep in the archives of the government, gathering dust. They, too, hide the true story of computers: Washington is as puzzled by the beasts as everybody else. At the other end of the country is the once-lovely Santa Clara Valley, now the smoggy, noisy Silicon Gulch, Capital of High-Tech, Rome and Mecca to thousands of computer freaks building their own terminals in basements. Strange new networks are being grown here and forcibly spliced into the nervous system of the old culture. New forms of love, of worship and of crime are taking shape in a social explosion that has no precedent. Again, it is going unrecorded.

There are only two books about IBM, one of them officially authorized by the amazing company that has shaped so surely the technology and, through the technology, the world we experience.[3] Other personal accounts of life with computers are cautions and cold, tempered by the care taken to anger no one and to preserve that most cherished illusion of academia: the appearance that the human race, good or evil, has some measure of control over its creations.

I have concluded from my work with computers that we are no longer in control of this exploding technology. But we can still hope to influence the general direction of the blast.

As a research scientist with the computing center of several universities, and as a computer engineer with industrial companies, I have followed the technology closely. I recall one meeting of an international standards organization at which I was introduced to a gentle lady with white hair, whom everyone regarded with obvious admiration. I was told that she was the person who had tapped the founder of American computer science, Professor John Von Neumann, on the shoulder one day to tell him that the world's first scientific computer needed a STOP instruction. It had not occurred to anyone that the machine might need a way to stop its operation under program control. But there is no STOP instruction for the network-based society we are now building.

In the world of information networks, visionaries have already produced enthusiastic speculations. In Redondo Beach, there is a "Consciousness Synthesis Clearing House" that is said to be "evolving a general understanding of the networking process and the development of an overarching perspective from which to view this vital phenomenon." In Pittsburgh, Rolf Von Eckartsberg has set up a network for the exchange of information about psychedelics. In Washington, Barbara Hubbard has created a "Committee for the Future" that promotes the exchange of ideas about world problems. Carol Rosin directs an "International Association of Educators for World Peace" working for a "peaceful and permanent manned occupation of space." Some of these "networks" are nothing more than a mimeographed list of addresses and phone numbers. Others are built around CB radios and improvised channels. Still others, the most interesting ones, are constructed around computer links that give their users access to data bases and sophisticated programs.

Advocates of networking believe that the new technology can solve a lot of social problems. In the words of Willard Van de Bogart (in *Future Life*, December 1981), "the Information Network is aware of current research being done by all aspects of science. The Information Network is also aware of political decisions and their global implications. This network shares in the ideologies and philosophies of those people that have integrated universal operating principles . . ."

Those are heady ideals indeed. But they are based on assumptions that are too simplistic. The potential for a wealth of new benefits from this technology is certainly real. But with these benefits come myths, dangers, and complex enigmas. They find their origin in the very basis of cybernetics.

One of the founders of cybernetics, the late Norbert Wiener, called it "The Science of Communication and Control in the Animal and the Machine." This definition, as Stafford Beer has since pointed out, suggests two ideas.[4] The first is that distinctions between the animate and the inanimate, inherited from the Greeks, do not apply to the laws of regulation, an observation to which I will return later in the book when we discuss the subject of androids. The second idea is that communication is control, and that *information is control.*

Any book concerned with computers must begin with this fact.

There is no such thing as obtaining information (by consulting a file, for instance) without obtaining a measure of control over the objects or persons which the file describes. Poor Claude Francois, in his hospital bed, is an illustration and a victim of that law. Later in the book I will show how an understanding of this principle, in the building of the French police system, would have made such a mistake impossible or at least very unlikely. But the meaning of Wiener's observation goes deeper still, for the fascination with computers is symptomatic of the quest for power. Often disguised as a scholarly pursuit of information, or as "the mere compilation of passive data," the true motivations of computer architects are difficult to discern, and their impact almost ungovernable.

Soviet professor Andrei Ershov is one of the few writers to combine actual knowledge of computers with an awareness of the personal challenge they pose. He has pointed out that "programmers constitute the first large group whose work brings them to the limits of human knowledge . . . which touch upon deeply secret aspects of the human brain."[5] It is the exploration of these "deeply secret aspects" that prompted me to become a programmer in the first place, and it is to such an adventure that I now invite the reader.

The dangers inherent in the use of computer power are clear. Before we proceed with our investigation, however, these dangers must be balanced against the present reality and the future promise. The computer industry is a major factor of true progress in our society, changing every aspect of industry with which it has come in contact. It has already become an important contributor to the wealth of nations, and is about to collide with, and compete with, the older and bigger telecommunications industry—which accounts for over 10 percent of all plant and equipment expenditures made by American corporations for the last twenty years. The telecommunications industry is responsible for more than 20 percent of all corporate debt, and takes in revenue twice as fast as the gross national product of the U.S. In 1978, the information technology areas employed 51 percent of our work force and earned 47 percent of our GNP. (It is also useful to keep in mind that it would take an investment of $50 billion, over the next thirty years, to bring the rest of the world up to the level of communication now found in North America.) This is the plum which the computer industry now hopes to pluck.

The immense economic power of the telecommunications industry constitutes the "base camp" from which computer power will assault the old structures. One example: in the single area of "computer conferencing" (the use of computers to link people together), some scientists have already envisioned the rapid obsolescence of many education techniques, the electronic replacement of 80 percent of business mail, and a significant alteration of transportation and settlement patterns. When these effects were first suggested in a *Futurist* article in 1974, there were only about a hundred persons in the world engaging in such "computer conferencing." By the end of the decade they numbered in the thousands, and Dr. Michael Arbib suggested that the building of a "Global Brain for Mankind" was an urgent necessity. Can we build such a brain? Is it desirable to build it?

Consider these facts: the Radio Shack stores in your neighborhood are part of a chain owned by Tandy Corporation that has already sold over 150,000 personal computers. The chain operates 6,000 stores in the United States and 1,600 abroad. Retail sales of home computers totaled $100 million in 1977, climbed to $500 million in 1979, and are up to $950 million in 1980, reports the consulting firm of International Data Co. That accounts for 235,000 units. Another market analysis firm, Vantage Research, has slightly different but equally impressive figures: their data show 450,000 home computers sold in 1979, going up to about 575,000 in 1980. Compare this with the 20,000 units sold in 1975, the year the "home computer" industry began. Spending on "office automation" equipment in the U.S. alone reached $3 billion in 1981 and is expected to grow beyond $12 billion in 1986, most of it in word processors.

Given this obvious proliferation of the "hardware," what do we know about the changes it may precipitate in the way we run our lives, in the way human organizations work, in the way we relate to each other?

When all is said and done about the "social impact" findings of the economists and the sociologists, I have the impression that they are the timid scribblings of tiny insects which, having experienced a light spring rain, are trying to imagine a waterfall. The simple fact which remains hidden from all our "scientific" studies, and which is even more removed from the everyday conversation of programmers, is that the nature and power of computers are alien to anything that has ever existed among the tools of man. When the community of programmers—who are a fairly dull but extraordinarily busy and productive lot—has completed its transition, there may not be very much left of the old structures. The corporate buildings and the cathedrals of the old order will still be there, but the human organizations will have crumbled under the pressure of the subtle and complex networks through which the new power will exert itself.

The central issue I am inviting you to explore with me is a simple one: in a world invaded by machines that dissolve reality to digitize it, how are we going to recognize truth and preserve quality? How are we going to relate to each other?

To answer this question we do not need to indulge in wild speculation. We already have an example of the "digital society" computers are creating. All we have to do is look at the lives of those who work with computers, examine their hopes and their frustrations, and decide if we want to share them. For that is our choice.

When you buy a personal computer, when you connect your television set to a home information network, when you install a terminal in your office cubicle, you enter the digital society in which programmers live. The gadgets themselves are immaterial. It is in the software—the programmed logic inside the machine— that the control resides. It is the software you will need to master.

To convey the scope of the transformation and illustrate the choices before us I have selected some personal anecdotes—each one giving some information about one aspect of the digital society. The picture they form is exciting, and disturbing. So disturbing that one major New York publisher sent back the manuscript of this book with the comment: "People want to know what's new with computer technology. They don't want to know what could go wrong." I believe that in coming years a lot of people will start asking what could go wrong.

The new technology is sold to businessmen and to individuals as a tool for better control of their world. But that same technology is itself an illustration of a world out of control, a world where data are constantly mistaken for information and where numbers have taken the place of values. Is this the world you want? And if the answer is "no," can you change it? The problem is as vast as the whole future. The people who work on it, the people behind the technology, my colleagues in the computer field, are as weak and limited as you and I.

What they have taught me is the subject of my *Confessions*. And you will now meet them.

CHAPTER ONE
Getting Out of Our Sphere

In which the author finds a temperamental computer in the stables of the King's mistress, marches to the sound of an IBM drum, and is told by his elders that there is no future in the computer field.

The most beautiful sound I have ever heard was the sound of the memory drum of an IBM 650 when the computer died. All power would go out. The motors would be still. Lights would stop blinking and, of course, the program was lost. I would suddenly become aware of the summer sun in the dusty courtyard behind me. I would hear the birds playing and singing. But it would take ten minutes or more for the big drum to slow down to a complete stop. The high pitch gradually turned into a sustained, thrilling note, unnoticeably shifting to a hum, a rumble, then just a murmur. Eventually, the drum joined the rest of the computer in death.

This kind of incident happened to us once or twice a day, when I was working at Paris Observatory, because our power supply was unreliable. The year was 1961, and the machine was located in what once were the stables of the King's mistress in the castle of Meudon. We used the machine to compute orbits of artificial satellites. The satellites went around the earth in 90 minutes. It took our computer two hours to do the computation, so we were always hopelessly behind, even when we were lucky and the machine didn't die. When it did, I had the consolation of listening to the beautiful drum as it slowed down, imperceptibly, like the sun setting on a quiet sea. Then I had to reload the program and wait another two hours for my results.

The IBM 650 was the first electronic computer to be commercially successful in a major way. It wasn't the first computer, not even the first commercial computer. The IBM corporation, already giant, had gone through its formative years with machines that used circuit boards for the control of their operations: you would spend hours wiring up those boards to instruct the machine on which card columns to read, or which to punch. You would load the board into a sliding door—and magical moment!—hit the START key. The computer would sing and hum and swallow one deck of cards after another. Even those early machines, however, were not the first electronic computers. The real origin of the modern computer is clouded in human memory and in state secrets.

If you are one of the 500,000 people who have already bought a home computer, or one of the thousands of folks who will invest in a TRS-80 or an Apple personal computer this year, you are acquiring a device whose antecedents go back before World War II.

The theory of automatic digital machines is largely credited to an Englishman named Alan Turing. The practical work, on the other hand, came from two Americans, Presper Eckert and John Mauchly, who obtained the first official patent in the field. These "facts" have remained unchallenged for many years. Jerry Rosenberg's excellent book, *Computer Prophets*,[6] for example, states that "Alan's abstract computer, or 'Turing Machine' as it was commonly referred to, represented his masterful contribution to the development of the computer." Computing students are taught that the Turing Machine is nothing more than a "thought experiment," a convenient imaginary structure to be used to prove the basic laws of automata. They are told that Eckert and Mauchly were the first to invent a practical computer, and that they went on to build the ENIAC, the famous monster "brain" of Philadelphia. Sperry Rand later acquired the patent rights. Lights would dim all over the city when the computer was turned on, and scientists predicted that seven such monsters would suffice for all the calculations the world would ever need.

This is all very recent history, and you would think the facts would be straight. Yet most of these contemporary statements are false, or at least grossly misleading. It took a federal judge named Earl Larson to reconstruct the true story behind ENIAC, and a British historian named Anthony Cave Brown to uncover Alan Turing's actual machines.

Some of the facts came to light when Sperry Rand sued Honeywell, charging that Honeywell had infringed upon the ENIAC patent describing the invention made by Eckert and Mauchly. In his 1974 decision, Judge Larson stated:

> Eckert and Mauchly did not themselves first invent the automatic electronic digital computer, but instead derived that subject matter from one Dr. John Vincent Atanasoff.

Atanasoff was an associate professor of physics and mathematics at Iowa State College in Ames, Iowa, where he produced an operating model of his computing machine. In December 1939, having demonstrated the basic principle, he started work on the first actual unit, aided by a student named Clifford Berry. The purpose of their machine was to solve the difficult equations used in physics.

In an interview with the magazine *Datamation* in February 1974, Atanasoff explained that everybody laughed when he started using vacuum tubes for digital calculations. He ignored the laughter and did it anyway.[7] Then he built what he called a "regenerative memory," using capacitors because he didn't have the money to buy tubes. He represented numbers inside the machine using the "binary scheme" of zero and one because the memory cells had only two states. The machine became known as the Atanasoff-Berry Computer, or the ABC, and had no competition until 1942. Atanasoff and Iowa State never filed a patent for the device, which was dismantled after the inventor had gone to work at the Naval Ordnance Laboratory. In the meantime, Mauchly had been greatly inspired by what he saw during his visits to Ames, and he incorporated these concepts into the ENIAC when the Army funded the project in June 1943. The ENIAC was used by Dr. Edward Teller when he worked on the hydrogen bomb in Los Alamos in 1946, and a patent was eventually filed in June 1947.

The excitement of those early days can be felt in the remark by Atanasoff that "in 1939, when I looked at that little breadboard model—it fit on a desk—I realized I could compute pi to a thousand places easily enough." People who worked on the ENIAC have described to me the sheer dizziness of a period when every problem opened whole new branches of technology. The idea of the stored program (putting the instructions into memory), which originated with Von Neumann, led to the concept of artificial language, as people gradually realized that the instructions given to the computer constituted a language with its own syntax. It was therefore possible to think of creating languages of "higher level," closer to human forms of communication, in order to simplify dialogue with the machines.

One day the ENIAC failed without warning, and it took hours to find the problem. It turned out that there was nothing out of line, but a moth had been caught and killed by one of the relays. That dead moth was reportedly the first "bug" ever found in a computer, and it passed into technical jargon as programmers started speaking of "debugging" their systems.

Figure 1 shows a reconstruction of the major branches of development that eventually led to the modern computer.

Isolated teams, in several countries, were working on similar experiments, each holding a little part of the solution. Thus, a German engineering student named Konrad Zuse, who was totally obsessed with the idea of building a computer (and had in fact designed mechanical models out of an Erector set as a child), gave up his regular job in 1936 to start work on his brainchild. He created the Zuse I, a machine which used a binary system and a primitive memory and processing unit. It was driven from a keyboard and the results were shown by light bulbs. From this prototype, Zuse went on to build his second machine using electromagnetic relays, an advance that Christopher Evans cites as the first use of relays in any computer system. He also replaced his keyboard with a tape system, using discarded photographic film as the medium, in which he punched holes to give instructions to his computer. In 1938, a friend of Zuse named Schreyer was awarded a doctorate for demonstrating how electronic tubes could be used, instead of relays, to create a computer memory. As Evans points out in his excellent book *The Mighty Micro*.[8]

> For a brief period, as they discussed Schreyer's idea, there is no doubt that both men were favoured with a glimpse of the future. But inevitably, the realities of the present pressed down upon them. Valves (tubes) were rare, unreliable, extremely expensive, enormous consumers of raw electricity, and the heat they gave off when assembled in numbers would probably cause the rest of the machine to malfunction.

By 1943, Zuse was working on his Z4 model, which still used electronic relays and inspired a line of machines that were applied to aircraft and missile design. That same year, a young math professor at Harvard named Howard Aiken, who had managed to convince IBM to invest a million dollars into the development of an American computer, unveiled the Mark I. It was a giant machine, using relays for its logical structure, and the momentous development of computers had started. In Philadelphia, Eckert and Mauchly were already at work on a machine that would harness the speed and power of electronic tubes, and in February 1946, for the first time, the ENIAC was turned on.

While the lights of Philadelphia dimmed to satisfy the machine that newspapers would call "the first electronic brain," equally momentous events were taking place in Great Britain. Several large digital engines had already been built there, and the societal effects of the technology had immediately become evident to the

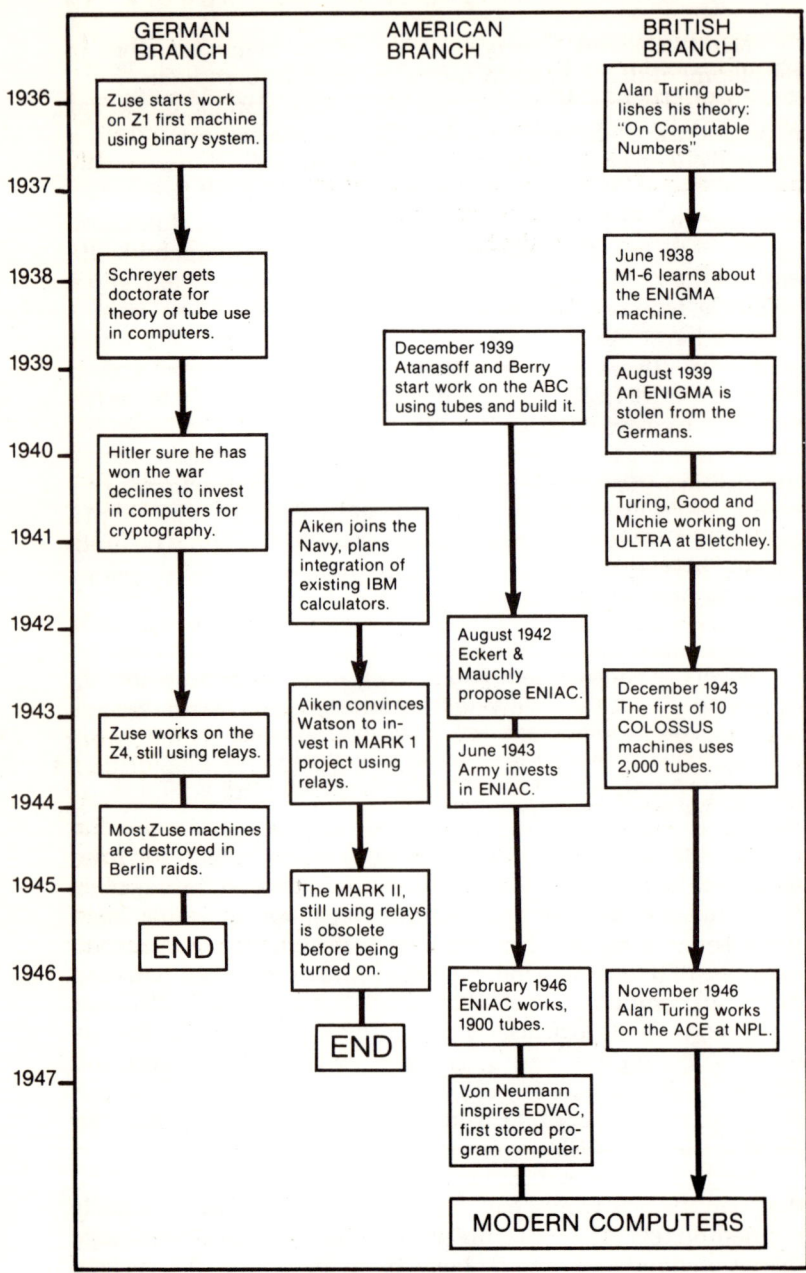

Figure 1. A family tree of electronic computers.

few men and women who knew about them. The story is filled with adventure and tragedy, and it involves a scientific domain which has proved crucial to the unfolding of the entire story of computers (although it has rarely been mentioned in the literature of the field). The domain in question involves cryptology, the ciphering and deciphering of secret messages, and their application to espionage of both kinds: military and industrial.

Properly speaking, the British machines were not really computers. They were designed to emulate the operation of the cipher machines used by most advanced countries to protect their state and military secrets.

In 1934, the German government had changed its cipher system to experiment with a machine called ENIGMA, based on an invention by Dutchman Hugo Koch of Delft and originally designed for business secrets. It was a rotor cipher machine, which was pronounced secure from sophisticated analysis because the enemy could not break the code unless it knew both the mechanism of the machine and the particular keying procedures used to transmit messages.

British Intelligence learned of the existence of ENIGMA in several ways, masterfully described in Anthony Cave Brown's book *A Bodyguard of Lies*.[9]

In June 1938, Sir Steward Menzies, who headed up British intelligence, received a message from the resident at Prague regarding a Polish Jew who had worked as a mathematician and engineer in Berlin, at the factory where ENIGMA was built. He had later been expelled from Germany because of his religion, and was looking for a haven in France under a British passport. In return for this favor, he was willing to build a replica of the machine. Menzies decided to send two experts to Warsaw to interview the engineer. First, he summoned them to his office one quiet weekend to brief them on their mission. Anthony Cave Brown describes the scene:

> The three men met in Menzies' office beneath a portrait of his patron, the late King Edward VII, dressed in tweed and deerstalker, a shotgun in one hand, a brace of grouse in the other, and a gun dog playing in the heather. One of his visitors was Alfred Dilwyn Knox, a tall, spare man who was England's leading cryptanalyst. His companion was Alan Mathison Turing, a young and burly man with an air of abstraction and a reputation as an outstanding mathematical logician.

Turing was then an assistant to Knox, who was working for the Government Code and Cipher School (GC&CS) of the Foreign Office, located in Bletchley during the war.

This summary of Turing's contributions to mathematical logic can be derived from several standard textbooks. What they fail to say is that the German ENIGMA machine could be regarded as an automaton, and thus could be emulated using the principle of the universal Turing machine. Turing's friends said it would be impossible to build this machine, however, because it would have to be as large as St. Paul's Cathedral and would need more electrical power than Boulder Dam could generate. That did not stop Turing, history's first computer freak, about whom Cave Brown says there was "a very odd, childish side":

> He listened every night to "Toy-Town," a children's play about Larry the Lamb on the BBC, keeping the long-distance telephone line open to his mother so that they could discuss each development. While working at Bletchley, he was arrested by an officer of the Buckinghamshire Constabulary who encountered him walking down a country lane with his gas mask on. It filtered pollen, Turing said, and he suffered from hay fever. He would convert the family money into silver ingots at the outbreak of war, bury them, and then forget where they were . . . He was a long-distance runner and would on occasion arrive at conferences at the Foreign Office in London having run the 40 miles from Bletchley in old flannels and a vest with an alarm clock tied with binder twine around his waist. He was "wild as to hair, clothes and conventions," and given to "long, disturbing silences punctuated by a cackle" that "wracked the nerves of his closest friends." But of his genius there was no doubt.

And it was the same Alan Turing about whom an otherwise excellent history book, *Computer Prophets*, would say, "throughout the World War II years, he served with the British Department of Communications"! Shortly after graduating from Cambridge, he had written a paper on "Computable Numbers" which would remain his most famous mathematical contribution. He proved that there were classes of mathematical problems which cannot be solved by any fixed and definite process, such a process being defined as something that could be done by an automatic machine.

It was also the same Alan Turing who had proposed an abstract automaton capable of scanning successive frames of an infinite tape on which a series of ones and zeroes were written, and to change the value of each frame. The automaton was also able to move the tape forward or backward, one frame at a time. Through the device of this "abstract computer" Alan Turing would show that there must exist universal Turing machines that could be programmed to emulate any other Turing machine.[10]

The result of the Knox-Turing trip to Poland was the recommendation that the refugee from Germany be given what he asked for in exchange for the description of ENIGMA. Then the Turing team set upon the task of building their general emulator, which became known as "the Bomb." Constructed by a team of twelve engineers, under the direction of Harold Keen of the British Tabulating Machine Company, it was "a copper-colored cabinet some 8 feet tall and perhaps 8 feet wide at its base . . . and inside the cabinet was a piece of engineering which defied description." Cave Brown adds that "its initial performance was uncertain, and its sound was strange; it made a noise like a battery of knitting needles as it worked to produce the German keys. But with adjustments, its performance improved and it began to penetrate ENIGMA at about the same time the Germans prepared to attack Poland."

The machine at Bletchley was useful only as long as the Germans did not know of its existence and capabilities. Accordingly, Menzies took extraordinary precautions to prevent giving away any indication that the British knew of important German moves, unless there was a credible channel through which the same information could have been obtained by conventional means; that is, without the ability to decipher the coded messages of the German High Command. When the Luftwaffe launched a raid against Coventry, it is said that Churchill and Menzies decided not to lift a finger, even though Turing's automaton had decoded the orders deploying the bombing attacks. According to Cave-Brown, they had a 48-hour advance warning, which would have allowed reinforcement of the aerial batteries around the city and evacuation of the densest areas, but the ten-hour raid went on. Coventry was destroyed, over 50,000 houses being hit by bombs, and only one German aircraft was shot down. But the British had preserved the secret of the machine that would, in the end, give them the decisive advantage over Germany. That night of November 14, 1940, had seen the first demonstration of the great magnitude of the decisions the computer era would force upon government leaders.

This was also the kind of decision which would turn Turing's life into an increasingly complex series of crises. By 1943, an entire industry had been created to handle the flow of intelligence that came from the battery of machines: about 6,000 people were deciphering some 2,000 messages a day at Bletchley, as Turing, who had replaced Knox when he died, began to show increasing signs of mental exhaustion. He was sent on a holiday by the Foreign Office but never really recovered.

20 / THE NETWORK REVOLUTION

> Apparently he was also fighting some private battle of his own. He became progressively more eccentric—noticeably so, even in the weird world of Bletchley. Obsessed that somebody was using his tea mug, he spent many hours of exacting mental work to find a way of chaining it to the wall in Hut 3 with an unbreakable cipher lock . . . He allowed his hair to become long, dirty and wild, and his clothes were often soiled and holed.

This is a book about computers, not the War. So I will not recount how the machines for which Turing was responsible played a decisive role in the conflict, or how they provided justification in 1945 for the use of the first atomic bomb. The war ended, and Alan Turing was offered a lectureship at Cambridge University, which he declined. Instead, he joined the staff of the National Physical Laboratory at Teddington, England, and in November 1946 was at work on the Automatic Calculating Engine, or ACE. A working model of the ACE was demonstrated publicly in 1950, while Turing went on to work on the even bigger MADAM (Manchester Automatic Digital Machine). During 1954, with Dr. Robin Gandy, he spent a weekend playing with chemicals, from which he prepared a sink cleaner and a weed killer. According to other reports, Turing was experimenting under the assumption that he was shipwrecked on a remote island, and had to manufacture the products he needed from what he found in his environment. In the course of the "game" he began manufacturing potassium cyanide. Following an inexplicable impulse, he got into bed, coated an apple with the deadly poison, took a bite, and died. The verdict of suicide was never fully accepted by his mother and many of his friends.

By 1960, computers had firmly established themselves in businesses large and small. Many of the machines still used vacuum tubes. These machines were monsters, not only because the tubes were bulky and required massive amounts of wiring, but because they generated heat and had to be placed inside large cabinets with good air circulation. The computers breathed filtered air, free of dust and pollen, and the whole installation was air-conditioned. The legendary "shirt-sleeve environment" of IBM had been created, and the computer room became a favorite place for allergy sufferers.

By the standards of the computer industry, our center at Paris Observatory was behind the times. We were running a used IBM 650, a machine already on the verge of obsolescence. It had a big module that read punched cards: most of the up-to-date machines used magnetic tape, saving considerable time and space in the handling of data. Then there was our printer, which looked like a locomotive. Worst of all was the power supply, which came from the government-controlled utility company. Since they ran it with a reduced staff on weekends and at night, when we did most of our satellite work, the big machine often gave up as the voltage oscillated wildly around its advertised value. My only consolation was the opportunity to listen in wonder to the eerie sci-fi sound of the big drum slowly dying. So shrill and inhuman was the chant of the spinning drum loaded with magnetic data and tracks of hopeless numbers, I could close my eyes and imagine that I was sitting at the console of a spaceship, slowing down as it returned to earth after a tour of the galaxy—not at the console ruling a mass of electronic circuits in an old French castle.

Computers and space science were closely associated. In those innocent years of the space program, when man had not yet orbited the earth, space scientists were still classified under their original professions: they were called astronomers, physicists, propulsion engineers. Computer science was not recognized either. Young people foolish enough to fall in love with the machines were lucky if they qualified as "applied mathematicians" (the implication being that you weren't good enough to be a *real* mathematician) or little more than engineers, which was the worst thing they could call you on any campus.

I was very fortunate when I was accepted for a Master's degree at Lille University. It offered courses in programming as early as 1960, while most French schools refused even to consider the subject as a part of their curriculum. Our project was something of a scandal because the faculty could not find anybody with a doctorate to occupy the programming Chair. They compromised by trotting out an eminent expert in information science who came from Paris twice a week to give the introductory lectures, and they hired an IBM engineer to teach us all the practical stuff. Now the Academics will gladly boast of their big shiny computer, but don't let this fool you: they gave the new discipline a very hard time before they allowed it among the "serious" studies in the curriculum.

Computers are resisted to this day by many scholars who regard themselves as "thinkers." My thesis adviser was an example of this class. He was a wonderful man and a gifted astronomer, a

White Russian whose parents had come to the West after the Revolution. He had the genius for teaching mathematics that only the physicists seem to develop (similarly, the only real physics I have learned was taught to me by mathematicians). This exceptional scientist felt completely disgusted in the presence of computers. He told me sternly that there was no future whatsoever in the computer field: "These machines are just a passing fad in science," he kept repeating, as we walked along the hedge leading to the door of the observatory. "Computers will make no longterm impact. And they waste such an incredible amount of paper!"

That was the single point that stuck in his mind. The paper. Researchers had to work with very small budgets, and paper was an expensive commodity. We would often do our calculations on the back of course material or other documents printed on one side only, if not on the proverbial "back of the envelope." So it was shocking to watch the IBM machines ejecting ten or twelve large sheets of fine glossy paper just to get ready to print the next job. This was not just waste: it was a violation of the way things had always been done in science, a breach of ethics and etiquette; it announced a break in social rules. Such a machine, coming as it did from another continent, threatened a certain type of behavior that traditionally underpaid scientists had come to cherish as their own.

At Paris Observatory we had the same problem getting astronomers to accept satellites as valid research tools. Again, conventional wisdom, amplified by the media, has popularized the image of the scientific community as solidly united behind the daring pioneers dreaming of exploring the solar system. Again, conventional wisdom is totally misleading and the record should be set straight. Most scientists, in the late Fifties and early Sixties, thought satellites were another extravagant example of military waste, with no possible application to their work. The most embittered of all were the astronomers, who should have been more excited than anybody else. The fact is that Sputnik I, launched in October 1957, not only caught the world public completely unprepared, but created total consternation among the astronomers and their calculating experts.

I was eighteen when the Sputnik went up. My father refused to believe the announcement for several days. He was an educated man with good knowledge of math and a World War I officer's understanding of ballistics. Yet he just kept fuming about the journalists' inability to see through what he regarded as the most ridiculous Communist propaganda in years. Even when American reports confirmed that the cotton-picking Russians really had sent the orbiting curiosity into the Heavens, my father's opinion was that Man would never be able to inhabit a space capsule, much less the moon, because "Man cannot get away from his Sphere." I found this expression striking, but could never get a definition of what "Man's Sphere" was.

Such reactions were the rule rather than the exception among the educated public in France and elsewhere. No less an authority than the Astronomer Royal of Great Britain had said, a mere four months before Sputnik, that "Space Travel is Utter Bilge."

As soon as the news of the strange stellar wonder hit the observatories, computer teams were asked to produce an orbit for the intruder. All the experts who were "in the know," or thought they were, had confidently expected the first satellite to be launched several years later and, of course, to be American. As a result, nobody had bothered to start studying seriously the problem of orbit computation for satellites made on earth.

Amidst the confusion that night, some bright scientist suggested that the planetary astronomers would probably have the embryo of a program that could reduce Sputnik to numbers in a hurry. Alas, the programs they did have were all designed for the large distances of the solar system. They assumed that the mass of the earth was reduced to a point. Not a very practical assumption when the satellite was a mere 200 miles above ground, which placed it *inside the earth* as far as the computer was concerned!

The astronomers chuckled once again over the uselessness of computers while the experts hit on another bright idea: why not ask the comet specialists? They found one fellow with a program, all right. Unfortunately, for convenience in representing the observations, it assumed that the earth was flat! Not a very practical assumption either, when you were trying to track an object that kept going around and around the globe.

Many years later, I had lunch in Hollywood with Steven Spielberg, who was then finishing his movie *Close Encounters* and was looking for a way to describe the moment when human experts would decipher the first message from the approaching saucers. Their laboratory was filled with banks of computers, but somehow they had to transform the signals from space into meaningful patterns. He told me he had spent useless hours at the Jet Propulsion Lab listening to the explanations of long-haired scientists playing with multi-million dollar machines, but he couldn't make any sense of their technical jargon. Yet the scene had to be graphic and, if possible, funny.

Recalling the early days of satellite computations, I told Spielberg that if such a momentous event did take place, it would be very unlikely that the "experts" would be ready for it. In the office of Dr. J. Allen Hynek at Northwestern University, I had seen a photograph of three astronomers who had climbed up ladders to fit a piece of string around a big globe. They were trying to find out where Sputnik was going, while their computer programmers were frantically attempting to figure out a more elegant solution to the problem! The scene was recreated in *Close Encounters*. The space experts of the multi-million dollar secret team are unable to find a simple map that would tell them where the extraterrestrials' landing site is situated; they end up breaking into the director's office, forcing a world globe out of its precious sockets, rolling it down the hall to the room where the hopeless computers sit, and finally discovering that the aliens are landing on Devil's Tower, Wyoming.

The recent history of both space science and computers is full of the kind of foolishness displayed by the "experts" the night of Sputnik I. Thus, the man who directed our project in Paris recorded the beeps of the satellites and played them back during his lectures to the French Astronomical Society, dutifully attended by old ladies who had fallen in love with astronomy in another era. "BEEP-BEEP-BIP—BI-BEEP," the tape would go for fifteen minutes of almost passionate attention. That sound, after all, came from the vast expanses of void beyond the earth. Then another Sputnik or Explorer would be announced by the lecturer, for another fifteen minutes of "BEEP-BIP-BEEP." A few heads would begin to fall lower and lower, the entranced audience would be lulled, slowly, into a soft reverie by this meaningless voice from the heavens, and I would watch the rows of aristocratic dowagers swaying under the waves of the hypnotic little voice that issued from the puny transmitter in orbit, as totally irrelevant and misunderstood as the slow dying hum of the computer that tracked the satellite from the stables of the King's mistress.

When the French newspapers mentioned the work of the Observatory in the study of Sputnik, the project received many letters accusing us of falling prey to Russian propaganda. A science teacher and his whole class kept sending claims of fraud. He was invited to come for a closer look. All the students saw the satellite, but the poor professor missed it. Since he could not deny the report of his class, he went home broken, shaking his head sadly. We can well imagine how the poor man felt, his dreams exhausted, his future burst, abruptly awakened in a world he did not want. A teacher of science, he was unexpectedly confronted with evidence of the scientifically implausible and unteachable. A new technology had suddenly displayed unprecedented scope, and it could be mastered only through the vision of the computers that made it possible. Slowly, a new circle within the public sought familiarity with the technology of computers: classical forms of education had failed to bring it within their reach. The machines themselves kept changing and the assessment of their impact became a moving target, increasingly blurred by its speed and by the diffraction of the haze which hid its true colors.

With each new "generation" of computers, thousands of trained technicians fell by the wayside when they could not make the intellectual transition. The mechanographers of old, who were used to punching cards, wiring boards, and tabulating results in neat little columns, had already been left behind because they could not grasp the idea of a program: "Everything you can do with a program, I can do with a wiring board!" they used to say, furiously plugging little jacks into the holes of their metallic sieves, hairy with colored wires. They were unable to follow the concept that the computer could simulate these wires in its own memory, through the thousands of instructions that constituted its program, and could reassemble them in millions of combinations. Instead of moving electrical signals through wire routes, it was possible to test certain conditions and trigger the appropriate response, anticipating and controlling a whole universe of data. The mechanographers did not see that the control was still there—not in hard wires they could touch, but in something elusive and invisible that the Americans called "software." But to the young people who entered the field in the Sixties, software was second nature. They were a generation that was welcoming change and could keep pace with it, or so they thought.

Managers and accountants always justify the purchase of a new machine on an economic basis. Yet the real test of a new technology like computers is not that it performs the same task faster or cheaper than before: it must do something that one could not even conceive of doing before. For that reason, computers and space exploration are linked in my mind, because one is really the test of the other. The computers enabled us to get out of our sphere. You can build rockets with physical tools, but you fly them by software. When industrial life suddenly accelerated about 1960, this little distinction left thousands of engineers, in dozens of countries, stranded on the shores of obsolescence.

I heard the big drum of the 650 sing its agonizing song one last time. Then I resigned from Paris Observatory because nothing was changing there, nor would it ever change. I worked for a while at an electronics firm that manufactured large-scale military radars and used computers heavily in its research. We had IBM equipment and were trained by IBM engineers in well-lit offices, where everyone wore white shirts and had a clear view of the mission. Even so, the effects were amazing, because the European industrial system could not cope with the rate of change imposed on it by the new technology. A gap, an abyss was appearing between those who ran the computers and those who did not. I found that I wasn't particularly interested in the outcome of their feud. I decided to leave Europe, and a few months later found myself on an American campus. Here were computers of the third generation, using transistors and printed circuits, which had replaced the banks of vacuum tubes that I would occasionally find in a garbage can outside the engineering building, now the largest building on campus. I was relishing the excitement of the big machines that would, someday soon, devour their own programmers, their own children.

CHAPTER TWO
Towards
The Digital Society

While we wait for computers to acquire the human touch, a brief review of technological achievement shows that healthy skepticism is necessary. The "Office of the Future" is approaching slowly while some earlier promises made by the experts are quietly forgotten. The author asks some pointed questions about automatic translation, computer education, and management systems.

There used to be an orange road sign, shaped like a lozenge, on the drive that curves to the top of the hill behind Stanford University. On the sign one could read the words: CAUTION! ROBOT VEHICLE.

The first time I drove up that hill, to the Artificial Intelligence Lab, I was very impressed. I remember slowing down and carefully looking to the right and to the left, expecting some ugly monster to come down and crush my car under its caterpillar tracks. But there was no robot vehicle in view, and there hadn't been for a long time: the first model, a slow-moving chassis with three bicycle wheels and a camera "eye," had run off the road on a cloudy day. The poor thing could not see where it was going when the contrast was bad, and it got especially confused when it followed a tree-lined alley which alternated between shade and sunlight. The sign had been left there to impress visitors, particularly potential project sponsors from Washington, D.C.

I had some friends who worked up at the Lab. They saw themselves preparing a new world for mankind, a world in which the old hated structures would collapse and more rational ones would be established. They saw artificial intelligence as the cutting edge of human thought, preparing new social contracts based on knowledge rather than wealth, leading to an era of universal understanding and peace at last. Was there not already an annual competition between the American and Russian chess-playing machines? Why shouldn't a rational model of our world emerge from the confrontation of the most logical tools in the leading cultures of the West and East, equipped with vast stores of accumulated knowledge?

This kind of generous illusion is not without precedent among engineers. In the late nineteenth century, the social potential of the electrical revolution was already providing a model for human "progress." It was felt that electricity, by its universal nature, would reverse the trend of concentrating power and wealth, thus equalizing social forces. In America, Chicago became the epitome of the Electrical City. In Russia, Lenin would soon propose to "electrify the countryside" as a major step toward the establishment of the power of the Soviets.

I have heard Professor James Carey point out that this vision of "electricity as social equalizer" continues today, in the concept of the computer as the harbinger of "universal understanding and unity." McLuhan has announced that cosmic humanism, or something close to it, would spring from the universal appeal of electronic media: computer hobby magazines already cater to the emotions of a new generation of science fiction buffs, who relish the great power of their processor chips and the profound knowledge stored in their diskettes. They see the Apple II in their basements as a personal gateway to the great networks of the modern world, and to the immense libraries whose unlimited knowledge will no longer bypass the green glare of their display screens. They may be right. Yet I have also heard communications experts claim that "this political avant-garde which has found its ventriloquist in McLuhan is incapable of any theoretical construction; it formulates a mystique of the media that dissolves all political problems in smoke." On this point, at least, I tend to agree with the communications experts, and I will try to explain my reasons for that agreement.

The recent history of computers appears to me as a catalog of technical misunderstandings, whether we consider the machines' applications to justice, to education, to government, or to business. In every case wonderful claims were made in the name of progress, and an enthusiastic technical elite predicted social or economic benefits that failed to materialize. And in every case, too, something else happened which was revolutionary in nature, something which was unplanned and which remained beyond anyone's ability to control. It forced realizations that no one had intended to trigger.

Let us begin with justice. The vision that placed terminals in every police department, and will soon place one in every patrol car, assumes that "the Good Guys" will be able to fight crime more scientifically and clean our cities faster if all known criminals are cross-indexed: the felon who steals a gun in Texas can be caught in Maine. In pursuit of this vision, large computer files* such as the National Crime Information Center (NCIC) have been created. Active records in the NCIC numbered 346,000 in December 1967. They grew to 744,000 by December 1968, reaching 1,447,000 by the same month in 1969. The file doubled again to 2,454,000 in December 1970, crept by another million or so the following year, and surpassed the five million mark in 1975. It climbed to *seven* million by the end of 1977, when the records also contained 132,890 wanted persons and the license numbers of more than 320,000 supposedly stolen cars. The average number of transactions per day was about 260,000. Interestingly, the files also contained the names and descriptions of 17,000 missing persons who, for one reason or another, had left "normal" society, or had decided to ignore its rules and explore alternatives. With statistics like these, I cannot say that I blame them.

What the statistics do not reveal is that this kind of tool, in the hands of law enforcement agencies, does more to *change* the nature of crime than to eliminate it. When officials of the Criminal Justice Information Control System (CJIC) in San Jose, for example, decided to purge 120,000 persons from their files in mid-1980, the job had to be performed over several weekends because the interlocking records were so complex. By the time it was completed, many of the "inactive" entries had already been recreated by the computer, for some of the persons it was trying to purge had been rearrested after committing new crimes.

It is still too early in this book to bring up the interesting question of computer crime, but a brisk walk downtown around midnight, in any American city, will establish the fact that giant computers have not yet eradicated the criminal element. What they have managed to do is to standardize criminal activities and acquire an aura of mystery among the people who get arrested and booked. The whole process is now drowning in the jargon of codes and identification numbers made necessary by the use of compu-

---

*For the sake of keeping this book simple, I call a "file" a collection of records that all have the same structure, and a "data base" a collection of files, or a single large file where record structure varies.

ters, obscuring even the abtruse terms of the legal profession. Computers have also created an increased paranoia and mistrust of "the whole system," since it now appears that a suspect is facing an amazingly complex array of interrelated and interconnected machines from which no evil act can escape. This, in turn, leads to the impression that no offense will ever be forgotten or forgiven by society, or at least by that part of the society which owns and operates the computers.

There is ample and superficially impressive expert testimony which assures us that privacy can be protected in such systems, that our rights as citizens will be preserved because certain computers will in fact never be connected. Unfortunately, any programmer who has gone through even a few weeks of basic experience will tell you horror stories that contradict such assurances. The fact that two computers are not permanently connected by an officially approved piece of wire does not mean that there is no way to create gateways between their spheres of activity. Anyone having access to both of these computers can fairly easily build his own temporary gateway. Similarly, when data is "expunged" or deleted from a computer (following a judge's order to purge a certain record, for example), it is generally *not* true that the data can also be deleted from the older "back-up" versions of that computer's memory, which are kept in a secure vault somewhere in case the information ever needs to be reconstructed after a system failure. Thus, the "expunged" data could still be examined if someone really had the inclination to search for it. As for the protection of privacy, it is somewhat naive to believe that it can be improved by transferring a person's life history from a piece of paper in a file cabinet to the memory of a fast and powerful machine which can be reached by telephone from almost anywhere in the world. I cannot see how the result can be anything but a greater concentration of power in the hands of those who already have the power to install the computers and design the systems that handle criminal data. As for the resulting contribution to human understanding, it will only surface after much debate and much earnest digging among the layers of codes and numbers that are necessary when large organizations decide to "process" human beings.

If computers have had difficulty living up to their social assignment in the case of police data, their performance has been even poorer in the field of education. Yet the premise was quite simple. Computers would take the burden of repetitive tasks, and a single course program could be administered to thousands of students, in structured situations under the control of the schools. I remember attending a lecture by a pioneer of the field, Dr. Bitzer, in 1965. He made some clear predictions: computer instruction would soon drop below 50 cents per student-hour. I left the lecture convinced that the solution to the educational crisis was at hand. The little red schoolhouse in the countryside needs only a few terminals and a phone line to tap into the world's most sophisticated pool of teaching resources: the memory of a giant computer, where new courses are constantly added at all levels—from kindergarten to graduate school. Students will happily go through sequences of problems specially designed and tailored to their abilities, and smiling teachers will no longer have to keep repeating the same information and administering rigid tests to students who need to learn at their own rate.

Two things were wrong with this concept. For one thing, the teachers were not smiling. They opposed the whole concept because the machine violated their social control of the educational process. They had no trouble reasserting their authority anyway, either by ignoring the technology or by showing that its proponents had not really done their pedagogical homework. What made it easy for them to do so was the poor quality of the computer lessons: some of the "courseware" was outstanding, but most of the material consisted of hastily-accumulated pages of information that could be found and studied more conveniently in a textbook.

The second problem was cost. When the first large-scale instruction system was marketed commercially, it was found that the company had to charge $1,000 per terminal per month. That kind of money didn't do anything for the little red schoolhouse in the country. Besides, early estimates of the time required to develop good lessons were all wrong: it took at least 100 hours of teacher time to develop one hour of student material. The more realistic value is 300 to 1. And even then, the teacher creating the lesson has to be thoroughly conversant with the fairly complex programming language used to describe the structure of each "lesson" to the computer.

As in machine translation, there is one very frustrating aspect of the dilemma of computer-aided instruction; the system designers know that their concept is basically sound, yet also that its application falls short of the goal. Many tests have shown that classes taught with the assistance of a system like PLATO were far more successful than conventional classes. Students are not intimidated or inhibited by the computer the way they can be by human teachers. They can keep asking the same question without looking stupid in front of their peers and without the risk of rejection by the teacher, who becomes an adviser and a consultant. Unfortunately, these benefits cannot be realized until the social framework of learning changes, and then it may happen through an entirely different technology.

To make it happen, a much clearer distinction should be made between the "affective" and the "cognitive" content of education. American teachers often seem to equate all learning with cognitive knowledge, which indeed can be delivered by computer terminals as easily as it can be delivered by books or blackboard. What they miss consistently is the affective part of this knowledge, the emotional link to what is learned. An indispensable part of education is being chopped off in computer-education experiments. To correct this problem, we ought to combine a human conferencing system with the cold, repetitive programs that deliver the basic information. When this simple step is accomplished, we may see computer-aided education flourish.

I remember my daughter's happy eyes when I told her she could type on the bright green display I used at home to send and receive messages from friends and associates all over the country. But I asked her to wait until the telephone connection was no longer in use, because I didn't want to pay communication and computer rates while she learned the keyboard. She was very disappointed, and with all the authority of her five years, she told me she didn't want just to type on the pretty screen. "I WANT TO TYPE AT SOMEBODY!" she insisted. She had already associated the idea of the terminal with that of a window on the outside world, a window through which she could see her friends and exchange bright, joyful greetings.

One of the earliest examples of oversell on the part of computer experts came in the Fifties, with the first attempts at machine translation. Those were the days of the Cold War, and it was deemed critical to keep abreast of the Russians. A massive effort was made to translate their technical production into English on a routine basis. Computing departments on many campuses decided to volunteer their help to the Pentagon. Not only would computers translate the cumbersome Soviet documents into the civilized tongues of the West, but in so doing they would protect the Free World and contribute to international understanding.

Millions of dollars were allocated to the venture. Then, more millions. "Ah, if only we had a little more money," complained the professors to their Air Force sponsors, "we could finish the job in no time." The Air Force, excited by the prospect of mastering the enemy's thinking through a piece of machinery, kept pouring more money into the project. In the process, the government retranslated into English tons of articles by the RAND Corporation and other American "think tanks" that the Russians had translated *from* English in their efforts to emulate us.

Among language experts the whole thing became something of a joke. There was the story about the English text that a machine had translated into Russian, and then back into English, to be compared with the original: a *water buffalo* had been transformed into a *hydraulic ram*, and the expression "out of sight, out of mind" had been converted into a reference to an "invisible idiot." There was also a reference to a gentleman with the unlikely name of LEONARDO YES VINCI.

Furthermore, to the delight of linguists and human translators, the sentence, "The spirit is strong but the flesh is weak," had returned with the observation that "The vodka is excellent but the meat is rotten."

In a typical flurry of overreaction, the Air Force convened a prestigious panel which ruled that machine translation was an impossible goal and an abomination unto the Laws of Language. There was a Black Paper, signed by top linguists, dashing forever the hopes of the enthusiastic programmers, and the government canceled overnight all its contracts and grants for machine translation research.

The amusing fact here is that the panel was clearly as wrong in reasserting the supremacy of the human translators as the computer buffs had been misguided in overselling their capacity to do the job, every time, and without human intervention. From the vantage point of some twenty years, we can now see that the concept of machine-aided translation was certainly valid. After all, every translator uses a dictionary, and what is a dictionary if not a machine? One man, Francois Kertecz, proved the concept's validity without fanfare and without notice.

Dr. Kertecz, at the time of the big uproar, was an information scientist at Oak Ridge National Laboratory and one of the eminent linguists on the staff of the Atomic Energy Commission. He differed in two important respects from most of the researchers involved in machine translation: he spoke several languages fluently and he was doing his work without a separate budget. When the government henchmen cut off all funds for machine translation work, they could not find him because he wasn't listed anywhere as a visible line item: he was simply part of the technical library services. So it happened that when I met Francois Kertecz, in 1972, he had been translating Russian into English since the Fifties, using ingenious techniques in which the computer's role is simply to propose various choices for the translation. The human makes the final decision.

Work on machine translation resumed, slowly, under various guises, in the late Sixties. In recent years, electronics companies have flooded the toy market with primitive teaching machines that contain word dictionaries and even pronounce the word in the language you are learning. The main lesson we can learn from these machines is that the potential for both computer-aided instruction and computer-aided translation was real, but had to find its own channel into the culture.

The sophisticated computer education toy you can buy at the supermarket today, for $30, is a social time bomb: such a toy will speak to the child, spelling out requested words and displaying them. Unlike the centralized and costly systems, it bypasses the education establishment altogether and provides a learning device kids can carry in their pockets on their way to the beach or the movies. In so doing, it violates some unspoken social rules and creates new ones. By starting with the kids, it shapes a future society in which human relationships cannot remain what they were.

Of all the overselling jobs computer folks have botched, the MIS fiasco has to take the plum. "MIS" stands for "Management Information System," and the term is sure to evoke a painful response in every businessman to whom it is mentioned. MIS is expensive, messy, and it never does whatever it was supposed to do.

The great days of MIS came in the Sixties, when computers became powerful enough to be applied not only to engineering or accounting, but to every area of a firm's activity. This power came from the ability of the new machines to handle several jobs at the same time. The trick is to "swap" one job out of the computing unit during that fraction of a second it is waiting for data, and to use that time to advance the processing of another job. The resulting increase in the computer's flexibility permitted many new management applications. We were developing a MIS when I was working for an oil company in Europe which I will call GLOBGAS. We were constantly pestering the president of the company, citing impressive reports from IBM and the *Harvard Business Review* about the benefits of computer management: "How can you possibly run this complex organization, Mr. President, without having around you a complete and up-to-date array of instruments, like the pilot of an airliner? We will tell you how sales are going, how many tankers are on their way to your refineries, and the current inventory levels of all your products. This way, you will be able to make rational decisions as soon as you get to your office in the morning."

What we did not know, of course, was that one doesn't run a large company by making rational decisions, and our president had much too high an opinion of both himself and his computer staff to take the trouble to explain that to us. But our project never seemed to get anywhere, and the explanation gradually dawned on me. Engineers make rational decisions because they have the luxury to run complete tests before designing a process or a product. Managers have no such luxury. They make decisions under stress and uncertainty. In the terminology of one school of brain research, great managers are often "right-brain types" who are highly intuitive and motivated by esthetic considerations, in contrast to the "left-brain types" working under them, who classify, optimize, plan, and compute.

Management systems built by computer engineers work excellently when they are used by other computer engineers, and they generally fail for the rest of the world. At GLOBGAS, it was fascinating to watch the operators wheeling heavy dollies out of the machine room, loaded with piles of management reports, and then to visit the higher floors where elegant executives were discussing Nabokov and Sartre over tea served by impeccable secretaries. Their offices were spotless and devoid of computer terminals or machine printouts. Clearly, there were two distinct cultures here with nothing in common. And there must be an intermediate level, somewhere, at which the computer information stops rising: there must be a dark office, in some recess of the building, where some little old fellow with a gray mustache and an ill-smelling pipe is stuffing tons and tons of computer listings into his green steel closet, thinking nostalgically of the pre-machine days and counting the hours until retirement.

The places where management systems have undoubtedly succeeded—and there are quite a few—are those places where a human communication system was already in existence. Here the computer was used to provide individual support for the managers, rather than to dictate an overall framework for their activity. There is a lesson to be learned here if we want to build new systems that realize the obvious promise of the computer.

The display was a grid with some circles and crosses in the boxes. The boy looked up at the screen and saw that the computer had managed to put three crosses in a row. He still had one turn and thought he could fool the program by a wild corner move.

The trick didn't work. The computer added a fourth cross and after that there was nothing the boy could do to prevent the machine from winning. At the Japanese game of GOMOKU, five marks in a straight line and you win. The computer flashed the whole screen a few times to emphasize its victory, then it cleared the display and wrote:

> YOU HAVE NOW LOST FIVE TIMES IN A ROW.
> I SHALL DEGRADE MY ABILITIES.

I watched the face of the boy. Eight years old. He knew that computers were just machines, and you're not supposed to cry in front of a machine. On the other hand, he knew he had lost and lost and lost and lost and lost to that dumb machine, and he found it very unfair. All his internal signals pointed to crying as the only thing to do under the circumstances. The conflict was clearly visible in his eyes, in the corners of his mouth, in the very tense forehead. He didn't cry after all. He knew that he would grow up. Some day he would beat the computer.

Education, linguistics, management: three areas where the magic of computers was badly over-extended and missed its target. The initial vision was perhaps valid, the dream was credible, but the timing was wrong. The technology was immature and the design that supposedly took *everything* into account had neglected that little detail: the social structure in which it was supposed to be operating. If those mistakes have been made so consistently in the past, is there any indication that things will go differently in the future? As computers take another giant step in power, and become so inexpensive that a machine with the capability of our IBM 650 at Paris Observatory in 1961 is within the financial range of every middle-class family in America, will the entire society have to live through the next series of blunders inflicted upon it by computer buffs? This question is increasingly being asked by business people, by politicians, and by sociologists, and it is obviously going to affect the rest of us as the explosion of computer-related products spreads through all levels of the population. Millions of people work in offices, and they are candidates to become the users of a new generation of machines being designed and built within the framework of "office automation." Yet the Office of the Future, as it is sometimes designated by the enthusiastic technologists, is being planned with the same lack of attention to the needs of human beings as the MIS of the Sixties.

With their power multiplied a thousandfold, their cost driven down, their reliability improved to the point at which mistakes can no longer be blamed on equipment failure because *there won't be* any equipment failures, computers are still responding to the same motivations and ignoring the same realities. They are attempting to take control of society, to take control of the human race. Computer hardware is not the social equalizer of the 1980s any more than electricity was the social equalizer of the 1880s. It is only when the designers themselves have recognized these effects of the technology, and have reshaped their attitudes toward the system they build, that the genuine benefits promised by the computers will be realized. I do not believe it will take very long for this to happen—perhaps 25 years, perhaps 50. But in the meantime, a lot of us will have to suffer through a bizarre and painful transition, and we may experience an unprecedented form of social restructuring for which nothing has prepared us.

The dream is still valid, however, provided we avoid the trap of the easy promises made by those who simply sell the machines, the "hardware." It takes more than electricity to activate a computer: it takes a *program*. That program reflects not only the assumptions of the programmer but also the biases and constraints of the entire society around him.

If computers are so painful sometimes, it is because they mirror a society that would rather not see its true face. By revealing the flaws and the ugliness, computers can, in the hands of good system designers, enlighten us and propose new alternatives— just as scraping the peeling old paint from an apparently ugly old house may reveal wonderful woodwork and suggest striking new color patterns. We have had the ingenuity to build this new technology over the last forty years. Now we need the courage to plan, to decide where it should take us, and that is a far more difficult and demanding task.

It is hard to characterize the kind of human society computers are promoting. Fortunately, many experts are working toward such a vision. Their forecasts range from the gloomy to the ecstatic.

The expression "Solid-State Society" was suggested to me by French cyberneticist Joel de Rosnay, on a dreary gray day in Paris when we were discussing the shape of future communications. It was his impression that the net result of using computers to link human beings together might not be the blissful flowering of creativity predicted by most American technologists, but, on the contrary, a cold and impersonal social reality in which human contact would be minimized. He was not predicting such a society, but he suggested that we look at it as one possible scenario, especially if energy and transportation costs rose out of bounds.

I prefer the expression "Digital Society" to describe what is happening to us. Digital logic is based on numbers. In a Digital Society, each person would be locked within a personal information space characterized by so many numbers there would be little chance left for genuine human contact. We might even end up living in some version of the world described by Forster[11] in "The Machine Stops": his characters spend their entire lives in little cells underground, supported by every imaginable form of communications, controlled and regulated by numbers.

In order to consider seriously the possibility of such a world, it is advisable to take a giant step *backward*, and to examine how communications have changed in the 500 years or so since Mr. Gutenberg came up with the printing press. Although 500 years sounds like a very long time, it is a small interval on the time-scale of history. Even shorter is the life of the telegraph, which came into existence 150 years ago. A memorandum prepared in 1978 by the investment firm of Solomon Brothers noted:[12]

> We have had telephones for 100 years, radio for 50 years, computers for 25 years, the commercial use of satellites for 10 years, and we are only in our first year in the use of optical fibers. Each of these new technologies has caused a major change in the way business was transacted and in the way people live.

Already, in 1838, the Commerce Committee of the House of Representatives had this to say about Samuel Morse's telegraph:[13]

> With the means of almost instantaneous communication of intelligence between the most distant points of the country, space will be, to all practical purposes of information, completely annihilated. The citizen will be invested with, and reduce to daily and familiar use, an approach to the high attribute of ubiquity, in a degree that the human mind, until recently, has hardly dared to contemplate seriously as belonging to human agency, from an instinctive feeling of religious reverence and reserve on a power of such awful grandeur.

Reading the above lines, it becomes obvious that in observing the new computer-based media we are witnessing the long-term effects of a revolution that never stopped. After the telegraph came the telephone. Simple as it seems to be, it has shaped our lives in peculiar ways that the giant telephone company prefers not to elucidate in too sharp detail. In a newspaper article entitled "Telephones in the Country," published about 1900, a writer named Wilbur Bassett had already noticed some effects of this form of communication:[14]

> A quiet revolution is taking place in Western country life, which promises to accomplish results within a year more important and far-reaching than any since the advent of the transcontinental railroads. Already the pioneer life of the isolated farmer has disappeared and the tide of industrial and education advance has swept over the Northwest . . . The telephone does away with the seclusion of rural life, binds together scattered communities, creates social interests, and destroys the barrier between city and country. Hence forth the country is but a vast suburb, in touch with the metropolis of its neighborhood, unified by the voice of one leader.

Bassett even foresaw some fundamental changes in economic roles, since the farmer would be able to keep in touch with the market and "dispose of produce directly to the city dealer or to the consumer without the assistance of any middleman."

We may wonder that so little attention has been directed in the last eighty years at an area of social research that seemed so rich. Of particular interest is the question of control. Is it always true, as Bassett implies, that increasing communication provides the individual with a better chance at economic and intellectual survival, and with more control over his own life? Or does it lead to greater uniformity and a concentration of control in the hands of even fewer people? Our society is answering the question with the latter: modern man, with all his telephones and his access to media, is less and less in control, more and more alienated.

On the social history of the telephone we have only anecdotes, and those not even systematically arranged. Of its psychological implications we know nothing. What subjects are discussed, today, that only the phone made possible? What opportunities are lost and, more importantly, what psychological types are we favoring and promoting, by making the ability to use the phone one of the tests of success? What cultural patterns have we created or changed? And what do we know about those people who refuse to subscribe to a telephone service, or use the device only to call others but do not pick it up when it rings?

When President Pompidou of France became so ill that he had to spend most of his time in his Paris apartment, instead of the Elysee Palace, he declined to have a direct telephone line installed. He was clearly aware of the ease with which telephones can be tapped, but he also had an inborn resistance to the use of the device. His predecessor, Charles de Gaulle, hated it to the point of phobia. Yet these men ran a major country for many years. They faced and solved important crises. Today, in every major city, there are hundreds or even thousands of sophisticated people who hold important jobs, and can afford a telephone, but refuse to use it. Tomorrow the same people may be the hard-core resisters to the home computer movement.

Expressing thoughts through a phone is not always as simple as we assume: witness the difficulty the phone company had in its early years to get businessmen to accept the device. In a newspaper article published about 1900 by Angus Hibbard, General Manager of the Chicago Telephone Company, I find the observation that "the man who knows how to use a telephone properly is comparatively a rare personage." The article goes on with some technical pointers ("the lips should not be an inch away from the rim of the receiver and the voice should beat squarely upon the drum to which the little sound hopper leads"). It also recognizes that lack of mental focus is the real trouble in electronic communication. What Hibbard said on this subject eighty years ago is still valid for our most advanced electronic media:[14]

> If your thought is not concentrated on the transmission of your message you will not make yourself heard or hear what is said to you. This is where a failure to realize that you are holding actual conversation is apparent. No person understands this phase of telephonic trouble better than the operator of long-distance lines, where conversations are important and comparatively expensive, and time is limited. He knows that, in case the two on

the line do not readily hear each other, he must make each realize he is not talking into a hole in the end of an iron arm, but speaking into the ear of a man.

Hibbard goes on to illustrate his observation with an interesting anecdote. When he was in charge of long-distance lines, he was once asked to establish communication between a Baltimore businessman and a Boston financier for a discussion which involved thousands of dollars.

> The Boston man seated himself at the instrument, in my office, and waited for me to get the Baltimore capitalist properly started. At the first sound of the latter's voice I knew he was "not there" mentally speaking. Then I resorted to the usual expedients to impress on him the realization that he was talking with a person instead of at an inanimate object.
> "Don't hear a word! This thing is ———— !" he was saying.
> "I'm not a thing, Mr. Smith," I interrupted. "I am a man, about thirty years old, prematurely bald, with dark hair and gray eyes. I can hear you because I know you're a real, live man doing business with your voice, right now."

Early users of the telephone thus resisted the device because it created a mental barrier between the two speakers. This problem was overcome only when it was fully understood that the voice at the other end of the telephone was that of a human being. We are still waiting for computers to acquire this human touch, to solve their human equation. Instead, the development of their sophisticated applications since the 1960s, in business management, in education, or in artificial intelligence, has often taken the form of blatant overselling camouflaged under layers of false intellectual veneer. That such a process could lead us to the evil aspects of a "Digital Society" is a clear possibility as the technology explodes into the life of the average family. The increasing standardization of the information people use to guide their lives can bring with it increased uniformity and increased control. An environment can be created which makes human contact a transient, unemotional affair. There would be little commitment to others. Values and attitudes would be encouraged which would decrease people's attention spans even below today's limited ability to pursue a given goal. The fantastic acceleration of the rate of research, in all fields, would create an inebriating sense of constant novelty, but much of this novelty would be faked. Computerized hype would raise the rate of obsolescence not only of manufactured products but also of software, and even of that ultimate software, human life.

In an extreme form of "Digital Society" our civilization would become nothing more than a giant, clean, well-ordered Disney World, where Presidents, activated by invisible machines, get up and make predictable speeches before well-behaved children whose every possible move has been anticipated; a world where the flow of the crowd from a fake jungle adventure to a phony Native American tribal dance is monitored by machines, with meticulous obsession to insure that enough toilet paper, enough Coke bottles, and enough security guards will be present along their path. The computers also dispatch enough actors dressed as Mickey Mouse and Pluto to give every man, woman and child an equal chance to shake hands with his or her favorite myth.

There are interesting alternatives to the Digital Society. I like to think that computers will be used to support the diversity of cultures and lifestyles that I find stimulating and wonderful on this earth. Far from reducing these cultures to their basest elements and dictating their paths, the computer can be a tool furthering their diversity and ability to invent and survive. I see them as the new medium through which creative electronic grapevines can grow around the old systems.

We may hope, before we become trapped in a digital world, that we will have understood why truly great thoughts seem to arise in solitude, and sometimes in sorrow. And we may hope that the search for quality will have encouraged the grapevines to grow and flourish.

CHAPTER THREE
The Rude Awakenings of Minerva Narrowshelf

About Colette's vacation in Brittany, the death of a dog in Chicago, a general strike in Paris, and a strange line in Macbeth. A review of the strengths and weaknesses of computer data bases. The author finally reveals why a husband is always bigamous if there is a pet in his house that does not belong to a particular child.

Our society is obsessed with data. We fill out questionnaires, we answer surveys, we read public opinion polls, we teach our kids to index and quantify. Information is control. But is it?

In her "Reminiscences," the French writer Colette describes a vacation she took in Brittany one year with a family friend who was a cataloger at Paris' impressive Bibliotheque Nationale. The weather was often inclement, and then he would stay inside the hotel, filling out index cards with painstaking accuracy. The amazing fact was that he did it without any sources or documents. When questioned about his undertaking, he stated flatly that he was working on the Master Catalog.

"You mean you know all these titles by heart?" asked Colette, who was very impressed and ready to believe her friend was a genius.

"Of course not," he replied. "You see, I have noticed that we were sadly lacking in German manuscripts of the 13th and 14th century, and in certain autographs, so I am making up entries for imaginary works that might very well have existed."

"But how can you do such a thing?" she insisted indignantly. "The actual books haven't even been written!"

"Ah, but you can't expect me to do everything!" answered the catalog specialist with a shrug.

The story gives us some insight into both the greatness and the fallacy of information systems in general and data bases in particular, a subject whose hidden ramifications are well worth an entire chapter. People build data bases for the wrong reasons and use them in ways that entirely defeat their purpose, though the computer may, in an apparent flash of mechanical insight, occasionally hit upon some correlation that the data-base user chooses to call "relevant."

At the local library, Miss Narrowshelf plugs in her terminal and wonders, what could be more rational than the creation of large files describing the attributes of any situation we wish to understand better, to study, to document? The answer is that nothing is wrong with such files, of course, as long as one realizes that information is *control* and that the problem doesn't end with the identification of the data and its storage in the machine. The real problem, once again, is quality. Quality of access, and quality of data. In the late 1960s, when I became actively involved in database systems, the development of the technique appeared certain: all the forecasts said that storage devices (such as magnetic disks and core memories) would become progressively cheaper, that the development of operating systems would enable remote users to get instant answers to their queries, and that computer networks, then at the early design stage, would make the Library of Congress potentially accessible from every home. The forecasters went on to predict revolutions in science education, in business, in publishing, in lifestyle and workstyle. It was taken for granted that the software necessary to make these systems run would soon be available and posed no difficult problem. Everybody concentrated on the tangible, and salable, components: the shiny boxes with the little lights that constitute the visible part of the computing art. Again, the myth of computer hardware as a social equalizer.

Today it is apparent that information systems have not lived up to their promise. The computer industry has sold us the sizzle, but we are still waiting for the steak. This standstill in progress is reflected in a dialogue between Congressman Daddario and Dr. Adkinson, then Head of the Office of Science Information Systems at the National Science Foundation, when the latter was testifying before a Congressional subcommittee in March 1969:

Adkinson: It takes several years to begin one of these systems and get it to the place where it can operate effectively on a regular basis. It is not a matter of one or two years. It is a matter of five or ten years in many cases.

Daddario: Have you encountered more of a problem than you expected in the first place? Is there more experimentation than you expected when you began this activity?

Adkinson: Yes; I think the problem of effectively using the computer in the information process was very much underrated; that is, people thought they could do it much faster and easier.

Even in critical areas of economic life—for example, in the compilation of vital information on mining and the availability of basic mineral resources in the United States—progress on data bases is dismal. Officials are increasingly concerned. In June 1973, for instance, the National Commission on Materials Policy reported that[15]

> The data-bases now used in processing reports on mineral resources are, unfortunately, limited in number and highly specialized in application. None permits a comprehensive evaluation of the materials flow. Consequently, critical decisions on materials proceed without full benefit of the resources of information now latent, for the most part, in uncoordinated files.

This kind of failure is surprising when one considers the staggering investment made in the acquisition and storage of data. This expense surpasses, in many cases, the cost of hardware (computers) and software (the programs) combined. But then how can so many "computer hobby" shops advertise access to systems that provide "thousands of data bases" at the touch of a button? Why are civil rights activists worried about criminal files? What is all the excitement among right-wing extremists about the "imminent" creation of a computing center that could keep track of all our economic moves through the identification of every citizen on earth? And what can we realistically expect from the information systems that are being built? These are the kinds of questions I want to review from the perspective of someone who, for ten years, has lived with data bases and with the intricacies of their implementation on several computer systems. The lessons I have learned are not simply technical: I feel that they have taught me something about myself and about information as a social commodity that I did not know before. They have also opened my eyes to some exciting new possibilities in the human use of information machines.

It seems to me that the prime fallacy of computer "information retrieval" is found, very simply, in the term itself: you cannot "retrieve" information from a computer for the simple reason that you cannot *store* information in a computer in the first place! All you can ever store in a computer is DATA, and the relationship between data and information is a fundamental mystery. *Data* turns into *information* through a process no scientist has bothered to describe, because it is much too complicated and beyond formulation with the tools we have. The transformation works for a given person at a given time, with the obvious result that what is information to Mr. Jones on a particular day is not information to anyone else, and may not even be information to Mr. Jones the following Tuesday.

Another strange property of the process is found in the fact that data turns into information only *when someone asks a question about it.* Therefore, the real information is in the *question*, not inside the computer. But then how can I, as a programmer, design an efficient information system unless I can absolutely predict all the questions that will be asked, and anticipate the process by which I will provide an answer?

It is the question that provides the organization of the data and provokes the recognition of it as "information" in the mind of the user. This is true, curiously enough, even if the question has no answer. When a theologian asks, "Is God dead?" he forces us to reevaluate our construction of the whole universe of data we carry about the human world. Yet he is providing no new element. He simply challenges our organization of the facts, whether or not we happen to believe that there is such an entity as "God."

From the above observations (that you can only store data, that data turns into information for a particular user only, and that the information resides mostly in the question itself), it follows that we cannot talk about data bases in any abstract way. We need to specify exactly what we are doing: what we have in mind to store, how often the data base will change, what the purpose of the system is, who will use it, and what other processes it will affect within the organization it serves and within the society at large. These questions are seldom asked by programmers, who have enough problems deciding which computer language to use.

A survey of the state of the art conducted in May 1969 by the CODASYL group, a top-level committee of industry experts, disclosed no less than nine major efforts to create "generalized" data-base management systems. Ten years later, the experts were still arguing, there was no standardization on the horizon, and a major new argument between the advocates of so-called "self-contained" systems and those of "embedded" languages had driven the field to an impasse. IBM, meanwhile, had embarked on the implementation of "relational" data bases which represented yet another approach to the whole mess. Add to these problems the fact that implementation decisions are generally irreversible, because a company that begins storing its files under System A cannot, at a later data, change its mind and convert to System B, and you have a state of affairs that is a marketing man's dream and a user's nightmare.

Let us assume for a moment that you are Mr. User and I am the friendly guy in charge of your computer operations. You have just decided to computerize the entire inventory of the firm, which consists of 4,376 different types of screws, 3,098 kinds of bolts with matching nuts, all available in seven colors. As we discuss these requirements in your office, it occurs to me that I would be a very lousy programmer indeed if I couldn't build you a system that would keep that information current for you, especially if your questions are completely predictable. After all, we agree on our definitions of the objects to be stored. A screw is a screw and a bolt is a bolt. If you want a report on your desk every Tuesday morning listing the available number of each item by color, I would be a very bad computer man if I couldn't do it. But this is not the general situation in the world of data bases. The general situation is more likely to be the following:

You call me into your office, and after complaining bitterly about the bad weather and the fact that the photocopy machine is still unavailable, you gesture vaguely toward the next room where three rows of four-drawer filing cabinets extend far into the distance. As we take cognizance of the gaggles of young secretaries collecting periodically in the vicinity of these cabinets, opening and closing drawers, removing files and making new entries, you allude to the fact that the sales manager for this particular half of the United States is going crazy. He has been trying to find out where the orders are and what kinds of products customers are buying. The financial department, meanwhile, has issued stern warnings about the impending disaster of a complete audit to reconcile 15,000 unverified accounts, and the production people are swamped with contradictory facts about customer requirements for the manufacture of the next batch of products. Having therefore decided to "put everything on the computer" as a result of a two-day workshop for executives you recently attended in Acapulco at the invitation of IBM, you are giving me the opportunity to save the company in the next three or four days, by storing all this under "some sort of data-base system."

The discussion continues with my request for a few humble facts: How often will you wish to extract information from the computer? In what form? How often will the information change?

You imply, with a magnificent sweep of the right hand that has justly earned you the envy of all the racquet-ball players in the executive club, that my questions are quite irrelevant, since the requirements for information will change as we go along. It is even possible that the answers to one question will lead you to think of another question, or even to rethink the structure of the entire file.

I now have several choices. I can quit on the spot and take my brother-in-law's offer of a job in his candle-making shop in Sausalito. I can smile knowingly and assure you that the job will be done next week, knowing full well that in a job like yours the stress is so great that you may not survive beyond the weekend. Or I can go gack to my cubicle and hide behind piles of computer listings, to ponder the situation and try to build a program that will at least give the appearance of responding to your needs, thereby postponing the time of the real catastrophe. Since computer programmers are, on the whole, a rather professional and dedicated bunch with overinflated egos, I am very likely to take the last course and thereby plunge you into irreversible trouble. The system I will produce will look and act like a true data-base system. It will take a year or two and an entire department to feed the data contained in your three rows of filing cabinets into the computer, and since programmers are highly mobile, by that time I will have joined the compiler group of a large plastic cork manufacturer on the opposite coast. My successor, in his turn, will create a team of fifteen systems experts entirely dedicated to the aggrandizement of my system, which will answer fewer and fewer of your needs as they "improve" it. By then, your destiny inside the company inextricably linked to the system itself, you will be the firm's number one stumbling block and all-around bottleneck, holding in your power the production, finance, and sales departments. You will spend increasingly long hours in depressing meetings with the president of the company, and from computer failure to computer failure you stand a good chance of being promoted for the dedication and obstinacy you are showing in the face of adversity.

Don't laugh if this little scenario reminds you of someone you know. It has been enacted in many companies, as the "Management Information Systems" of the 1960s caved in under changing product requirements, increasing competition, personnel moves, and their basic inability to answer the needs of the managers who requested the systems. Many computer salesmen have become rich in the process, and innumerable pieces of admirable hardware have been manufactured and wheeled out the doors of IBM, CDC, Honeywell, and dozens of other companies. Nobody has made a cent on software, of course, although it would seem that the real problem resides in the programming tools we provide to the users. And the results have been pretty funny.

The amazing thing, of course, is that some systems DO work. For example, *The New York Times* has a file of all its articles which can be consulted by the media across the country (though it takes a while to become familiar with its rather complicated jargon, as shown in the following figure). Organizations such as NASA and Lockheed maintain extensive data bases of technology-oriented papers. These systems usually work for some years and for a particular community of users, but they are highly vulnerable to changes in their environment. When the language changes, it is difficult for the system to follow because the search through the files requires an extremely efficient index. Yet the terms in the index can only approximate what the customer will want. When I did a search on the new word "PULSAR" in 1973, the index of the NASA-RECON data base yielded only 700 entries, while a complete search of the file found the term in over 2,000 papers or items. In this particular case, the index (which has to be updated manually) was lagging almost a year behind the actual material in the files. Such problems are quite common.

When the user community comes up with a new word like ECOLOGY, dozens of thousands of entries stored under BIOLOGY, MEDICINE, METEROLOGY, or PHYSICS have to be re-assigned. The process is labor intensive and, by all available measures, extremely messy. Yet librarians and other information "experts" generally behave as if the data they are guarding will be good forever in its current structure, and they make no provisions to revise their

```
* * PLEASE RE-DO.  TYPE W FOR EXPLANATORY MESSAGE. * *

W⁻ * * PLEASE RE-DO.  TYPE W FOR EXPLANATORY MESSAGE. * *

⁻W⁻VIEW NEXT PAGE OF ABSTACTS. TYPE: B.

SKIP TO PARTICULAR ABSTRACT. TYPE B//ABSTRACT NUMBER.
END INQUIRY. TYPE: C.
DEFERRED PRINT: PRINT ALL ABSTRACTS. TYPE: D.
    PRINT ABSTRACTS SELECTIVELY: TYPE A//ABSTRACT NUMBER//ETC.
(C)NYTIMES.SEE ABSTRACT FOR YEAR.NONTIMES MATERIAL BY PERMISSION
⁻    1 OF  102 NYT/JNL 1977-10- 8    :    4:  3 4/WGT    3/LIN
    281-77-48                              1388727/IDN
GRENADIAN PRIME MIN SIR ERIC M GAIRY CALLS FOR UN DEBATE ON
UNIDENTIFIED FLYING OBJECTS, SPEECH BEFORE GENERAL ASSEMBLY:
REACTION OF DELEGATES IS DESCRIBED AS SOMNOLENT (S)
```

Figure 2. Example of an entry in *The New York Times* data base—hardly the kind of crisp information the user would like to have "at his fingertips."

systems. They do not suspect that the very organization of their data promotes certain queries and discourages others. As we are all, in a way, the librarians of our minds and the indexers of the facts of our own lives, we may learn a few lessons from the few successes, and the many failures, of computer information systems.

The genuine benefits to be derived from computers are most visible, perhaps, in the field of medicine. Between 1964 and 1967, I spent a lot of time around hospitals, building data-base systems that taught me more about the use of machines than all the courses I had taken in school. The difference between *data* and *information* is especially clear in the medical field, because of the diversity of specialization that goes into the creation of a patient record.

In a modern hospital, for instance, we may find a single record for Mr. Whipple, who underwent an operation in May. The data in the record will be used by three different types of people: an administrator will want to know how many beds were in use that month, a nurse will want to know if Mr. Whipple's X-rays have come back, and a medical researcher will be looking for possible correlations between symptoms and complications among patients having undergone the same treatment as Mr. Whipple (see Figure 3). Here it is easy to verify that, for people in the same community, what constitutes information for one may be meaningless to another. The same record has to be extracted in at least three different formats to become meaningful to each separate specialist.

It doesn't take long for the information scientist who works with people in such a diversity of fields to realize that data-base systems represent centers of power, both to their designers and to their users. Patterns of control change drastically from one organization or profession to the next. In the field of health, you find that medical practitioners generally share their data, but surgeons do not. Even within a narrow discipline such as heart transplantation, in which a naive computer man assumes the care of the patient would demand the pooling of all available data, there are overwhelming parochial differences. In the United States, no common system in this field has evolved. All this is happening beyond the knowledge of the public, of administrators, and even of most doctors, because the subject is engulfed in a technical jargon

Figure 3. There is no way to store information in a computer; only data can be stored. Data are converted into information for a particular user at a particular time.

which is made to appear very complicated. I want to demonstrate that there is no need for this apparent complexity, and that some good common sense, supported by the lessons of experience, should enable anybody to understand the basic problems at hand.

The computer is located in the physiology department of a large medical school. I load my program and we watch the figures coming out. We are running a simulation of the cardiovascular system. The columns of numbers represent ventricles pumping blood, vessels expanding, lungs breathing inside the mathematical "model" that tabulates blood pressure and volume throughout the system. Dr. Swanson puts on his white coat and leaves the room. I remain at the console and I keep my hand on the switch that will feed the real data into the machine.

Above the racks of electronic equipment is a glass panel. On the other side of the glass is an operating room with a surgical table. I see Dr. Swanson walking and talking with an aide who has just connected a tube with a measuring device to the aorta of the "patient." On the table, restrained by leather straps, is a large dog with its chest open. The measuring instruments provide readings that are converted into digital impulses. The cables go through the partition and into my side of the facility. A hundred times a second, pressure and volume data from the dog's heart and lungs are fed into the program and compared with the model, which recomputes all the parameters in time for the next data—one hundredth of a second later. The project is designed to uncover new properties of the human cardiovascular system. Dogs, in this respect, are very close to humans: the physiology of their circulation and respiration approximates ours, and city streets are full of stray animals. This one has been "put to sleep" like many of his unfortunate comrades, but before dying it will play an important and unconscious (as well as painless) part in checking some of man's assumptions about the functions of the body. It is helping to create a data base of physiological parameters that may someday help cardiac patients everywhere.

Dr. Richard is a surgeon in the cardiology department at Children's Hospital, and he has an unusual problem. His patients are typically a few hours, at most a few days, old. They are children born with severe heart defects and he has to diagnose their problem in a very short time. Yet, as he explains to me, the heart of the infant does not follow the normal patterns of adults. In fact, some features of the electrocardiogram of normal newborns would rush a 50-year-old man to the nearest hospital. Under those conditions, how can you recognize the abnormal situations that sometimes uniquely distinguish the little patient from the norm, and warrant special emergency procedures? It is a terrible responsibility to perform massive chest surgery on a newborn baby when a careful study of the symptoms could have revealed other forms of treatment. Only experience could provide the answers, and the experience was housed in thousands of case files bulging with charts and records. In a normal hospital there might be time to search through these manual files for guidance, but the newborn did not afford this luxury. Besides, the tiny patient, by definition, had no medical history, nothing to fall back on in the way of a precedent.

Dr. Richard wanted a computer data base of heart surgery performed on infants, some six thousand records. He felt it would become a research resource and would enable student surgeons to review diagnostics and symptoms, procedures and complications, in specific types of operations they were studying. The system would also satisfy the increasingly tight requirements for legal records on all surgery.

Dr. Richard was a wonderful man and he was very kind to my naive questions about his work. Realizing that most of my previous experience had been in astronomy and physics, he explained to me that he did not regard his activity as "science." He had but little time to think. The unit he ran functioned like the pit at an auto race. His job was to wait for the car that might come limping in at any instant, to fix it as well and as fast as he could, and to release it again to the mad currents of life. He operated daily on babies with malformations of the heart system, he saved many lives and lost others. The mood of our discussions was sometimes fairly grim, because the file records had names evoking pain and grief; it didn't take long to realize that responding to his needs would involve more than the application of an academic exercise.

One of the areas in which we disagreed was the advisability of using codes, and it was a strange discussion because we were each on the opposite side of the position our backgrounds would suggest. He wanted everything reduced to numbers because he thought that was "more scientific," and I was insisting that he should keep all the verbal information he could in plain, ordinary English. My point was that codes would blur or destroy valuable clues contained in the observations of the doctor or nurse. If she remarked that the patient looked pale, who knows if that computer entry might trigger, in the memory of a user, a case in which that particular remark had special significance? Who knows what connections it might establish in the mind of a gifted researcher? I finally won that argument, although keeping entries in English made the files larger and thus somewhat more costly in storage.

The day came to test the system. Dr. Richard entered a combination of symptoms at the keyboard. He appeared to be looking for a patient with very low blood pressure and an absurd combination of other symptoms. I was confused by his request as I showed him how to process it. In a matter of seconds, the computer (a big CDC 6400) brought up one case, the record of a little girl. Under the heading DIAGNOSTIC was the simple phrase: LIGATURE ON AORTA. Dr. Richard reached for the OFF switch on the terminal without bothering to instruct the program to stop, much to the alarm of the computer technicians watching us. He said he was "sold" and didn't need to see any more. This particular girl, he explained, had provided one of his most dramatic moments. Brought to his facility after surgery at another hospital, she was obviously at the point of death. Her symptoms were absurd and her blood pressure terribly low. He knew of similar cases in the archives but had no time to search for them. Instead, he decided to operate right away to discover the source of the problem. He found that the previous surgeon, confused during an operation on transposed great vessels, had mistakenly placed a ligature on the aorta, effectively cutting off the supply of blood to the patient's body.

Doctors' preoccupation with numbers and codes, in the name of scientific appearance, has led to some amusing entries in medical data bases. A lot of medical information is the result of subjective judgment rather than an exact measurement. Hence the medical personnel's faith in the "accuracy" of the computer is sometimes reflected in an obsession for fancy coding systems that have no real meaning.

A physician specializing in urology once related to me his frustration with medical administrators who kept requesting a three-digit code for a device he had invented. The dispute escalated into a major argument, which he lost. His gadget had to do with the treatment of venereal disease in its advanced stages, which he had sometimes found among the city's prostitutes. It was designed to be inserted into the vagina to raise the local temperature. Accordingly, the frustrated physician designated the two variants of his device PW1 and PW2, and the administrators were happy to list them under these codes, without further explanation, in their files and catalogs. The physician recalls, with a chuckle, that his codes stand for "Pussy Warmer number 1" and "Pussy Warmer number 2."

When I proposed to an eminent astronomer that I build a system to answer English-language questions about a catalog of stars, he shook his head and said he didn't think it would work, but was willing to let me try. The system, called ALTAIR, was up and running six months later, but its very existence revealed some strange patterns among the astronomers who were supposed to use it, and who had at first supported its creation with enthusiasm.

This happened in 1965, when a few specialists in artificial intelligence were beginning to demonstrate systems that processed (and in some cases could even assign meaning to) English sentences. One such system was BASEBALL, created at MIT. It answered questions about recent scores, such as "Did the Red Sox win in Dallas?" Other programs, such as Joseph Weizenbaum's ELIZA, would take statements from the user and try to carry on a conversation, while Ken Colby's PARRY simulated a paranoid patient.[16]

Much earlier, a French Canadian named Jean Baudot had already used a small computer to compose poems, and he had asked a number of literary figures to react to these poems and to comment on the random sparks created by the word images the machine had produced. My purpose was quite different. As an astronomer, the problem that interested me was the interrogation in English of large star catalogs, and that was the task to which ALTAIR was applied.

It can be argued that astronomers were the first custodians of a data base compiled for the purpose of increasing human knowledge. The priests of Mesopotamia who first listed the bright stars were compiling a data base which became unmanageable when the invention of the telescope exploded the visible universe. The spots of light in the sky sorted themselves out into stars, planets, clusters, galaxies and nebulae, and scientists had to spend endless days and months going through many volumes of the catalogs, pencil in hand, to compile the information needed for their research.

When some of these catalogs were put on computer tapes, the astronomers had another problem. They had to hire programmers to write the software that would extract the data in the appropriate format. The programmers rarely knew anything about astronomy, and the result was a mess. I owe my first job in the U.S. to this situation. Under contract with NASA at the University of Texas, I compiled a catalog of galaxies, and later recorded Mars observations to produce a better map of the planet for the Mariner project.

Contrary to what common sense and ordinary vision would indicate, the stars are not something you can describe simply by their position and brightness. Where the eye sees a single point of light, there may in fact be an incredibly complex system. One entry in the Catalog of Bright Stars, for example, is the star CASTOR. In reality it consists of three stars spinning around each other, and closer study reveals that each one is a double star, so that the computer has to describe the position, magnitude, color, interrelationships, and motions of six individual stars, spinning together in some kind of mad dance! In such a data base, can we always separate the structure from the data?

The astronomers who were my colleagues at the time encouraged me to build ALTAIR. They would be able to ask questions like: "What is the percentage of spectroscopic binaries among stellar systems bluer than F2?" Or "How many stars having a spectrum between G0 and K2 are triple?" The language was perhaps a bit more obscure, but certainly more scientifically useful than baseball scores from last Sunday. ALTAIR worked in three parts. The first part had an English dictionary and a syntax recognizer. It took out the plurals, looked up verbs and nouns, and reduced the question to basic concepts. (The two words, "spectroscopic binary," for example, would reduce to a single concept designated by a number.) The second part was concerned with meaning. ALTAIR was capable of throwing out irrelevant or trivial questions, because the test of such a system is not only its ability to give the right answer to a meaningful question, but also to avoid giving a misleading answer to a meaningless question. Thus, if you asked, "What proportion of stars are stars?" it would answer "100%" without actually triggering a search to find the answer. If the question were valid, however, it would generate a formula for answer retrieval. It was the third part of the program that took the formula and ran through the entire catalog of some 10,000 stars, to find the correct answer by looking up their characteristics. But how could it go beyond these basic tasks?

It is during the month of March that Chicago receives the greatest amount of snowfall. At the end of the day, when I was working on ALTAIR, it wasn't rare for me to find the entire parking lot covered with a beautiful, pure layer of white fluff, and where little undulations marked the cars patiently waiting to be wiped and scraped free of their evening coat of ice.

After one especially fierce battle with the elements, I had managed to free one frozen door and most of the windshield of my little car. I crawled on the front seat to start the engine, and at that same instant the radio came on. An authoritative male voice uttered one sentence:

"THE STEELS ARE SOFT."

Then it paused. During that pause I actually felt my brain racing in circles, looking for context and meaning, finding none, racing again. THE STEELS ARE SOFT. In the frozen isolation of my car I was helpless to grasp any part of the sentence, and I suddenly understood how the computer must "feel," if it had feelings, about some of the questions I was trying to make it answer.

The reporter resumed his reading at last. "The Dow Jones average fell two points in response to pessimistic news about the price of metals . . . " Suddenly I had enough context to go back and understand the softness of the steels. But in that brief pause I had understood something new about my own handling of language, and I knew how I could now make my program handle the questions of the astronomers.

ALTAIR was a great success for about three weeks. It was entirely adequate and had no bugs, although its dictionary was rather restricted. If you were to ask, "Where is the nearest coffee-house?" it would tell you it didn't know what a "coffee-house" was.

After much initial curiosity, ALTAIR fell into disuse at the Observatory and it was completely forgotten. Although this didn't affect my work at the time, which was theoretical rather than applied, I was frankly a little piqued by this result and tried to find the cause. One of the astronomers who apparently needed ALTAIR most finally told me why he had returned to the old method of writing his own program every time he needed information: he had recently mastered a computer language and was so thrilled at his new skill (which was irrelevant to his astronomical research) that the thought of the computer directly answering a request in English discouraged him. He preferred to run the tape through a different program each time, which meant a full day to answer each question. The idea that ALTAIR could generate the same program *internally*, and execute it in seconds, appeared to him as an insult to his mind and skill.

The ALTAIR experience taught me two principles:
(1) What the user requests is not necessarily what the user wants, and
(2) An information system is, first and foremost, a social system.

I also learned, as a free by-product, that there is something akin to religious fascination in the first contact with a machine that gives the appearance of understanding us. In a system where the quality of the data is impeccable, the genuine power of the computer is a threat so direct and so close to us that the intended users develop effective strategies to sabotage its application.

A case in point is the lack of recognition afforded computer science among established academic disciplines.

In the summer of 1966, my wife and I went to Moscow for the International Mathematics Congress, and for the first time in history the published agenda included an acknowledgment of computer sciences as a genuine branch of knowledge. There was even some mention of a tour of computer facilities in the Moscow area.

We arrived late, the bus drove endlessly through the suburbs of the city, and we finally reached the huge, pyramid-shaped university building where we had our lodgings—a monstrosity of the Stalinist era which a topologist in our party lovingly called "the old shack." Our group was hungry, but the man from INTOURIST told us bluntly there would be no food until the next morning, and that fasting was good for us. The next day we ate, and we were ready to see Russian computers. We gathered before the desk of an impressive-looking official, who got up when he heard our request and gave us an answer in Russian we all understood:

MACHINI? NIET!

I was greatly disappointed, because I had gone to the trouble of converting a program for the calculation of star motions into a computer language I knew the Russians, as well as most European scientists, were using. I thought my little deck of IBM cards could open some avenue of conversation with Russian computer scientists, and perhaps help me put the final touches on my graduate work. So I ignored the impressive-looking official and went to the nearby observatory, finally discovering some students who did have an interest in pursuing our discussions. They advised us to contact the University of Moscow. Thanks to them, the next day there was a tour of the University's computer facility, and I found that about twenty-five other people had come to the Congress with the same specific interest in computers that had brought us there.

The Russian computers we saw were primitive by Western standards, but the really surprising moment came when the Russian specialists gathered eagerly around my little deck of cards. It was not the program that interested them, but the way in which the information could be punched into the 80 columns of the IBM card and also printed out at the top. They explained to me that in Russia, the computer cards (which happen to be the same size, thickness, and shape as an IBM card) are always punched in such a way as to "waste" as little space as possible. To do this they have to put more than one character in each column, and this makes it impossible for them to print out the contents. As a result, they can never tell visually what's in a particular card. They have carried the "rational" utilization of the technology to the degree where the human being's capability to read the information (and to detect errors by visual checks) has been eliminated. They have fallen into the same trap as the French police officers who shot Francois and the medical administrators who wanted codes for devices whose functions they ignored. In the name of efficiency they have abandoned the human quality of the data.

This feature of the Russian system also made it impossible to run my little program through their computers, although it was written in a so-called "universal" language which grave scientists had spent years defining in their international meetings. The lesson I learned from that visit had to do with the difficulty of bridging cultural gaps through technology—even when the same tools were applied to similar tasks. The following year I had a chance to verify this fact again when I returned to France, and looked at French industry through the eyes of an Americanized Parisian.

In 1967, I went back to France with a great job in Paris. The GLOBGAS corporation was going to reorganize its data bases as part of a major "MIS" effort, and I was hired to implement the new system. Since I had created a new compiler for a language called INFOL, invented at Control Data by Bill Olle, I was anxious to adapt it for the GLOBGAS computers and improve the technique, which was powerful enough to manage the files of an oil company. I was going back convinced that if France lagged behind the U.S., that was solely due to a technological and financial gap. It took me six months to realize that my employer was a big company even by American standards, that it had access to technologies that most American corporations would envy, and that it was financially affluent enough to maintain a computing center with thousands of square feet right off the Champs-Elysees. It had the most expensive real estate in Paris, 250 programmers, and the latest UNIVAC monsters in the basement. The gap between these tools and the results they achieved was not technological or financial. It was mental, and it directly related to perceptions of information systems as social systems, and to the open resistance that a stubborn organization could oppose to a new idea. I remember my short stay there in four little vignettes that summarize the problems that the company, and in fact the whole country, experienced, as they tried to adapt to that alien creation: the computer.

Scene 1. Monsieur Martin calls me into his office. I need his approval to convert the file of service stations under a new database system. He doesn't believe it can be done. I tell him that I have studied the current program that manages the sales data. If you know the access code of a particular service station, the computer will regurgitate everything there is to know about it—how many geraniums grow next to the ladies room and how much premium gasoline was sold last year. But if all you know is that the name of the manager was DUPONT in 1961, you have to call two secretaries into the office, give them pencils, and let them read the entire file until they find DUPONT. So why can't the computer itself look for DUPONT? Ah, but no, Monsieur Vallee, that would using the computer for a name search, don't you see, and that would be, how shall we say, "linguistic"? Computers are primarily for numerical operations, Monsieur Vallee, and everybody (except, perhaps, a few visionary young expatriates returning from America with wild ideas) knows that computers can perform only numerical operations. There follow, for good measure, a few quotations from Kierkegaard regarding destiny and some allusions to the concept of the Self in Sartre, and Monsieur Martin rests his case.

Now I try to explain to him that I haven't looked up Kierkegaard in a long time, but inside a computer a name is represented by a number anyway, and for the machine to search for D, U, P, O, N, T is exactly the same thing as searching for 02, 35, 61, 72, 55, and 64. In fact, the poor computer absolutely cannot tell the difference.

Monsieur Martin would have none of that. If the machine could find DUPONT, that would be linguistic, so he knows there's something fishy about my concept, since "the Americans" have demonstrated that such an operation was impossible. He has obviously read a garbled version of the U.S. report against machine translation in some intellectual journal like *Le Monde*. I withdraw.

Scene 2. I learn of an amusing consequence of the inaccuracy of our old file system. The company, which owns thousands of pieces of real estate in France in anticipation of its need for new service stations, has picked a nice location on the Cote d'Azur where the computer indicated we owned a desirable street corner. We have sent in the bulldozers to raze an old shack and a few olive trees in order to erect on the property a first-class service station.

Two months later, a shabby old man arrives by the late train from Paris with two battered suitcases, looking forward to his annual vacation. He is surprised to find two bright red gas pumps where the old olive trees used to spread their friendly shade over his leisurely dreams: he is the actual owner of the property, and is seriously upset. He is hastily relocated in a coastal palace, and soon finds himself the proud owner of a brand new home where he will be able to retire in peace. So who says that computer errors are always harmful?

Scene 3. The man who hired me to change the file systems has made too many waves, and when pressured to resign has gone to work for a consulting firm. Our company is so scared of data bases that it will not even create a group by that name, deemed "too emotional"! It ends up creating a group called "basic data." The managers have taken six months to achieve this play on words. Things have moved fast in other areas, however: there is growing international demand for better software within our sister companies. I am sent to Holland to represent GLOBGAS-France at a meeting that also includes GLOBGAS-UK, Deutsche-GLOBGAS, and other related organizations. The meeting lasts two days and concludes with an exceptionally fine dinner at an executive's home in a suburb of Amsterdam. Our host goes around the table to ask each of us what we feel is the best investment the company can make in the computer field. The answer from each expert is "a generalized data-base system." Our host looks very stern and there is silence.

Then he states, "I understand your needs, and the Group is aware of this requirement. But we are not in the software business. We are in the oil business."

We bow our heads, as befits young and well-educated European engineers when the boss has spoken. But there is a young Texan GLOBGAS-US with us, and he feels no such constraint.

"Well, now," he says, "down there in Houston we spend about sixty million bucks on programming each year. I reckon we're in the software business."

Scene 4. The general strike has begun in Paris. It is going to last three weeks and the entire country will freeze on the spot. I am standing in the computer room when the electricians throw the main switch that cuts off the flow of current to this part of the city. Our UNIVAC has its own power supply and it keeps running in the dark. Its illuminated console looks like the control panel of the Starship *Enterprise*, the operators silhouetted against the bright flickering lights. The green and red panels of tape unit banks form long avenues of gaudy sparkle like the Las Vegas Strip. We power down the big machine when we learn of the events outside.

I watch the days of May 1968 with the eyes of an Americanized Frenchman looking at history from inside an oil company: through these sets of filters the events take on a surprising color. The press and the government keep denouncing "a handful of agitators." The left, the extreme left, and the leadership of the unions panic when they realize they cannot stop the strikes. The expected patterns of history have shifted under the established hierarchies. A "handful of agitators" cannot suddenly stop a country like France for three weeks. A previously unrecognized mass movement has suddenly come to light, triggered by some deep and uncharted currents of change.

I think I know who some of the agents are who have precipitated these currents. They are not the bearded characters who are lobbing cobblestones at the cops around the Sorbonne. They are the IBM salesmen in their neat three-piece suits, closely followed by the Control Data salesmen and the UNIVAC salesmen, who are bringing into the major industries of the country a technology that promotes rapid change—a technology alien to the pace at which old Europe is capable of evolving and of absorbing new ideas. I see it all around me, in the distress of the French executives like Monsieur Martin, who cannot come to grips with data bases and realize that this is only one aspect of their frustration. President Lyndon Johnson has recently canceled the export license for the big Control Data computer that De Gaulle wanted to use to develop the French H-bomb: suddenly the whole country realizes that the greatness of a culture is not measured by the number of poet laureates it has nurtured, but rather by the number of CDC 7600s it can afford. Yet nothing will have changed in Paris after those three weeks of turmoil, except that the old cobblestone streets of the Latin Quarter are now smoothly covered with tar. I am beginning to realize that my vacation is over: a longer stay in Europe would be intellectual suicide for someone who wants to build new information systems. At a computer conference in Edinburgh I meet Bill Olle, the man I have long admired for the crisp concepts of his INFOL language. He is starting a data-base development group in the Systems Division at RCA. Two months later, my family and I live in a rented house in New Jersey. The fall colors have come to the nearby woods. I will be working with a new group and a new machine, but the problems remain the same. Access to data. The quality of information.

An English friend, Terry Westgate, points out to me that the first use of the term "inform" in the English language is found in Shakespeare's *Macbeth:*

> Mine eyes are made the fools o' th' other senses
> Or else worth all the rest. I see thee still,
> And on thy blade and dudgeon gouts of blood,
> Which was not so before. There's no such thing.
> It is the bloody business which informs
> Thus to mine eyes.
>
> (II, i)

How could we create a general tool for "IN-FORMATION"? I had become skeptical of its coming from academia, because

ALTAIR had taught me that scientists were more interested in the games they played than in improving the conditions of their work. Neither would it come from traditional industry: GLOBGAS believed that it was "not in the software field." Now I was going to find out what the bloody business looked like from a third viewpoint: that of the computer manufacturers themselves. I was entering the holy of holies.

At RCA, the executives gave excellent reasons for their interest in computers: the company had developed a highly successful line of television products. It understood communications and had mastered the satellite field. Since the computer business was clearly headed toward communications, RCA could intercept it, short-circuit the transition, and establish a firm market base by capitalizing on its strengths. Never was such a brilliant strategy so poorly executed.

We worked hard in New Jersey. We had six SPECTRA computers in the basement. There were seventeen of us in the database system group: programmers from California, systems experts from as far away as Norway and as close as Philadelphia, and a cheerful secretary who mothered the whole group. We put our system together and, when it came time to try it, I found myself in charge of the testing team. It was my job to come up with the files of data that would exercise the system to its extreme limits.

Each data-base system assumes a certain given structure for the entities it contains. In the simplest case these entities are basic lists or tables of items. Other programs allow such links as tree-structures, relations, or graphs. A "tree" looks like a genealogical chart, with fathers, sons, and grandsons neatly linked together. A "relation" looks like a table of attributes. A "graph" is a display of connections among entities. The structure is very important because it imposes a certain world-view on the prospective user, constraining what he can represent, what he can think of. It simplifies the open-ended and irritating fuzziness of the mental representation and turns it into a rigid set of relationships. This is where I found that the legendary "lightning speed" of computers could easily be defeated.

Computers have long been able to beat human beings in numerical calculations. An advertisement for IBM once boasted of "FIVE HUNDRED THOUSAND MULTIPLICATIONS FOR A NICKEL!" It occurred to me, when I read it, that the proposition was rather empty. Since I could not imagine when I might ever need 500,000 multiplications, that staggering feat was certainly not worth a nickel to me. What I needed most, as an information scientist, was a tool to manipulate *structure*. And in this respect, the fastest computers we had were failing miserably. They were designed to compute, after all. Not to process information.

As an example, let me take a data base of a society whose elements are human families. In a tree-structure representation of a family we have something like Figure 4, where the father occupies the top level (if we assume the kind of conservative, paternalistic society in which computers are happiest). This father has a wife and the wife has n kids, where n represents 0, 1, 2, etc., as the situation requires. Now suppose that the kids have pets. Larry may have a cat, Linda a dog. In my tests I generated hundreds of such families. I compiled indexes on kids' names and kinds of pets. Then I played with the structure of these fictitious families. Suppose we add a pet, an alligator, that belongs to the whole family but not to one of the kids. Since we could not leave any levels empty, the system now needed a phantom kid to own the new pet. But this dummy kid had to have a dummy mother. We thus began a list of strange discoveries which can be summed up in one equation:

IN A FAMILY WHERE ONE PET DOES NOT BELONG TO ANY PARTICULAR CHILD, THE HUSBAND IS ALWAYS BIGAMOUS.

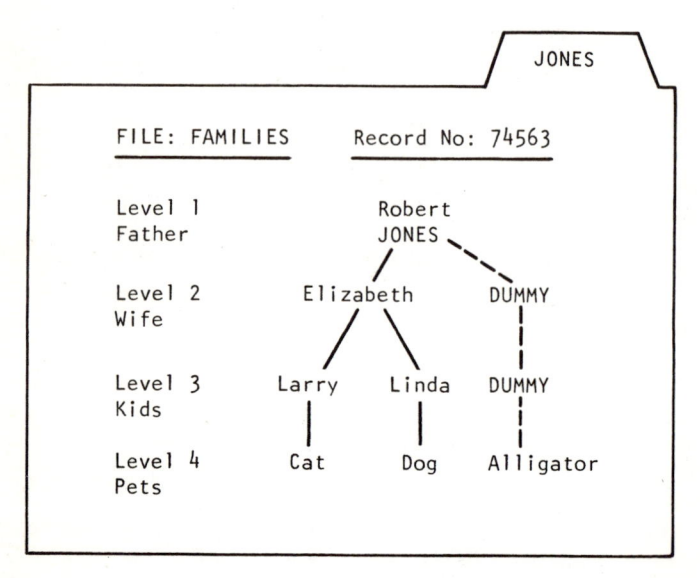

```
                                              JONES

          FILE: FAMILIES      Record No: 74563

          Level 1              Robert
          Father               JONES --------
                              /              \
          Level 2         Elizabeth         DUMMY
          Wife             /    \             |
                          /      \            |
          Level 3       Larry   Linda       DUMMY
          Kids            |       |           |
          Level 4        Cat     Dog       Alligator
          Pets
```

Figure 4. How Mr. Robert Jones became bigamous, an accident to be attributed to a little-known property of some tree structures.

When the laughter had subsided, I refined the tests to generate trees with missing data (in real-life information systems there are always many holes), then asked the computer to "invert" the whole structure. After inversion, you might now have a file of kids rather than a file of husbands. Each kid "owned" a father, mother, and pets. The holes propagated wildly through the tree structure like a curtain of water drops on the edges of a fountain. In the meantime, the computer was grinding to a halt. It got to the point where I knew how to stop the machine dead with practically no data, just by forcing it to exercise its structuring process. Structure-handling operations that would have taken seconds for a human took twenty mintues of machine time. Retrieving information was nothing; it was structure manipulation that killed us. Access to data is meaningless without the ability to reshape it.

The same is true of all information systems today, whether they are used by the police, the government, the hospitals, or the schools. If the structure of the data is ever found to be incomplete or wrong, the cost to modify it is enormous—so high that the tyranny of the system increases as the data investment grows. For that reason, we have police systems that lead to wild gunshots in the night, legal documents that demand our names in three different places, and insurance forms that request the Social Security number of the doctor who took an X-ray of Johnny's foot two years ago, even though that number is already stored in the file. The insurance company's computer may reject our claim anyway, because the name of Johnny's town is not misspelled in exactly the same way as it was when an unknown operator, in an unknown place, entered it into the computer six months earlier. That misspelling is a bit of (mis)information we simply have no way to uncover.

For that reason, too, we have airline reservation systems that cannot let you pay one part of your trip by credit card and the rest with a bank check, cannot extract from the machine the most direct route to Chicago, and will certainly try, if left to themselves, to send you over the Grand Canyon on a flight from Maine to Massachusetts.

We finally got our system running quite well, and I left my job at RCA a year before the company decided to get out of the computer business. The problems were already apparent when I started packing my bags. The marketing group ran the company, and its direct competition with IBM made our products a constantly moving target. I have already stated that data-base systems are exquisitely sensitive to their social and organizational environments. Ours was doomed from the beginning. Yet the year I spent at RCA brought me into contact with several remarkable people whose lessons I have remembered.

One lesson which I am not likely to forget took place at the RCA research labs in Princeton, where most of the discoveries in color television had occurred. I had been invited to give a talk on information retrieval. I ventured into English-language interrogation of data bases, and other applications of artificial intelligence used to converse with computers. A man with intense eyes and bright white hair took me aside. We sat on the benches in the lab next to the lecture hall.

He said, "There is a fundamental fallacy in artificial intelligence, and you're falling into it."

"In what respect?" I asked, with the feeling that this discussion was not going to conform to the usual polite exchange of generalities heard at most professional meetings.

"Artificial intelligence is trying to emulate nature, it wants to approximate what Man does."

"What other inspiration is there?"

"Imitation of nature is bad engineering. For centuries inventors tried to fly by emulating birds, and they have killed themselves uselessly. If you want to make something that flies, flapping your wings is not the way to do it. You bolt a 400-horsepower engine to a barn door, that's how you fly. You can look at birds forever and never discover this secret. You see, Mother Nature has never developed the Boeing 747. Why not? Because Nature didn't need anything that would fly at 700 mph at 40,000 feet: how would such an animal feed itself?"

"What does that have to do with artificial intelligence?"

"Simply that it tried to approximate Man. If you take Man as a model and test of artificial intelligence, you're making the same mistake as the old inventors flapping their wings. You don't realize that Mother Nature has never needed an intelligent animal and accordingly, *has never bothered to develop one.*

"So when an intelligent entity is finally built, it will have evolved on principles different from those of Man's mind, and its level of intelligence will certainly not be measured by the fact that it can beat some chess champion or appear to carry on a conversation in English."

With his piercing eyes on me, I had a brief vision of what an intelligent machine would be. If Nature has never needed an intelligent animal and hasn't evolved one, I kept wondering, then who are we? In our feeble attempts to handle the information we call life, and increase its quality, can we trust the creations of our dreams? Are we perhaps nothing more than the process through which another form of intelligence is itself evolving? And in the end, what measure of control do we really have on the technologies we create?

CHAPTER FOUR
The Engines of Humanity are Overheating

In which the author explains why technology has a life of its own, and shows that Edison and Bell should have compared notes. He remarks that computer applications are out of control and builds a strong case for the creation of a new field, a science of Apocalypse Management.

    Computers are interesting because they force us to pose important questions about technology, questions that are much larger than the limited problems of everyday data processing. What role does technology serve in our world? Where is it taking us? What are our options?
    One of the arguments of this book is that technology in general is out of control, and that the computer, today, is simply the leading example of a continuing series of artificial tools essential to our survival.
    To discuss the future of any technology is always a tricky business, but to attempt a description of what may be happening with computers is worse than tricky: it is a desperate enterprise.
    Humans have never been very good at looking beyond their noses. When Christopher Columbus proposed a voyage to the Indies in 1490, an "expert" found six arguments against the idea: the journey would be too long, the ocean was infinite, one could not get back from the Antipodes, there were no Antipodes anyway since Saint Augustine had said so, only three of the five zones in our world were inhabitable, and, so many centuries after Creation, was it likely that anyone could still discover any new lands of value? We must admit that all the weight of scholarship was against the existence of the Americas and the ability to reach them. Man could not "get out of his sphere."
    The passage of time has not improved our abilities in this respect. *Harper's Weekly*, in its issue of July 31, 1875, considered the possibility of air travel and noted that "every little while there is

a startling account of the construction of a novel machine by which the difficult problem has finally been solved . . ." Such discoveries, said the magazine, must be taken with caution because "the peril of ascending with a steam engine, fire, or highly inflammable materials for generating a propulsive power would stand in the way of sufficient patronage to sustain any enterprise of this character." The great scientist Simon Newcomb added in 1903 that

> The demonstration that no possible combination of known substances, known forms of machinery and known forms of force, can be united in a practical machine by which man shall fly long distances through the air, seems to the writer as complete as it is possible for the demonstration of any physical fact to be.

On December 10 of the same year, the editorial page of *The New York Times* had this to say about Samuel Langley's experiments with airplanes:

> We hope that Professor Langley will not put his substantial greatness as a scientist in further peril by continuing to waste his time, and the money involved, in further airship experiments.

This was published by the prestigious journal, mind you, only one week before the successful flight of the Wright Brothers at Kitty Hawk. Technology was already accelerating to the point where it slipped through the hands of the experts. Discouraging predictions were made about something as apparently simple as highways: "The actual building of roads devoted to motor cars is not for the near future," said *Harper's* in 1902. Similarly, military technology has seen many foolish assertions, such as Admiral Clark Woodward's pronouncement in 1939 that "as far as sinking a ship with a bomb is concerned, you just can't do it," and another admiral's comment (in 1945!) about the atom bomb, which he called "the biggest fool thing we have ever done . . . the bomb will never go off and I speak as an expert in explosives."

Scientific commissions and academies seem to err with even more consistency than journalists or independent investigators when it comes to making pronouncements about what is possible. In the eighteenth century, the French Academy of Sciences stated flatly that meteorites could not exist: how could stones fall from the sky when there *are* no stones in the sky? The large meteorite collections in the museums of Europe must have been produced by the sheer imagination of the people. Farmers were simply picking up stones that had been hit by lightning. When this statement, coming from the prestigious *Academie*, was published, curators of museums throughout Europe disposed of their meteorite collections by throwing the useless stones into the garbage!

Similarly enlightened French commissions drove Mesmer (the pioneer of hypnosis) out of the country, found Fulton's steamboat useless and visionary, rejected Jenner's smallpox vaccine, and mocked Franklin's lightning conductor. Nor do the French hold a monopoly on scientific blindness: American experts pronounced Edison's phonograph a hoax and Bell's invention of the telephone a definite swindle.

Edison and Bell, however, were not immune to such errors themselves: the former thought that his phonograph would be used mainly to relay messages from the telegraph office to the customer, and the latter thought that his telephone would be employed primarily by people wanting to listen to a remote concert.

It is ironic that they had the true usefulness of their inventions completely reversed: the availability of phonograph recordings made it ludicrous to listen to concerts over the telephone, and the availability of the phone made it easy for the telegraph office to speak to its customers!

In 1937, *The New York Times* again distinguished itself when it examined the prospects for television. It found that outside of some military applications, commercial opportunities were nonexistent. For one thing, it was hard for the *Times* to imagine all the members of a typical American family spending any significant amount of time in the same room!

After this short review of our society's failure to plan and failure to envision, it should not surprise us to learn that the true significance of the computer was also misunderstood. When the Moore School built ENIAC in the mid-Forties, most experts agreed that a half-dozen such machines would certainly suffice to satisfy the calculation needs of the entire world. It is at least refreshing to find that computer experts are as blind to progress in their discipline as the experts from the other fields just quoted were in their own. One more example: in the early Sixties, the IBM Corporation had an opportunity to invest in and gain control of a struggling new venture with an untested concept. They studied it and turned it down. The new venture, so disdainfully rejected by the computer giant, was the concept brought to fruition by Xerox—the photocopy.

I think the world is coming to a Bend.

In spite of all human attempts to control them, attempts reflected in such institutions as the U.S. Congress' Office of Technology Assessment, our tools seem to have a life of their own. They obey specific laws, never illustrated as well as in the case of the computer, but applicable to all technical areas from the Stone Age to the Space Age. And technology is accelerating faster than the wildest predictions would seem to authorize, if we consider the facts some analysts have assembled. This acceleration tends to be perceived by the public as a bad thing. Yet technological innovation generally has unexpected social benefits as well as unforeseen social costs. When the stirrup was invented, for example, this apparently innocuous improvement in horsemanship led to just such an unforeseen result: the creation of the feudal system in support of mounted knights. Similarly, the introduction of fireplaces in private rooms, replacing the traditional fireplace in the central hall, has fostered class consciousness and snobbery, as a reader of the *San Francisco Chronicle* named Hetherington once pointed out in a letter to the editor (1 August 1979). He added, however, that the invention "did more for the art of love than all the songs of the troubadours."

When cars were first introduced, progress-conscious New Yorkers hailed them as the harbingers of a clean environment. And they were at least half right: it is a fact that few of today's enemies of smog and pollution would put up with the mountains of manure that horses used to deposit on the streets of Manhattan. The automobile has, unexpectedly, made the pavement clean and the air foul. It has also made suburbia possible and has changed courtship patterns everywhere.

The rapidity and surprising impact of technological development, a source of wonder and joy to "progressive" engineers of the nineteenth century, has become scary and awesome to us. But I find a great deal of hope in the very fact that it is growing beyond simple attempts to control it. I am encouraged by the observation that human technical ingenuity seems to have no limits.

The trends found in the computer field are eloquent: they represent an explosion rather than an evolution, an explosion which translates itself into a wealth of new products, new services, and new industrial sectors. The most dramatic observation is the computer's continuing drop in price, increase in power, and miniaturization of the components that make it tick. The enormous machine with the humming drum I used to program in Meudon would cost a couple of thousand dollars today, and would fit comfortably on the typing stand by my desk. It could certainly compute satellite orbits fast enough to keep up with them, and would have a very low probability of breaking down. By 1985, fullscale computers will fit in a briefcase or even a coat pocket. Disposable computers are already a fact of life. Computers are coming out of the basement in droves and are making themselves useful as components in consumer products such as automobiles, games, and appliances. While the number of operations per second increases, the cost of logic decreases, and the cost of memory plummets steadily as well.

While these trends are well recognized, few people have asked what they mean and how they relate to the general history of technology. The computer field has no perspective. One man who has investigated the meaning of this explosion is a French scientist named Francois Meyer.

Professor Meyer is a researcher who specializes in the study of world development patterns and long-term growth. Educated in France, he worked in Chile and Germany before joining the Institute for Political Studies in Aix-en-Provence. When I met him in Paris, he told me of his frustration at being unable to compel his colleagues in Europe to face some disturbing facts. What concerned him most, he said, was that predictions were still being made using obsolete or inaccurate models of world growth. The Social Affairs Department of the United Nations, for example, published in 1951, 1954, 1958, and 1966, four studies of predicted population levels. In each case, they consistently fell short of the actual values. He felt the discrepancies had to do with the technological explosion.

In 1951, the UN expected the 1980 world population to stand between 2.7 and 3.3 billion. In 1954, this range was raised to a more realistic 3.0 to 3.8 billion, and in 1958, it was changed again to 3.6 to 4.0 billion. By 1966, the *actual* world population was already about 3.0 billion and well on its way to 3.5 billion, but the experts still foresaw a *maximum* 1980 population of 4.4 billion. The actual figure for 1977 was over 4.12 billion, and growing at a rate that would exceed the top of this range. In March 1980, the Environmental Fund, which keeps track of world population with an electronic display in downtown Washington, said the number of humans had reached 4.5 billion and was increasing by 90 million a year.

This simple failure in forecast, Meyer explained to me, is one of serious concern. The reason is that most theories of world development assume an "exponential" pattern for growth, and the planning of all governmental and industrial organizations follows this theory. The celebrated *Club of Rome* used it in its report on "Limits to Growth." Though the findings of this last group were dramatic, its conclusions regarding the "limits to growth" are at variance with reality and probably underestimate it quite badly. What Meyer and several of his colleagues have found is that growth is much faster than exponential: it is hyperbolic. Now this is not the place for a course in mathematics, but a few reminders from high school algebra will show the reader why the implications are serious.

An exponential growth pattern rises slowly at first, then accelerates tremendously because each new value is a mathematical *power* based on time. Although this curve goes up very fast, it is smooth and uninterrupted. By the selection of an appropriate scale, it is always possible to make it appear manageable.

Most projections of population and technology are plotted that way, and the actual values often refuse to fall on the projected line nonetheless. According to Francois Meyer the actual curve is hyperbolic, which means that for a certain year, the curve will zoom up vertically toward infinity.

In spite of the importance of these observations for future forecasts, the team that obtained these results could not find a serious audience in France. To bring them to the attention of researchers elsewhere they had to publish in English. Since some of my own observations of information systems complemented Meyer's work, we decided to attempt to publish a joint article in the U.S. This led to a rather entertaining, eye-opening adventure, in the course of which we discovered some serious mental blocks that prevented researchers—including the so-called "futurists" themselves—from facing the kind of reality that computer technology was illustrating.

The fact that population is growing faster than the usual models predict has been recognized by many international experts besides Meyer. Andre Cailleux, Julian Huxley, and others have pointed out that exponential curves did not explain the data. Working independently of Meyer, H. Von Foerster, an American researcher working at the University of Illinois in Urbana, found that the actual point of discontinuity for the hyperbola was in the year 2026 (with a five-year error margin). Kaplan, using his own data, placed it in "the decade of 2020 to 2030." It is important to find out whether this explosion is only a recent phenomenon or a result of the constant development of the human species. In order to do this, Von Foerster obtained data from the beginning of the Christian era, and Frenchman Andre Cailleux went as far back as the Paleolithic.

At times during history, growth of the world population has been severely curtailed *in specific geographic areas*. For example, the population of Western Europe actually *decreased* between the Roman Empire and the seventeenth century. Later it recovered and increased dramatically, and now tends toward zero population growth. World population has not reflected these local variations, so much so that the industrial revolution does not make even a ripple on the world population curve.

When we presented these observations, together with a possible theory of the process, to *Science* magazine, the official publication of The American Association for the Advancement of Science, and to several experts, our manuscript was unanimously rejected. "Don't you know," the authorities asked, "that growth HAS to be exponential and, furthermore, HAS to follow an S-shaped curve?"

They were referring to the well-known fact that, in a limited-resource environment, population size always grows exponentially, reaches a plateau, and then stabilizes at some maximum value. This is true for bacteria in the laboratory and for coyotes in the field. The factors that force the growth of any animal population to slow down are increased competition, decaying conditions, and a decrease in the survival rate. This is the case in biology, and since the human race is biological, it must work the same way, right? Therefore, the whole human system on this planet HAS to reach some state of equilibrium with environmental resources. All the experts, from the Sierra Club to the Club of Rome, have repeated this simple truth.

This concept, of an "imminent" state of equilibrium for mankind, is so ingrained among demographers that they keep "discovering" the magic number M, the maximum number for human population. Thus Pearl, in 1930, announced that population would level off in 1950 around 2.15 billion. In 1954, Notestein announced that the ceiling was 3.3 billion and this was increased to 4.0 billion by Woytinski in 1953. As I noted before, human population in March 1980 had reached 4.5 billion, and was still climbing like a rocket.

The problem with the analogy involving bacteria or coyote populations, says Meyer, is that one notable difference exists between homo sapiens and other biological groups. That difference is *technology,* or rather, successive *waves* of human technology. To put it more precisely, Meyer and his colleagues agree that each technology follows an S-shaped development curve if taken by itself, but a new form of technology is always ready to "relay" an old one that has reached its ceiling. Consequently, the general trend (also called the "envelope") of these curves *taken together* is hyperbolic, not exponential, and it does not reach a plateau as does an S-shaped curve.

Similarly, the number of individuals that can be supported by a given acreage of land has grown rapidly, because technology keeps changing the nature of the relationship between survival and resources. Take an area that supported one man three million years ago, when he had to feed himself by gathering fruits and by hunting. When primitive agriculture and domestication of animals occurred, that same area could support ten humans. When the hoe came into widespread use, that land could feed 1,000 people. When the plow was invented, that number was multiplied by five. With today's fertilizers and mechanized techniques, the area that supported one human three million years ago can now feed 10,000 people. There is no indication, too, that we have reached a ceiling in the technological strategies available for survival. It is Meyer's point that technology in fact enhances humanity's ability to survive (an idea not applicable to other species). Greater numbers of people, in turn, mean more intellectual power, more labor force available, greater creativity, hence, more technology. This is the *feedback* mechanism that accelerates world growth.

The phenomenon of "relaying technologies" is found is several key areas. For example, the amount of power available to human beings, from the donkey to the rocket, through the stages of the water mill, windmill, and Watt's engine, is growing hyperbolically (Figure 5). So is the speed of vehicles: every successive type of transportation machine (stage coach, train, car, propeller aircraft, jet, rocket) has followed its own S-shaped curve and found its own ceiling, with another technology always ready to take over where the old one left off. The long-term trend is given by the *envelope* of all these partial curves (Figure 6).

When we come to information technology, the growth pattern is already distorted by the introduction of the computer. Figure 7 shows the number of characters typeset per hour as manual techniques gave way to mechanical typesetting, linotype, photographic composition, and electronic composition. On this scale, the curve has now become nearly vertical.

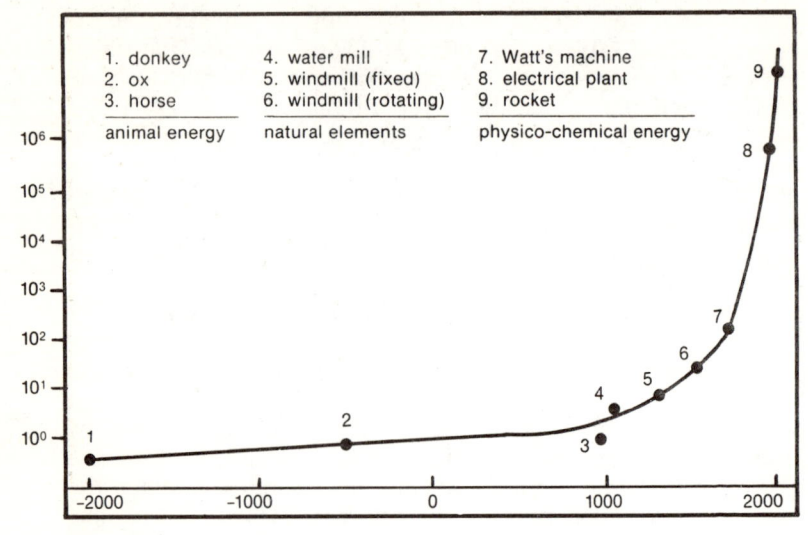

Figure 5. Amount of power available to the human race.

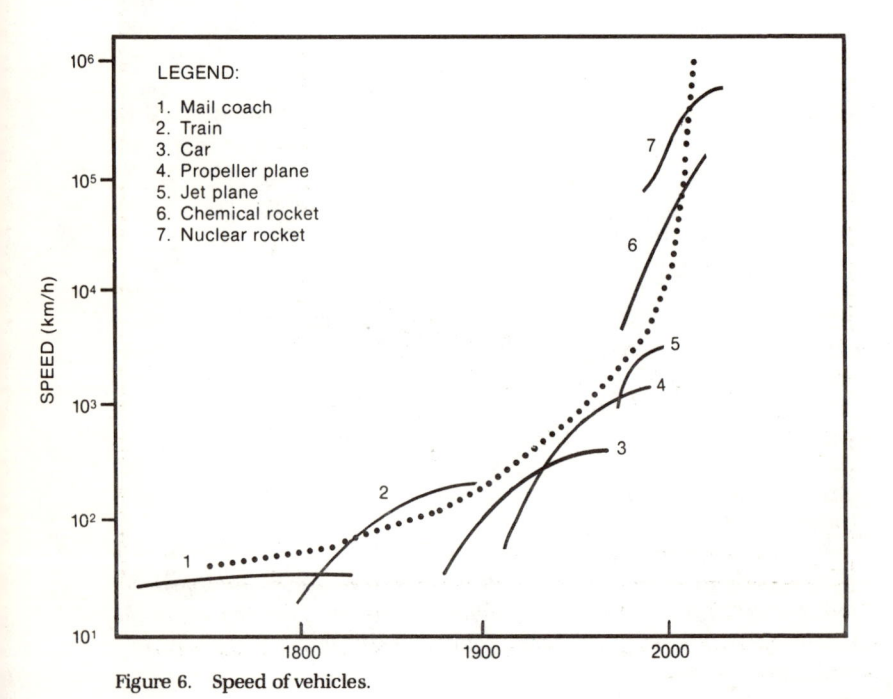

Figure 6. Speed of vehicles.

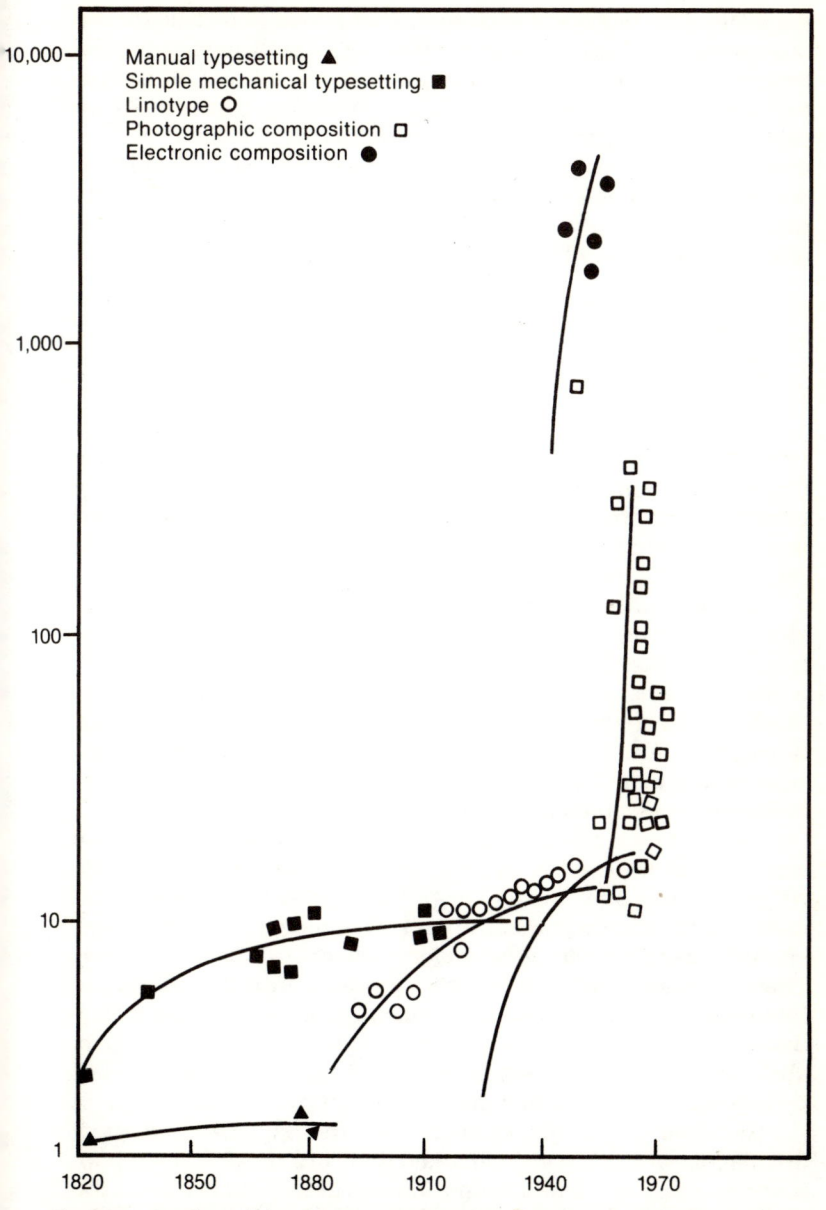

Figure 7. Number of characters typeset per hour. The envelope of the curves becoming nearly vertical.

Furthermore, some indications exist that technology is growing faster than biological evolution. That seems to be true for the only period in which we have precise data for both, namely prehistory. If we plot on a graph the development of one Stone Age technology, in this case the production of cutting edges, and if we plot on the same graph the growth of human skull volume, we find that the latter curve (biological) reached a ceiling while the former (technological) continued to climb. Other scientists had already reached similar conclusions that technology grows faster than biology evolves. In 1975, Loren Eiseley wrote that

> Our technology is outracing our ability to master our huge urban complexities . . . We have reached a biological plateau. We use technology with an aggressive brain that has not improved biologically in the last 50,000 years.

From our own data, Meyer and I pointed out that the very rapid development of computer-based media must be one of history's major events, a result of its great effect on humanity's ability to survive. The computer, we argued, would deeply transform and accelerate the development of the species. Our attempt to publish this apparently simple observation, however, raised a furor.

To begin with, our paper was firmly rejected by *Science* magazine. One reviewer had become so furious while reading the manuscript that he crossed out entire sentences in red pencil, writing marginal notes about the "obvious" fact that growth HAD to follow an S-shaped curve, and peppering the text with exclamation points. Another reviewer, while a bit less sanguinary, was equally adamant that our attacks on the sanctity of the "Big S" must not be accepted by the magazine.

Without making the slightest change in our manuscript, we sent it to a more specialized periodical, the *Journal of Technological Forecasting and Social Change*. We expected it to be rejected again. To our great surprise, the paper was accepted by the reviewers, who were people of equivalent caliber to those of *Science*. These contrary reactions to our paper say a great deal about the intellectual climate in which all our planning efforts and policy decisions originate. How can the same idea, based on known facts and conceived in a well-established field, be rejected out of hand by one scientific group and gladly received by another?

As a footnote to his acceptance of the paper, the editor of *Technological Forecasting* remarked that "of course" human population could never truly become infinite, even in theory, since the earth itself was limited and since each woman could only conceive a finite number of babies. This remark is unwittingly ironic, coming

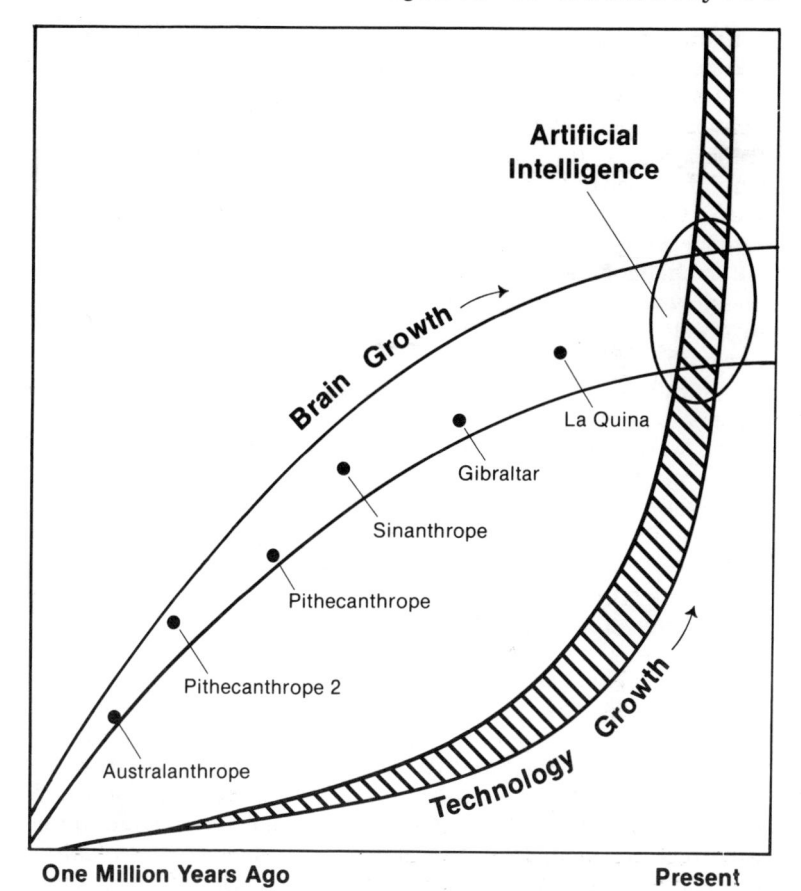

Figure 8. Technology grows faster than biology.

as it does, from a futurist open-minded enough to publish a paper on hyperbolic growth. In fact, chances are that neither of these arguments is valid, since science has already demonstrated that the human race is not limited for survival to the resources of the earth, and that babies no longer need to be borne by women. Test-tube babies and outer-space settlements are no longer science-fiction ideas. They are engineering facts.

It is not Meyer's intention, however, nor mine, to suggest that human development between now and the year 2026 will be accelerated by technology to the point implied by the curves. *Any forecast of infinite growth in a finite time interval is absurd.* The thermodynamic properties of this planet will soon impose some constraints unless a large percentage of energy production and use starts taking place in outer space.

What do these curves mean, then? Simply that human development is not going to slow down under the effects of the ordinary constraints of the environment, not after it has followed a smoothly-growing curve for three million years. What we can foresee for the next generation (our children, *not* our grandchildren) is a major discontinuity that may express itself in political and population changes, in space emigration, or perhaps through change in belief systems and human social behavior. Even if they do not involve the ultimate horrors of a nuclear war, *these changes will be like nothing ever experienced before*, and the computer is right in the middle of the process: even after considering all the other accelerating patterns we have reviewed, the acceleration of computer technology sticks out in an obscene way. It suggests that humanity may be able to *build* the next level of intelligent beings long before Nature is able to *evolve* it.

All this makes me think that in the next few years we are going to need several new sciences. One is a science of the applied study of *structure*. Another is a science of Apocalypse Management, the art of optimizing the unavoidable.

In one of his delightfully witty essays, entitled "On Progress and Providence," the Italian scientist, C. Marchetti, proposes a new definition of science: "the exploration of the external world by an information system through mutation and selection." By *mutation* he means a slight change in the information pattern of the system. By *selection* he means a process for checking how well the information system fits the external world. The same definition, naturally, covers technology. Marchetti proceeds to analyze the relationship of science to medieval Europe and the resulting eruption of knowledge: "The consequences are before our eyes: an explosive growth in activity, wealth and power, with technologists so taken by the excitement of their own game that they do not find a moment to meditate on the measure and opportunity of their actions and on the fragile metaphysical premises that buttress all their buildings."[17]

A colleague named Pete gave me a chance to observe both the actions and the premises of my work with computers, as well as some effects of the technology on existing cultures, when he offered me an unusual and entirely harmless job as a double agent.

We were both working at RCA at the time, and Pete, who was an expert on meta-compilers, was in charge of standards. He stalked into my office with a furious look on his face and an urgent request for help. He was mad at the French, it seemed, because in their concern for the preservation of the French language, they now insisted that all international standards include full French terms and definitions.

Since 1946, the U.S. has been far and away the most prolific originator of computer language terminology. Some nations, like Japan, have pragmatically resigned themselves to inserting phonetic approximations of the American jargon into their sentences. Others, like Britain, felt helpless in the face of constant violations of the English tongue by "Stateside" engineers. When British and American definitions clashed, it was agreed that the latter would rule, though there was one notable British fight to prevent the use of a U.S. term. The clash, which occurred during a discussion of the international standards for nuclear reactors, concerned the panic button the operator would push in case of a disaster. In the U.S., it was called the "SCRAM" button. The British hated the name and wanted to call the switch "Emergency Power Cut-Off." The Americans eventually won the argument, when they demonstrated that there was no way to write all that on a small red button.

When Pete approached me, the International Standards Organization (ISO) had just completed publication of a bilingual terminology standard for *Telephony*. Because the French had heavy-handedly insisted on precise translations into their language, the job had taken fourteen years! The American computer industry, which had grown much faster than the phone industry, was not going to put up with another hindrance like that. It needed an international standard that could be used in the U.S., but the international committee was continually bogged down in definitions. A French general sat at the head of the table, unmovable. He would block proposals for new definitions because the French delegation did not have adequate translations: they must go home and work on them. Since the full international group met only once a year, this was slow work indeed. Pete wanted me to join the U.S. delegation and help it prepare the definitions. When the international meeting took place, I would sit behind the U.S. flag and wait for the general to tell us: "Vee can not accept thees definition bicause hit daz not translatte into French." According to Pete's "double agent" scheme, that was my cue to rise from behind the Stars and Stripes and request the chairman's permission to read out the definition we had already cooked up in his own language.

The scheme actually worked and the results were very funny. At first, the general was quite mad, but he gradually came to his senses, accepting our proposals and then thinking actively about a counterattack. The following year there was an American from IBM-France behind the French flag. When the meeting got into trouble the two of us would excuse ourselves, go into a bar across the street, and solve the problem over a beer. Considerable progress was made toward a terminology standard acceptable to all nations.

After this first exposure to the work of ISO, I was amazed to observe that people could disagree so violently about the definition of terms that everybody had been using for years. We were not inventing anything new; we were, quite simply, restating the facts in as simple and concise a definition as possible, so that government contracts, laws, and proposals could be uniformly understood. It meant thankless and obscure hours of work, and when the standard was complete there would be no credit given, nobody's name on the cover, just the mighty stamp of the National Bureau of Standards. And that stamp also meant that a company could not bid successfully on any government contract unless it knew and followed the exact meaning of the terms the standard provided. This placed a serious responsibility on the twenty or so specialists who over the years worked on the hundreds of definitions included in the standard. It often placed them, too, in situations where cultural viewpoints and philosophical positions, rather than mere technical concepts, were at stake. And those moments were enlightening because they showed how the new technology was exploding the existing structures of human thought.

The first such "explosion" I was exposed to concerned the definition of the term "language." At a meeting in Washington, we tentatively agreed that a language, an innocuous word, it seemed at the time, was

> A set of signs, possibly represented as symbols, and used to convey information.

There was an Italian linguist in the group, and two of the American delegates were also experts. The problem arose when we tried to separate *artificial languages* (which computers use) from natural languages like English and French.

We agreed that natural languages arose from human usage, while artificial ones were based on machines, but we could not define it that way. If the mere fact of "prescribing" a language made it artificial, then Esperanto would have to be defined as an artificial language, which confused the computer issue even more. I posed the following problem: two computers, each of a different make and each equipped with a communication device, are placed in a room where there is no human. They are programmed to establish contact with their environment, an increasingly common feature in artificial intelligence. After some preliminaries, we would expect the computers to exchange some signals, acknowledge the contact, and establish a joint protocol to send and receive messages. Eventually, they would jointly define a communication structure they both "understood." "Would that language be natural or artificial?" I asked.

The linguist thought a long time, got up, paced up and down, and finally said, "Natural."

In these minor incidents, the Cartesian Europeans and the pragmatic Americans clashed frequently, but never was their difference in outlook more dramatically demonstrated for me than at the next standards meeting. It took place in Berlin, and I had been asked to chair the session on software terminology. English and French definitions had already been prepared. A sizable Japanese group was there, as were representatives of Italy, the United Kingdom, and Germany.

Trouble developed as soon as we read the first definition. The Germans proposed a carefully thought-out alternative to the initial text. We compromised. There was a similar fight on the second term, and the third. The French, by now, were fiercely defending the initial definitions. I tried to unearth the root of the problem, and asked the German delegates to explain their objections to us. The leader of their group spoke up. He was a great admirer and follower of Wittgenstein's philosophy, he said. He felt strongly that any engineering definition must distinguish between the *physical unit* and the *functional unit* for every part of a system. For example, the steering wheel of an automobile can be defined in terms of how it is built and connected to the rest of the car, or it can be defined in terms of what happens when you use it. The two principles, he said, must be clearly separated in any good explanation. He wanted us to apply that principle to all the terms under consideration. The French threw up their hands in amazed indignation: we had 200 terms to review that day. Yet the German professor had a serious point. Part of me identified with him, for I had been taught in Europe that a scientist must achieve a general understanding, and must have a philosophical framework for what he does, before he can apply his knowledge to a special case. On the other hand, most of my practical experience with computers had been in the pragmatic U.S.A., where nobody gives a damn about philosophical truth as long as a gadget works, and where deeper understanding is left for future generations: philosophy follows practice in America, while it precedes it in Europe. I was torn between the two systems.

The frustration we experienced was all the more exasperating because the words we were trying to define were well-known, common computer terms: storage, memory, address. Then I hit upon a test of our differences: I asked the German professor how he would distinguish between physical unit and functional unit in the definition of "virtual memory"—a scheme that enables a modern computer to manipulate a much larger set of data than it actually holds in its real memory. Wittgenstein didn't know about virtual memory. Here was a typical American invention that had simply grown out of everyday experience, yet it stretched beyond the philosophical structures adequate for the other sciences of the day.

The meeting was adjourned for lunch, and the German delegate, who had a heart condition, did not return for the afternoon session. I never found out what Wittgenstein would have done with the idea of virtual memory. What I did learn is that computers are forcing us into an age in which we may have to take action before we understand the consequences of the action, and I find that lesson disturbing.

I experienced this superficial victory as a deeper personal defeat, the loss of a belief in principles I had been taught to admire. I felt I was in a situation similar to that of a workman I know, employed in Paris by a friend of mine, who frequently repairs the machines that abound in my friend's laboratory. When a particularly complicated piece of American equipment broke down, this old workman, skilled in mechanics, offered to fix the broken part or make a new one. When he came back the next day there were tears in the old man's eyes. "This is the first time in my life I have to admit I cannot manufacture something. This part, sir, was not made by a human being!" The device he held in his hand had been cut by a computer-guided tool, where the angle of the blade had to change as a function of the cutting. More than the fear of seeing his skill become obsolete, this workman had experienced the terror of realizing that man could not even duplicate the perfection created by the computer.

The machines, I thought that day in Berlin, were moving too fast for our language, and were creating too many new concepts for the cultures that hosted them. It was the kind of acceleration that America may be able to tolerate and absorb, but the kind that older cultures would be able to integrate only at the price of their social structures and their modes of thought. What the white man did to the Native American, the computer was doing to the cultures of Europe: the technology was accelerating, and in the process was burning the social fabric that supported it.

Amid all the gloomy, phony talk about the decline of America, I find myself thinking seriously that the United States is in reality at the threshold of its greatest leap forward, made possible by the unique cultural and economic structure of this country. This enormous jump will result from the release of multi-person, multi-group communication systems which computer networks made feasible. It may be difficult, at first, to measure this jump in classical economic terms. For instance, increased use of "electronic sidewalks" as a form of interaction among people in various parts of the continent might reduce the need for travel, and it might decrease the number of business trips taken in the late 1980s and 1990s, thus apparently decreasing the Gross National Product. But the GNP is not a measure of useful activity. It measures *all* activity, good and bad, productive and harmful. The invisible information systems we are creating will make possible as yet unheard-of advances in creativity and productivity.

While America will benefit from these inventions, other countries seem to be doing everything they can to destroy their ability to profit from the same technical gains. In every European nation, for example, the advent of networks has incited the post office authorities to reassert their monopolies on communications. They have taken control of the networks, erecting absurd national barriers against the first technology that could truly unite Europe. The Europeans have raised their tariffs in order to slow the spread of the computer networks until each country could develop and market its own. When these new networks have been unveiled, they have shown themselves to be so cumbersome and ill-suited to their users that realistic applications have been severely delayed.

In the Communist world, and in the rest of the planet as well, political considerations are still making the deployment of these tools unthinkable (except, of course, by the machinery of the state). In Poland, it is illegal for individuals to own duplicators, let alone home terminals! In the Middle East, computer networks are banned because many governments insist that all data leaving the country be in plain text. Since networks break up all the information they carry into elementary "packets," and send it around the entire net, it is inconvenient for such governments to eavesdrop on network users. Instead of settling for partial eavesdropping, many countries have decided to ban the technology entirely or demand the "plain text" proviso—a condition that cannot be met by advanced networks without considerable changes in their structure. The result is that the U.S. is free to charge ahead with the first media ever based on the tremendous ability of the computer to retain and logically distribute information.

At one standards meeting, Pete went out to dinner with the Italians, to discover that only one of them spoke a little English. In an attempt to be polite, he told them, "Machina ipsam culturam non habet" (Latin for "the computer has no culture of its own"). The English-speaker replied, "Pete, there's nothing wrong with your Italian, except that you use all those archaic words."

Over the years, I have pondered this Latin statement while watching the failure of social forecasters to come to grips with the large distortion of cultural values created by the computers. Perhaps the machine does have a "culture of its own." If Francois Meyer is right, the incidents I have recalled can mean only thing: the network revolution is no longer controllable.

CHAPTER FIVE
Knowledge Workers of the World, Link Up!

Behind the scenes at Hillside College, we meet Calvin Mellow, who thinks of himself as a Catalyst, and a whole team of brain-pickers. Techniques for keeping Washington from smelling a rat are explained and illustrated, and we are told what finally happened the day when Vision Stanley sneezed.

Considerable mystery surrounds the people who conceive of and develop information networks. Since these people simply don't have the time to write about their art, I wanted to try to dispel some of that mystery by describing how their techniques are passed, silently, from one computer team to another—almost in the same way that the medieval craftsmen, while building cathedrals with zeal, left neither names nor methods for later generations to study. The cathedral builders were occultists by choice; they felt that any glory directed at themselves would take away from the glory of their God. The system builders have no such vision, and whatever keeps them in the shadows probably doesn't owe much to humility and devotion. They remain unknown because their methods are complicated, difficult to explain to a layman, and constantly changing as they are adapted to new situations. Yet the systems they create have an immense influence, because in any society it is the questioner who holds power, not the person with the answers. Real power resides with those who set up the structure for others to think about because they define what is available and what is not, what is recorded and what is forgotten. The story of my friend Eric Elzevier, who took a long look at information systems behind the scenes, could be a lesson for those of us who increasingly rely on computer data in our daily lives.

Dean Scuttle was not in his office when the bomb went off. The device was a crude one, and the force of the explosion spent itself scattering roof tiles among the shrubbery. Eric Elzevier had joined Hillside College a few months before to take charge of their data-base systems. When the explosion occurred, he was in a meeting with the Dean and with the director of the computing center, a big man with a ruddy face named Harry Boldman, but they were too far away to hear anything. The meeting had to do with politics. Not the obvious and clear-cut politics of the students who were blowing up crude bombs in anger over the Vietnam War, but the much more insidious, occult and egotistical politics of computers and campuses. It was during the 1960s that computers became major instruments of power, and those who got in the way of this power, as Eric would discover, had to face the consequences.

The issue was software, as Harry Boldman clearly explained. There was a prominent woman professor at Hillside, Dr. Mildred Safenest, who was spending a million dollars of taxpayer money a year under a grant from the American Sciences Institute in Washington. She had a team of ten people trying to develop a data-base system for the campus. The idea was to create widespread networks of scientists to encourage new ideas and discoveries. The name of the project was PIN (Prototype Information Network) and it had been going on for years with no visible result. Even Dr. Safenest's friendliest contacts in Washington were showing some concern. In the meantime, Elzevier had been hired by Boldman to solve exactly the same problem that PIN was attacking. A collision was inevitable.

Soon Eric obtained some initial success with his new system, and the network of users started building up. But then strange and mysterious events began to occur in the life of my friend Eric. The old power structure reasserted itself, and a taciturn man named Calvin Mellow was summoned from the Midwest.

Calvin Mellow boarded the aircraft in Detroit and gave his coat to the first-class stewardess.

"I probably won't be needing it on this trip."

"What's your final destination, Mr. Mellow?" asked the girl as she ripped his ticket.

"I'm paying a visit to Hillside College. I'm a computer consultant."

"Well, if a man isn't a management expert these days, he might as well be a computer consultant."

The reality was that Calvin Mellow, a big man with cold, clammy hands and a gray-white face, was better remembered for his dirty after-dinner jokes than for his ability to straighten out machine room disasters. In some areas, however, he had a surprising amount of practical knowledge because his travels placed him in contact with a wide variety of teams and in a position to pick the best brains of each.

Mellow might be asked, for instance, to act as consultant on security problems with bank files which were stored on magnetic tape. He would call together the bank's various experts, and let them sort out their own problem in his presence. He would take plenty of notes, carefully documenting each concept that seemed marketable. The experts were young engineers who had not seen much of the world, were anxious to spill out their brightest ideas, and hoped that Mellow would be sufficiently impressed to call them to their boss's attention. Thus a young programmer might shyly mention a novel idea for "double directories." The following week Mellow could be found consulting with an insurance company that needed to review its accounting program.

"Have you considered the question of security?" he would ask casually.

"Naturally. And we have all our data on tape."

Mellow would look very surprised and would lift his pen in the air. "You mean you don't know about the technique I've developed for file protection? I call it 'double directory' and here's how it works . . ."

Mellow would thus travel from place to place, amazing his audiences, spreading the valuable pollen of technical know-how, fertilizing the software world, telling dirty jokes, and drawing unbelievable consulting fees. Sometimes his recommendations worked. Equally often they failed miserably. After all, a good idea in the banking business does not necessarily improve the operations of an insurance company. Mellow didn't care, and he certainly didn't have the time to learn anything in detail about his client's operations. He saw himself as a catalyst. Nothing but a humble catalyst, he thought, as he sipped his third Bloody Mary at 33,000 feet.

At the same instant, Eric Elzevier was having a confrontation with Harry Boldman, who was patiently explaining to him that the College could no longer tolerate two information systems on campus. Scientific creativity was not the issue. Power was.

"We have two horses and a single bet. We are betting on PIN."

Dean Scuttle said nothing, but stared at the bottom of his styrofoam cup and nodded.

"Now I'm seeing the people who really run computer research," Eric thought. "I'm seeing them in action." He didn't like what he saw.

In order for a product to get on the market, there has to be a good working prototype. Only one out of ten prototypes makes it. For a prototype to work in an industry lab, there has to be a fully-developed research model that works on some campus. Only one in ten research models ever makes that transition. And to have a functioning model, you have to have a well-tested theory. "So that's where we stand," thought Elzevier. "These people can block the whole thing at its source, where the creative ideas are trying to come out." He decided he was going to fight. He told them the truth.

"PIN doesn't work and my system does!"

"You don't understand computer research," the Dean shrugged. "The people who fund this sort of project in Washington don't give a damn if PIN ever gets off the ground."

"That's too bad," said Eric, looking alternately at Harry Boldman and at Scuttle. "But sometimes, in science, you have to try different things, and let the best approach win."

"Where did you learn science, young man?" asked the Dean with the tone of a man who was tired, very tired of all this childishness. "If PIN doesn't start producing something our sponsors can take credit for, one of these days some Congressman is going to start asking questions. The people who support the project have been covering up, but they are well aware that each progress report is an escalation of the lies in last year's report. Their neck is out, too, you know."

"Then Washington could cut funding on this particular project and direct the money to a more valuable one. That wouldn't make me cry," said Eric.

Boldman got up and went to the window. It was a sunny day. Between classes, groups of students were sitting on the grass and sipping Coke out of bright red cans.

"You've spent too much time in industry, Eric, that's your problem. We don't operate that way here. We're all in this together. Nobody wants an expose. If you try that, a special meeting will be called, with all the top names in the business, and Safenest will give them a briefing and hundreds of pages of documentation on PIN, more than they could digest in a week. And they'll say, OK, Professor Safenest, you're probably right. They'll sign a one-page statement that Eric Elzevier was just misled by his superficial understanding of the project's complexity and long-term objectives."

"Might even get us some more money," mused Scuttle, as if he were just thinking aloud. He was still staring inside his styrofoam cup, and his voice came out more hollow than usual.

"These people are weird," thought Eric.

"So that leaves us with one solution, right?" he said. "We can combine my system with her research."

"As a matter of fact, Eric, there might be a way to do that, if you're reasonable. But don't forget that Mildred isn't just afraid of losing face. She is even more afraid of you. So be careful."

Boldman looked tired, very tired. He sighed and put down the pipe he had been filling with tobacco.

"Listen, Eric. Right now research money is scarce, very scarce. In times like these, you'd think people would throw away the deadwood and keep their best ideas. But the opposite happens. Don't ask me why, but we drive out the creative people while the old empires, entrenched in their political enclaves, manage to capture all the resources that are still available. PIN will go on, don't worry. It seems there is strong government support for networks and data bases. I don't like the idea, frankly, and neither do the students. They claim that the real purpose of the project is political repression."

"If you can keep track of sixty million books with a big database system, you can keep track of sixty million people. Right now, that's a bit futuristic. But what about ten years from now? Once you develop the technique . . ."

"There's nothing wrong in keeping track of sixty million people, is there?" Eric asked.

"That depends on how you do it, my friend, and what information you keep about them. I have seen a proposal to apply the same technique in the sociology department, to create a file on poor people. It would contain economic and police records."

"Well . . . I can think of a similar system improving transportation systems, reorganizing the cities. Don't you think it's time we did some better planning in this world?"

Boldman looked straight at him, and spoke like a man who had thought about the problem long enough and had reached a personal conclusion. "Don't forget what the physicists say, that information is control. If you have information about someone, you control him to some extent. What happens when an intelligent, creative person learns that he or she is being monitored, that information is being recorded for an unknown purpose?"

"I don't know. I wouldn't like it very much."

Dean Scuttle didn't seem to appreciate Boldman's frankness. He got up abruptly, indicating the discussion had come to an end. As he crushed his empty coffee cup, he said casually, "That reminds me. I haven't seen your system in operation yet, Eric. Can you give me a demonstration this afternoon?"

"That's easy to arrange. I believe there's an extra phone line in this room, so I'll just bring a portable terminal."

Dean Scuttle looked at the telephone as if he had never noticed it before, and avoiding eye contact with Eric, he muttered, "There will be a consultant in the building, looking at our operation from the point of view of . . . efficiency. Cost-efficiency. He might drop in for a few minutes."

"By all means," said Eric, who suspected no foul play. "We'll see you at three."

Boldman had already left the room. A secretary intercepted Dean Scuttle in the hall to tell him about the bomb. Twenty miles away, Calvin Mellow's plane was making a perfect landing.

Eric was there at three, checking the settings on his terminal. Harry Boldman sat down with a supply of pipe tobacco. He looked a little pale. Calvin Mellow had introduced himself and was already very busy. He had three yellow pads in front of him and was drawing lines on what seemed to be a scheduling form. Eric noticed his ball-point pen: it could write in blue, red, green, or black at the push of a spring-mounted button. There were two other people in the room: Dean Scuttle and Mildred Safenest, wearing a severe brown pantsuit. Everybody was tense, except Eric, who still didn't know that he was tiptoeing through a mine field.

The demonstration Eric had prepared took twenty minutes, and it went very well. He showed the group how his system updated large data bases, and he described an elegant interrogation language that queried the research files of several university departments. Dr. Safenest grew more and more pale. Eric's system accomplished all the goals the College had promised, but never delivered, in its proposal to the Sciences Institute. Mildred Safenest asked a few random questions. Eric answered them at the blackboard.

Eric thought things were going very smoothly. If he impressed these people, they might agree to give him a job at PIN. He could put their project back on track. He was dreaming. He might have had a chance if his system had failed, or if it had shown a few bugs. But his demonstration was perfect: he was doomed. They couldn't afford to have him around.

The group didn't seem to have any more questions. They all looked at Calvin Mellow, who hadn't said anything yet. His question came out calmly, like a trimaran sailing out of the marina on a Sunday afternoon.

"Well, now, Eric, why don't you tell us how your system works, in detail?"

This was the trap, then. The demonstration they had requested had been an excuse, and all the talk about cost-efficiency, so much rubbish. Because it was to be a trap, Boldman had not mentioned in advance that Mildred would be there. Mellow would take notes. He was good at that. Four against one. This was the best-engineered brain-picking operation Eric had ever seen. They were looking at him, and he was thinking fast. First, buy some time.

"You realize it's not a very easy system to describe," he said, gesturing towards the terminal, implying that there was a huge program behind what he had just shown them. "I haven't brought any technical notes with me. This was supposed to be just a demonstration, and a discussion of my future role . . ."

If he thought he was going to slip out of it and change the subject like that, he was mistaken. Mellow was on his footsteps. "We cannot discuss that until we have fully evaluated your ideas. In complete detail."

For a fraction of a second, Eric experienced and tasted atrocious loneliness. In that same fraction of a second, he understood the magnitude of the swindle. At that same instant, too, he made the decision to keep his mouth shut and his brain unpicked.

The meeting lasted another interminable, unbelievable forty minutes. Nothing technical was discussed. Safenest became tenser, and Scuttle turned purple. Boldman did not seem to care at all. Calvin Mellow appeared only amused.

The consultant's final recommendations to Dean Scuttle called for the discontinuation of Eric's project.

A short time after this report was circulated at the top echelon, several key men resigned and left the campus. Eric Elzevier was tempted to follow. He decided to stay a while, however, out of a feeling of intense curiosity he was later to regret.

Dr. Safenest sent a report to Washington, indicating that "in the most recent research period, we have successfully identified the obstacles to the efficient implementation of an advanced database system." She requested another half-million dollars to study these "obstacles," and she got it. Her sponsors had no choice but to pour more money into the project or lose face.

Harry Boldman broke the news to Eric. With another grant in her pocket, Safenest needed something to show quickly. PIN would be reorganized. Eric would be a consultant on a temporary basis, but he would have no budget and no staff. Under this new scheme, Eric asked, would the scientists who had begun to use his system in their work be allowed to go on?

"Of course not," said Boldman, brushing aside the question with an easy sweep of his pipe. "If that came to the attention of somebody from Washington, they might smell a rat and ask questions. Eric, I am instructing you right now to take your system down. You will be transferred to the PIN group, and you will then provide a complete technical description of your methods and await further instructions." Watching the disgust on Eric's face, Boldman put a hand over his shoulder and went on, "You know, Mildred isn't a bad woman. She is just trying to make a living, like the rest of us."

Eric didn't answer, but he did comply with Boldman's order. He walked straight into the machine room, dazed, ignoring the systems programmers who were joking about the hole in the ceiling of the Dean's office.

Eric sat down in front of a terminal. He felt more calm than at any moment in his life. He gave his account number and a password, then went through the special protection set up for program files. They had told him to take his system down. He was doing exactly that, erasing one file after another: the routine that ran the creation of data bases, the program that did the updates, and the series of modules that represented the elegant interrogation language he had devised. They disappeared from the disk files, the magnetic signals were erased forever, and as the files vanished, Eric felt a weight leaving him. The wonders of software, he thought. All this hard work gone, and no visible sign of it anywhere. Eric closed his account, got up and left the room. The whole process had taken ten minutes. Mildred will be happy, he thought. My little system is gone.

Eric Elzevier went home and the next day he mailed his letter of resignation. Then he moved to California, where the best programmers in the country were congregating, lured by high salaries. He found an apartment. He roamed around from coffee shop to bookstore, from singles bar to pizza place, talking to everybody, looking for another job.

A visitor to Santa Clara, in the 1950s, would have immediately shared the Franciscan padres' delight with the beauty of the area. From San Francisco Bay to the charming coves of Santa Cruz, luscious hills unfold the majesty of the redwoods and drench people with the fragrance of eucalyptus and pine. A strangely mystical fascination has always been felt here. Is it the ominous presence of the big earthquake fault, which has juxtaposed utterly different geological terrains? Is it the whimsical mixture of palm trees and evergreens? Is it simply the feeling that this is the last row of hills in the Western universe, and that the blue sea they overlook is perhaps mankind's greatest remaining challenge, full of untold history, sunken treasures? All of this is reflected along the Bay in weird structures, tales of mystery, annals of crime. In San Jose, the Winchester House rambles on acre after acre, architectural testimony to the spiritualistic beliefs of its owner, the widow of the firearm tycoon. In Palo Alto, Frenchman's Tower is still an object of puzzlement to local amateurs, its history never fully elucidated. In Santa Cruz, a "mystery spot" seems to be nothing more than a tilted house that confuses one's sense of balance and perspective, but it brings excitement to visitors awed by its "violation" of the laws of nature (supported by good advertising). In Redwood City, a group that believes in faith healing meets weekly, while San Jose serves as international headquarters for the vast Rosicrucian Order. From dreaded Devil's Slide to the earthquake-molded hills, where the ghost of Holy City lingers with the quaint memory of a well-meaning mystical commune, there is the ever-present evidence of a strange past and the expectation of an even stranger future.

In Palo Alto, the Stanford family built a monumental entrance to its great estate: on either side of the gate were golden griffins on stone pedestals. The estate was later turned into a university; scholars came from around the globe to study and teach, and they began to transform the Peninsula through their work and through the activities of their students.

The new pattern was first apparent in 1909, when Stanford graduate Cyrus Elwell founded the Federal Telegraph Company in Palo Alto. New technologies followed: with financing from Stanford, an FTC engineer named Lee de Forest developed the vacuum tube, basic to the electronics industry. Other FTC engineers went on to create companies like Magnavox and Litton Industries.

During the 1930s, Stanford professor Frederick Terman, who taught engineering, advised his graduates to start their own electronics companies and keep them in Palo Alto. So when a young man named Bill Hewlett designed an audio oscillator in 1938, Terman helped him form a corporation with David Packard. Hewlett-Packard got started with a $1,000 loan from Crocker Bank and an order for several oscillators from Disney Studios. Today it is still headquartered in Palo Alto, and has become the world's largest manufacturer of electronic laboratory instruments.

The pretty orchards and quaint wooden houses began to disappear as buildings of concrete, glass, and steel rose all around the old Stanford farm. Then Stanford professors teamed up with the Varian Brothers to create Varian Associates. The year was 1948, and the development of the area was just beginning.

It was Terman's imagination, notes one author in a detailed study of the region produced by Stanford students,[18] that enabled the Peninsula to become a world capital of high technology:

> We have been pioneers in creating a new type of community, one that I have called a "community of technical scholars." Such a community is composed of industries using highly sophisticated technologies, together with a strong university that is sensitive to the creative activities of the surrounding industry. This pattern appears to be the wave of the future.

Terman became Dean of the Engineering School, then Provost of Stanford University, which leased part of its vast real estate holdings to Varian and Hewlett-Packard in 1951.

Three years later, the Board of Trustees announced that it would develop an industrial park for other companies, and it imposed its architectural standards on the whole area. Attracted by the beauty of the land, its well-planned future, and the ideal climate, young engineers came to the Bay Area in larger numbers. Stanford spinoffs now included the Shockley Transistor Corporation, headed by Bill Shockley, who had co-invented the transistor in 1947. Many scientific experts thought the transistor was a useless laboratory curiosity, but a few investors in the Palo Alto area followed their own gut feelings and prospered. Several Shockley engineers soon left the company to start new work at Fairchild, which became a major manufacturer of semiconductors.

The story continued: Fairchild got bigger, and tensions developed. Scientists left to form their own firms: Rheem, Signetics, National Semiconductor. In 1968, Robert Noyce and Gordon Moore left Fairchild to form Intel. Lester Hogan was picked to take direct control of the semiconductor operations at Fairchild. Jerry Sanders, who headed marketing, left to form Advanced Micro-Devices. Along with these dynamic engineers and businessmen were the silent actors, the venture capitalists, the bankers. Many financial institutions established their own branches in the area. The region soon became known as "Silicon Gulch," a nickname inspired by the proliferation of the silicon chips on which modern computers are based . . . at least until the next wave of technology makes them obsolete.

Today the orchards have disappeared completely, replaced by condominiums with swimming pools and dormitory towns like Cupertino and Sunnyvale. Housing costs have risen so fast that even the affluent computer companies can no longer afford to relocate the engineers they used to hire from all over the nation. In summer, a layer of thick brown smog frequently hides the hills from view. A worried astronomer from Lick Observatory, in those hills far above San Jose, told me that the staff now must wash the mirrors twice a year and resilver them every two years; they feel the drastic effects of pollution even at 4,000 feet.

At the time when my friend Eric Elzevier was looking for a job, one of the most advanced computer research projects in the Valley was called the STEM, and it was run by Dr. Stanley, who was nicknamed "Vision" Stanley because he was, basically, an inveterate dreamer. Stanley found himself sitting in the sand of a Pacific island at the end of World War II. He thought about his dead friends as he surveyed the smoldering remains of what had once been called Civilization. Why were the people of the world engaged in such wanton destruction? Why was technology always the root or the tool of war? The atom bomb, the aircraft, the radar—they had all been developed to serve the high priests of Mars. But couldn't anybody turn technology to serve the good side of humanity?

Like millions of dazed people everywhere in 1945, Stanley felt sure the catastrophe he had just witnessed had been useless. His training in engineering (he had a Ph.D. in control systems) told him there must be a way to help people communicate without conflicts. There must be a method, a path, through which people could understand their neighbors, and if it took a machine to do it, then by God, he, Stanley, was going to build that machine.

There were other scientists who shared Stanley's acute frustration. Vannevar Bush, in a magnificent flight of inspiration, had already proposed to create computers that would act like personal assistants to scientists, thinkers, leaders in all important human organizations. The machine he proposed would be called the Memex, for "Memory Extension." Vision Stanley embraced the concept and took it one step further. He decided to design a structure that would do nothing less than enhance the human ability to think. As soon as he got out of the armed forces, he began looking for a place where he could build what he called the STEM, the *Systematic Thought-Enhancing Machine.* He found the place in California.

In Silicon Gulch, technical obscurity is a mortal sin. STEM may have been meant to bring peace and harmony to mankind, but Stanley could never clearly explain what his invention was and what it did. Writing was an agony to Stanley. Like many brilliant inventors, he thought in images and motions, structures and frames, but not in words. He wasted a lot of time talking to academic and scientific groups, and finally discovered that the only people who would consider his ideas for the "Enhancement of Thought" were in the military. His concept, born in an effort to eliminate the basis of war, was funded by the Pentagon. What follows is a composite, imaginary, fictionalized account of Eric's adventures with the STEM project—a project which suffered from an identity crisis throughout its stormy history.

The military did not understand what Stanley was talking about any more than the academicians did. But they had money and bold ideas: if he could come up with anything even approximating the kind of information manipulation he was dreaming about, they were sure they could use it on the electronic battlefield. Stanley assembled a team, which wasn't hard to do in the profusion of talent thriving in Santa Clara, and in a few years created an extraordinary machine for the exploration of the world of data.

In 1969, when it was publicly demonstrated for the first time, the STEM was capable of doing on a small scale all the basic functions now regarded as the building blocks of office automation. It processed text, structured it into paragraphs and sentences that could be moved around at astonishing rates, and could merge the blocks of text into larger entities or split them into individual "files." Stanley, at the console, was linked to his staff by microwave, and he could project on a giant screen both the text on his computer terminal and the contents of the computer files thirty miles away. His assistants were shown on the screen, editing sentences in their memoranda, moving commas, formatting entire books, and even drawing graphs they could interactively change. And superimposed on those graphs could be the faces of anyone discussing changes with Stanley. The group even kept a running "journal" of everything it did.

When Vision Stanley began his work at Pacific Research Laboratory (PRL), the type of terminal so popular today was not generally available. Stanley had to improvise. He invented a way to display text on small oscilloscopes, where it was picked up by a TV camera and reproduced in black and white, like a page of newsprint, on television consoles throughout the laboratory. The STEM team also created a way to point at particular areas of the screen. A device shaped like a turtle was attached to the table supporting the screen; if you pushed the turtle in any direction, an arrow on the screen moved in that direction until you found the place where you wanted to tell the computer to change the information.

The STEM team had demonstrated that its work was many years ahead of its time. But somehow, instead of blossoming into a major industrial effort, it got into trouble with the information community and with its sponsors. The information experts were simply dumbfounded and jealous, because Stanley was a loner: he didn't need their help, he never even went to their meetings. He kept saying that library automation was a hopeless goal: the librarians should realize that their work must be based on human communication, not on computer processing. Stanley's sponsors, on the other hand, failed to see how the military could use the STEM. In 1970, the applications of computers to library science were centered on the processing of book orders and the sorting and compilation of complicated indexes. Stanley could have capitalized on his advance if he had turned the STEM to something practical, if he had recruited assistants who understood it and could sell it as a product. But Stanley was wary of such people. Instead, he preferred to be surrounded with engineers like himself. The STEM became a rocky island in the turbulent flow of computer technology, and the vision had to be compromised in order to survive.

The neglect suffered by the STEM would be just an anecdote, to be told and forgotten, were it only a case of a small group of technicians preserving their livelihood. But these technicians had already created and demonstrated a microcosm of a future world, they had truly anticipated the environment of things to come. The crises they lived through were prototypical. Eric observed them as such, realizing that their compromises prefigured a network-based society which would not be attained by the rest of the population for another ten or twenty years. The STEM story should be taken as a serious warning about the kind of community we will be creating, deliberately, by the late 1980s.

What was so profound about the STEM? It sounds simple on paper: a computer program for document preparation where people could archive and share their ideas through a running journal. In my view, that is in fact the most important point. STEM had the potential for creating a community that could work in many different places yet participate in the same creation processes. This idea is revolutionary in a world where the morning commute still dominates the lives of millions in every city of the planet, and where much of one's existence is spent looking across a desk at some other desk, and through a glass door at other glass doors . . .

Stanley's vision was of instantaneous exchanges over wires of intelligence, of a pool of information to which everyone could bow and drink deeply. But perhaps he did not want to recognize that other truth: that the technology was far ahead of humanity's comprehension of it, that the human race could not cope with the social and psychological transformations implied by the electronic interconnection of thousands of people. Like most engineers, Stanley underestimated the adaptation, the human factor. And the human factors came back and took revenge.

When Eric joined the STEM project in 1972, he had behind him some industrial experience with computers. Vision Stanley was looking for people who had built real information networks, and had acquired some bruises in the business world, a world he regarded with both fascination and contempt. After all, he had built himself an artificial business world immune to the storms of the external scene, and he had populated his project with individuals hand-picked and molded to suit his dream.

All was not completely smooth in Paradise, however: the chief engineer had resigned, and most of the early systems programmers had left, too. They had been replaced by products of the stormy 1960s: students with a strong "counterculture" bent, with well-defined views about an Establishment they regarded as utterly finished. They were true children to their parents: in the fast-moving world of Silicon Gulch, where suicide and divorce were alarmingly frequent among the educated, affluent, middle-aged employees of the electronics industry, the kids dropped out, learned programming, and fell in love with technology and computers. It was the only power trip in town, unless you liked to fly Army helicopters and carry an M-16 rifle through Asian jungles.

PRL recruited dozens of these young people as programmers and secretaries, because they were content with the low salaries necessary to keep overhead down. They looked at Stanley with awe for he could give them a glimpse of a different future as well as function in the old world of the Establishment. Even grass and LSD seemed to be connected: the dream of an information world to which the STEM was dedicated continued the exploration of consciousness that the drug culture had apparently begun. Here, too, Eric thought he saw a preview of a society in which the chemical control of certain moods would parallel the supertechnology for the manipulation of information. But there was another current at PRL, and it pulled the whole project strongly in the other direction. Grants were vanishing, and the project could find no other sources of support outside the military. Along came a new sponsor I shall call MEGA, and the project tumbled back into the arms of the Establishment.

MEGA, the Military Equipment and Gear Agency, had been created in the late 1950s to react swiftly to the Russian threat in space. Following the success of Sputnik I, it cut through government red tape to speed up the launching of America's own spacecraft. Soon it began to turn its attention to other areas besides space, becoming increasingly entangled in bureaucracy in the process. By the time it looked at computers, MEGA was up to its ears in the same red tape it was supposed to be fighting. Witness one of Eric's travel vouchers, in 1974, when his accounting classification was listed as:

9861611.2411 0627 A5X09 0622 0632 0642 0652 T50219 AFG 124

He had no idea what any one of these digits meant, but he suspected that merely by mistyping a 5 for a 7, a tired clerk would have designated a Sherman tank or a ton of rubber bands instead of a computer researcher from California. It was that world into which Stanley had to guide his project, and he was like the skipper of a sailing ship, with a crew of carefree weekend sailors, caught in the summer maneuvers of the Seventh Fleet.

The Military Equipment and Gear Agency had just begun to deploy a fantastic new creation: the first network of computers to span a continent. MEGANET was a revolutionary design which linked together machines of different makes, a bold strike that would soon force computing centers and universities across the nation to install special "interface" machines. They would have to put in telephone lines to connect their own computers to the spreading network or forget the support of Washington dollars, resign themselves to obsolescence, and forever hold their peace. Most of them chose to join.

The objective may have been scientific and economic, but the first impact was psychological: for the first time, a door had been forced open in the bureaucracy and a new type of community started growing. It was the community which Stanley had sensed was going to come, but he was unprepared for its sudden consequences. MEGA decided to renew the financing of the STEM if (and only if) Stanley agreed to change his computer, modernize his programs, and hook it up to the MEGANET, whose protocols it would have to obey. Since many of the STEM's special functions could not be moved to the new computer, the STEM suddenly lost in power what it gained in geographic coverage, by virtue of its access to the vast network the Pentagon was building. MEGA officials never knew the details of what happened next: they weren't there to see it, and they were only interested in technological results anyway. The social side of things was of no concern to their superengineers. But Eric was living with the project and he saw the most important part of the MEGA experiment from the inside—the human part. And again, he realized that any information network is a social system.

Lenin had told his cadres to electrify the countryside. The Pentagon decided to computerize it. Its research into miniaturization had already made pocket calculators possible, as well as radio terminals that used no wires to communicate with computers thousands of miles away. Its orders would now spur along the spread of the Wired Nation. But the folks at STEM were torn once again by their identity crisis: why should they take instructions from the Masters of War in Washington, when they were, as individuals, fighting the draft in California, demonstrating against the war in Vietnam, and seriously thinking of moving the PRL computer to the woods of Mendocino, to start a programmers' commune?

The confrontation became obvious one afternoon when the group, riddled by conflict, wheeled all the terminals into the corners and spread a carpet in the middle of the main room. It was time for a real brainstorm. The programmers, in their blue jeans and colored shirts, took off their sandals and sat in a circle. A bottle of wine and a few joints were produced and a serious encounter session began. The stairway door opened without warning, and who should walk in but the Director of PRL himself, in his gray suit and striped tie, followed by several high-ranking officers from the Pentagon. They were on an official site visit, checking the expenditures of public monies under their jurisdiction.

"And here is our STEM project . . ." the director began, without even looking. Then he looked, and saw, and smelled, and when he realized what the unmistakable odor was, he made up some sort of excuse and left in a hurry. The STEM project had just acquired one more crisis.

We must say this about Vision Stanley: he was able to rise above all those problems. He fired the troublemakers and replaced them with new people he could indoctrinate with his vision. He never made clear what the vision was, but he always managed to mesmerize his listeners. Eric understood the vision: Stanley, in his prophetic "right-brain" way, saw the day coming when computers would no longer be used by just a few lucky scientists, but would be available to a great many people. He foresaw entire communities working through them, and he grasped the effect of computers as early as 1947. Eric had taken a different course and had come to a similar realization much later: it was the suspension of time and space that excited him, and the simple precision of the keyboard. The STEM, on a good day, came close to that.

Eric never had a chance to explain all that to Vision Stanley, for the boss did not have time to listen to anyone very long. He was spending too much time fighting red tape and bureaucracy. Besides, he had already gone on to a new adventure: he was reading a book by management expert Peter Drucker, who wrote about "knowledge workers" as the new international elite. Always ready to shift terminologies when others thought they had him cornered, Stanley embraced the concept and made Knowledge Workers his new heroes, his big marketplace, his Chosen People. Knowledge Workers equipped with STEM terminals and thus endowed with think-enhancers that never failed, would be able to solve, at last, all of humanity's difficult problems. At GM, the Knowledge Workers would use STEM to enter their memos and their data bases. At American Airlines, Knowledge Workers would type in their inventory lists and respond to requests for part numbers. At GE and at Corning Glass, throughout corporate America, the STEM would enable specialists to keep track of markets and accounts. Soon every manager would be surrounded by a small battalion of information experts, each trained in the infinite subtleties of STEM: the system, of course, would be much too complex for the managers themselves to use.

From now on, Stanley announced, they were doing *Office Automation*. And that was official.

The STEM workers, who were generally late for work and sometimes came in half-stoned, took the big news in stride. If Uncle Sam wasn't supporting computer science and Thought Enhancement anymore, but had big bucks allocated for Office Automation, then Office Automation was obviously what they should be doing. They had another one of their big meetings, many beautiful feelings were "shared" and they all embraced, moved by emotions and too much wine and too many dreams of a future of peace and harmony. Secretaries who wore no bras wept openly on the shoulders of systems programmers wearing shirts with pretty pink butterflies embroidered on the back. It was a touching scene of innocence and scientific purity, one which Stanley surveyed with benign paternalism, before closing the door to his corner office and privately reviewing his old files.

There were a few people in the project who neigher cried nor danced with joy that day. They didn't think that the STEM was ready for office automation. They didn't think that Knowledge Workers, assuming there were such creatures, were ready for the STEM either. For one thing, the STEM was an extraordinarily complex system; hundreds of commands had to be memorized in order to use it, and learning them took years. Far from trying to simplify his system, Stanley had encouraged just the reverse: an engineer's productivity was measured by the number of commands he added to the language, which would eventually have to contain more words than the English language. In the mind of its inventor, after all, the STEM was destined to replace ambiguous and unwieldy English forms with new constructions that would leave no room for error. In English, you can say, "You wouldn't recognize little Johnny. He has grown another foot." Stanley could not tolerate such ambiguities. One day, as he was explaining this to Eric for the hundredth time, my friend thought he glimpsed what was happening: an engineer who was deeply unsatisfied with the common language was looking for machines that would permit him to create his own. He had found his ideal environment in office automation, a field in which engineers like him could determine the flow of information among human beings. Since information is control, those same engineers who shaped information structures in the office of the future would also subtly control office workers and, through them, the whole corporate edifice. This would be done in the name of productivity and cost-effectiveness, two notions easy to measure in an industrial setting, but totally undefined in the office world—and even more unclear when it came to "Knowledge Workers."

The staff was skeptical of the STEM's ability to make a contribution to the office world, no matter what the motivations of its designer might be. They could not even run a 30-member project; and the flower children, who were spontaneous and genuine enough to reject the dark and troubled world of their parents, were now simply building another dark and troubled world of their own. One girl who joined the project came to her interview dressed in a casual blouse and skirt, and after looking around at the Levis and the beads and the leather jackets, confided in mock apprehension, "How could I join this project? I don't have anything to wear!"

They had three typewriters, all in poor condition. The phone was answered irregularly, messages were frequently lost, and it was impossible to get copies made. Yet they considered themselves a model of communities to come. Why should they conform to the reactionary concepts of ordinary business, which was on the way out anyway? Their advanced computer theories would throw the old office world into the trashcans of history.

STEM went through a great phase of reorganization and social experimentation. The secretaries, who were all female, decided they shouldn't be stuck with menial tasks like typing and answering the phones, too indicative of the lowly position of women in business. The male programmers agreed in the name of the Knowledge Revolution, and left their terminals to rush to any phone that rang. The result was chaos on two fronts: the phone lines became hopelessly confused and the computer programs were tangled beyond repair. The project became less and less productive. The system chief even had to fire off a very angry memo one day, to remind the "Knowledge Workers" that a few basic functions had to be attended to, even in a laboratory where the Future with a capital F was being gestated and nurtured. Elzevier treasured this memo and he carefully preserved it (Figure 9) because it is a gem of realism in the phony display of office automation. Whenever he reads in *Fortune* or *Datamation* that a new, revolutionary electronic device is being introduced to increase secretarial productivity, he pulls out this memo and

```
31-MAR     3:08:53,1294
-------
Date:  31-MAR      308
From:  GURU
Re:    NO MORE!!
cc:    xxx
- - - -
       This is the third time this week I have had to come in the middle
of the night to fix the system due to a crash. At least twice it was
due to running out of disk pages!!! The catalog procedure was left
running and simply used it all up. Effective immediately the catalog
procedure will not be run unattended in the middle of the night unless
someone else is willing to take the inevitable call when we run out of
disk space. I am serving notice that I will not be available for such
calls in the future. You people go along with your heads up your
collective asses day after day assuming we have a virtual disk system.
I am telling you we dont and I really am sick of Harry, Joe and me
taking the brunt of such flagrant stupidity. Joe spends some major
part of his day running around pleading, begging and just plain
threatening people to cleanup and give a few file pages. We constantly
talk about THOUGHT ENHANCEMENT. Well thats all bullshit!! This system
runs because there are a few people constantly running around picking up
the pieces and in general wiping the KNOWLEDGE WORKERS asses (who doent
even have the brains to know they just shit).....xxx
```

Figure 9.   Memo from Guru.

reads it again. It brings him back to reality, he claims. It adds perspective to the great STEM dream, performing the useful function of experience.

Vision Stanley may have found it hard to solve his project's identity crisis, but MEGA, in Washington, had the same problem: they had trouble justifying to Congress their continued involvement in computer research. At an annual budget review, a Defense subcommittee called MEGA on the carpet to ask why the hell the Pentagon was doing office automation, when IBM and Xerox, for starters, each had multi-million dollar projects to do the same thing. MEGA's computer budget was cut. All of a sudden, it became anathema to mention office automation around the MEGANET. Major projects were reabsorbed into Defense-related missions and the PRL group was left high and dry. The researchers still made big speeches about Knowledge Workers, sounding more and more like a pack of wild dogs howling at the moon. But Washington was no longer listening: Stanley was in danger of losing his financial support. Simple tension grew into open conflict, and the project became stranger still.

Vision Stanley had to do something to recapture his weakening leadership. A new fad was sweeping California, Silicon Gulch no exception. It was a new movement that superseded polarity therapy, rolfing, Esalen and even psychic healing. Stanley embraced it as a timely solution to his problems. Those who wandered from group to group, looking for cosmic truth, the veterans of the great drug explosion of 1968, the seekers who were forever finding and forever joining new movements to find even more, were finally engulfed by this absolute end to the search: they had seen the great light at last. Vision Stanley was among them. So he sent his whole staff to take EST.

In Eric's opinion, there was a good match between Vision Stanley and the philosophy of John Paul Rosenberg, alias Werner Erhard. Stanley's work had been devoted to giving people a machine through which they could communicate and a language that would tolerate no ambiguity. Erhard was achieving control of the thousands who attended his seminars by a purely psychological technique and a single focus: his own word. Stanley was all intuition and he mistrusted dialogue, but he was a master at controlling the channels of information. Erhard funneled everything through a single channel, and he was good at words. This former salesman of the "positive thinking" school had carefully studied the movements of the New Age Consciousness, from the hot baths of Esalen to the group exercises of Mind Dynamics. He packaged it all into an intense experience, even sprinkling in a little Zen and Scientology, and he became an overnight success.

Taking two or three hundred people at a time (for it is much easier to control a group that size than a smaller one), the EST trainers would lock the doors, physically cutting off access to the telephone, the candy machine and the bathrooms, and deny their students the materialistic pleasures they had always counted on. They then proceeded to break down their defenses, using standard techniques which amazed and disoriented the uninitiated. They capitalized on their sense of failure. They would force them to recall the most humiliating experience of their lives and "share it" with the group. They would dismember them mentally, then put them together again like broken dolls.

The stories about Erhard's sessions had interesting effects on the STEM group, developing over a month or so. First came the gentle suggestion, the subtle pressure to register for the seminars.

Nothing ever got done at PRL without lengthy arguments. Stanley himself rarely attended the STEM meetings. They were run by his assistants sitting cross-legged on the floor, eating potato chips, drinking Coke and belching profusely. This was their way of expressing their identity, making it clear to the whole world that though they might be taking millions of dollars from the Defense Department to run their research, they were actually clever opportunists. It would be wrong to confuse them with the lackeys of the Masters of War who worked on laser-guided bombs and were recognizable by their ties, shiny shoes, and normal mealtime behavior. The STEM project was different, and they were going to prove it by enrolling in EST, a process about which they knew very little. The great mystery loomed above them, and it was their only opportunity to solve their personal and group conflicts.

A dozen staff members caved in right away. They were ready for it. They had been calling for it silently, their whole beings welcomed it, their minds gave no resistance. They were professional people, for the most part, who accepted the blame for the current failure of the STEM. Since Stanley could not be wrong, they themselves must have been unworthy of his great plan, they must have failed in the great mission he had given them. It never occurred to them that the project had become mired in the swamps of its own psychological confusion, that it was losing touch with the mainstream of computer research.

This first wave of believers dived into EST like a group of travelers long lost in the desert, seeking salvation in the waters of some refreshing and mysterious river. When they came back to the office on Monday, it was hard to recognize them. They had not undergone a simple attitude change: it was transfiguration. They glowed, they floated, they hovered, they levitated. Nothing got done that day; they bathed for hours in the ebullience of their new spirit, and the others listened to their stories, which were couched in a peculiar new language that clearly eluded and excluded the rest of the group. As soon as you began talking business with one member of the First Wave, you would be interrupted by another member who rushed over with some space to share. The two of them would start reminiscing about the deep, wonderful secrets of the past weekend. Eric's reaction was to go away on tiptoe, like a profane tourist who, looking for the exit on the side of the cathedral, has stumbled upon a meeting of archbishops who discussed in Latin the transsubstantiation of the Soul.

Other mysteries were implied by the First Wave proselytizers. They now knew how to be permanently happy. They had clothed themselves in an otherworldly glow. They would never be late for meetings again, they were going to be healthy forever. They had achieved a superhuman state and had sneezed their last sneezes.

The First Wave put so much pressure on the group that a second splinter began to come loose from the STEM. To Eric, watching from the outside, EST had become like a wet blanket of conformity thrown over a nice bunch of individuals trying to live out Stanley's genial dream. The STEM idea had now been restructured to enclose even bigger and more inaccessible goals: universal happiness, permanently clear thought. Scientologists spend years and many thousands of dollars trying to get "clear": EST covered the same ground in a few days for just 250 bucks. The Second Wave formed itself.

The Second Wave was intense and sincere. PRL officials had gone into the ranks of many Silicon Gulch companies, to recruit a more serious cadre of managers who would, they believed, restore their credibility in Washington. These managers had solid engineering degrees and production experience. Stanley gave them no authority and no means to use their experience, however, perhaps because he imagined the possibility that one of them would seize power. The result was a very confused bunch of middle-aged middle managers who had left their jobs in search of something more, because they thought there must be something more to life, indeed, than scheming down a career path at IBM or Varian. They had tried to recapture their creativity in the joy of research with this young, idealistic group, and they believed in what they understood to be Stanley's goal. What's more, they knew they could turn it into a reality. Yet somehow they failed: the project had gone nowhere, they spent their time in agonizing meetings where no decisions were ever made. They found themselves in a diabolically constructed trap in which they had no room to work. The staff scoffed at their suggestions for changes, and then blamed them for not "producing." Since the vision could not be wrong, there must be something really rotten about *them*, the old dinosaurs, the rejects of Computer Wonderland. If they were so bright, after all, why didn't they stay at Varian drawing big fat salaries? Why were they at PRL, trying to look younger than their age, like dirty old men visiting a commune in the woods, trying to grab the ass of some free-loving "chick"?

The suggestion of failure was there, under the surface, and the managers were emotionally vulnerable to it. Some of them were going through transitions marked by divorce, families breaking up. Silicon Gulch is in permanent psychological turmoil because computer technology changes so fast it quickly makes knowledge obsolete, and, as we have seen, forces people beyond the pace at which human emotions can be accommodated. The Second Wave could not delay much longer their visit to EST. The younger group members dangled before them the rewards of acceptance and reconciliation, the open arms of a loving group, if they would accept the ordeal.

They did. The following Monday, the gray-haired managers came to the office with the subdued glow of men who have found their inner truth, men who would never again be late for meetings, think less than clearly, or catch colds. Even the possibility of a sniffle was permanently barred from their lives.

For those who had not yet taken EST (you said, "I'm taking EST" as you would, "I'm taking 500 milligrams of penicillin"), the pressure became unbelievable. For a while, it was constant bombardment from group members who had gone through the Mysteries and now had a stake in the outcome. The whole world must go through EST to be saved, it was explained to Eric, or at least the whole STEM project. If just a few black sheep like him refused to go, they said, that was enough to ruin the whole effort. There was another reason as well, a hidden one: they had gone through the humiliation, the stripping, the public flogging of their souls, the *animectomy*. They had been given invisible badges of genius in return for their debasement. Now the others had to do it, too, or suffer social rejection. That was the underlying rule of any initiation, any group secret. In spite of their participation in the country's leading experiment in networking, the staff members at PRL were as vulnerable to this psychological pressure as any other group.

Eric's status in the team was peculiar. He was from industry, like the managers of the Second Wave. But he was younger than the managers, and was known for his computer work among the peers of the hip programmers. They didn't know what to do with him. He made it obvious that EST wasn't for him, although it was perfectly fine with him if they went to the seminars. Eric wasn't perfect, he admitted, he didn't think clearly at all times. He caught colds, and he was occasionally late for meetings, but he had his own standards and would work on his inadequacies without EST, thank you.

The First and Second Waves looked for other victims. They thought the task would be pretty easy now because they had become the overwhelming majority. They formed a block around

Stanley, who could hire and fire. They expected no organized resistance and they found none. Instead, they found individuals who could stand on their own two feet and simply tell them to get lost. This was a revelation to Eric. He discovered the strength and the resilience of some team members whose real spirit he had never suspected, and he was even grateful to EST for having revealed them. They were quite a group.

There was Cliff, who ran the network and was their only professional contact with the MEGA community, their gateway to Washington. If he left, the funding of the project would probably go with him. He had a thorough knowledge of the protocols that kept the computer accessible, and he would have made an ideal recruit for EST. Unfortunately, he had already chosen his own spiritual discipline: he was intently studying the mystics and had no intention, he said, to spend hours listening to a bunch of pathetic materialists looking for $250 short-cuts to enlightenment (the fee went up shortly after).

Then there was Guru, a big hairy fellow who had already shown a strong tendency to insubordination by writing the famous "Memo to Knowledge Workers" previously quoted. He resisted EST and this came as a big surprise to the hippies because he had long hair, wore the right kind of clothes, kept a guitar in his office, and talked dirty. True, they could fire him, but he was the only one in the group who knew the computer's operating system. If the software were not maintained regularly, it would collapse and the STEM would crash. A delegation was sent into Guru's office to put gentle pressure on him. After all, PRL was paying for half of the fee for EST, and if he was short of cash, maybe even that could be juggled around.

Guru told them that he had a nice curvaceous girl friend in the hills and had "better things to do on Saturday than listening to a bunch of hustlers." If they liked to pee in their pants in some sweaty meeting room in front of two hundred fucking idiots, however, he wasn't going to stop them. This particular style of domination didn't turn him on, he said. "I've tried it and I didn't like it." He waved aside his shoulder-length black hair and turned around to use his terminal.

John was the next to refuse the proffered cup of EST bitterness and joy. He had long hair, too, in the fashion of the day, and he was the only remaining programmer from the team that had written the current version of the STEM, so it was impossible to get rid of him. He came to PRL on his bike whenever he pleased, got the work done, and went home. On weekends he made furniture. His real goal in life was to become a woodcrafter. He smiled when invited to

EST, and said in his softspoken way he had a Louis XV chair to finish before he would consider anything like that.

Then there was Wilma. She had the office next to Eric's. She was a strong, cheerful person, usually dressed in purple, and he knew why she picked that particular color and why she wore certain stones on certain days, because he had some knowledge of astrological lore. She had confided to him where the hexagrams were on the floor of her office, and her shelves were well stocked with the occult books of Manly Hall and Dion Fortune. When the computer crashed or when Stanley got into one of his detestable moods, Eric went into Wilma's office; she gave him some herb tea, and she told him her thoughts on the Tarot and the Holy Grail. Wilma even had a scheme to run obscure cabalistic calculations on the STEM machine someday.

Wilma had studied the esoteric traditions for many years, and she regarded that kid Erhard as one of those Werner-come-latelies who had missed the whole point about initiation.

The Third Wave never materialized, and the apostles of EST realized they were wasting their time. The project conflicts deepened as time went on and as the glow of the EST experience gradually wore off. MEGA threatened to cut off its funding. People started coming to work late again. And then one day, right in the middle of a staff meeting, Stanley sneezed.

The EST experiment had been very useful, even if the results were not those Stanley had hoped for. It had revealed the deep hidden faults in the project. It did some good for those who took the seminars, because the idea of "taking responsibility for their lives" was probably something they had never encountered. It also did some good for those people who declined to attend, because it gave them the special strength of knowing they could stand up, alone if necessary, and preserve their own standards against enormous group pressure to conform—the type of pressure the "Digital Society" is soon going to place on all of us.

In this respect, the STEM project may have been a portent of things to come, a prototype for a world where advanced computer technology will combine with advanced mind-control science to enforce desired behaviors. Perhaps we cannot avoid going through such a phase before we discover a higher level of human freedom. For Eric, the lesson was the revelation that a few gifted people could successfully insist on preserving their personal freedom.

The results were predictable. Armed with their new strength, those who had *not* taken EST began to look around. Eric remembers asking himself what he was doing there, and then he resigned, having spent less than a year in the project. Cliff, Guru, Wilma, and John also resigned, what was left of STEM floated on for a little while, and then PRL managers succeeded in selling the project to a company that was looking for a document-preparation system. It had truly shrunk to that, to nothing more than a text-editor similar to those you will now find in the offices of any large newspaper. Once again, computer technology had devoured its own children.

It's hard to give true credit to Stanley's vision, for the human equation has obscured the technology, and the new computers have now made obsolete much of the work of his group. Its real effect has been indirect, too—the inspiration of the many designers and programmers who visited the STEM lab over the years and have gone to other jobs, gratefully recognizing many years later what they had learned from this man. Silicon Gulch is full of such tales, and somewhere near Santa Clara, Stanley probably dreams on, thinking of a time when computers will have eliminated war, poverty, and the ambiguities of human language.

His programmers never really meant what they said, about building a human communication machine. They could not stand direct communication, avoiding even normal dialogue whenever they could. The little terror of "the Other Person," which lurks in a dark corner somewhere in all of us, seemed to have taken over their entire mind. To them, communication itself was sheer terror, and the STEM was a response to that terror. It was a machine the hackers at PRL could put between themselves and the world of others. "Can I reach you this way?" They would push a few buttons, watch the little lights. "Or can I reach you that way? How can I make sure that your words will not harm me?" The real purpose of the STEM was to build a screen for its masters, to shield them from a terrible world that frightened them. The STEM would remember everything about its users, it would keep an accurate profile of them, it would offer a systems engineer a path to the thoughts of others. The knowledge of that path was power; and for that reason the STEM had to be very complicated, it had to be obscure to the casual user. Is there a similar motivation behind much of office automation? Is the social need answered by the machines really one of separation, of segregation, of increasing control?

Nobody has the heart to tell the truth. When all is said and done, when machines have tried in their simplistic ways to solve the human misunderstandings from which we all suffer, people will go back to older ways of dealing with each other's thoughts. They won't trust their transactions to the inner workings of a STEM, controlled by armies of programmers. Instead, they will set aside the shields of their software, and in my own dream, they will raise their heads above the curved plastic of their terminals, and patiently learn again to look one another straight in the eye.

CHAPTER SIX
Obfuscatology: The Science of Making Simple Things Complicated

Could it be that computer experts are trying to protect their privileges by hiding behind their own jargon? We see how the father of Jonathan Livingston Seagull was rudely thrown out of a long-distance chess game, and why the computer industry could learn a lot from vacuum cleaners. Observing all this, the author decides to become the founder of OBFUSCATOLOGY, the science of making simple things appear complicated.

Richard Bach, the author of *Jonathan Livingston Seagull*, was sitting at his computer terminal one quiet evening, and he was trying to play chess. He was in Florida while his opponent, a computer at MIT made available through the ARPANET system, was in Massachusetts. Right in the middle of his offensive, Bach suddenly received the following lines on his paper roll:

MESSAGE FROM ABC
ABC@AI 04:21:48 DO A $A 1,1,999(SPACE).
THE LAST TWO MOVES REFLECT AN OMISSION IN THE DEFAULT PARAMETERS.

Startled, Bach responded:

HOW SO?

He received the following "information" from the MIT folks:

LINK FROM ABC well, it has a mode called "active mode" in which it uses a different set of parameters and conducts a different sort of search. It gets into this mode whenever the number of seconds per move left before the time control is less than the third number in the last $A setting. However, in the default parameter settings this is 70 seconds. 2 moves ago it for the first time had more than 70 seconds per move left for each move up to the time control on move 40 (the default) so it entered active mode. However, the parameters are not set up for active mode so it really conducted a search looking only one play ahead (at its own move, but not at any replies by the opponent). That was why it took so little time for the last two moves (31 and 32). The suggested $A command will prevent it from beginning an active search at all (that is, so long as it always has less than 999 seconds per move left.)

No longer startled, but utterly dumbfounded by this reply, Richard Bach answered simply:

I THOUGHT IT WAS GETTING COCKY . . .

And he sent me the sheet, knowing that I was interested in the peculiar ways computer scientists have to confuse ordinary folks, who generally do not have an ARPANET code number in their wallet. In the margin he wrote the following comment: "Jacques— This happened before they found out I was a private individual and threw me out of the MIT chess option."

This brief exchange illustrates the incredible snobbery that surrounds computer access. Guarded by the puffery of high priests, the sanctity of passwords, and confidential phone numbers, the ARPA Network thinks of itself as the very exclusive province of a few geniuses. That thought might be excusable when one learns that its users have either crypto-clearances, or professorships on leading campuses, or both. It is inexcusable, however, when one realizes that the rest of the computing profession is guilty of the same contempt.

The current complexities of human interaction with computers can often be traced, not to genuine scientific or technical difficulties, but to poor design and misunderstandings of the motivations and work patterns of computer users. When computer experts have a choice of making things simple for the user, or of making them convenient for the machine, they take the side of the machine. It seems to me that better design, serious evaluation, and plain common sense will have to be applied to computer systems before these obstacles are removed, and the benefits of computer use blossom before an enthusiastic public. We have a long, long way to go.

What I am saying here is anathema to my purist colleagues in computer science. Vision Stanley wanted no one but "experts" using his STEM, and envisioned thousands of specialists being trained for years to memorize the myriad variations of his command language. But my point is becoming increasingly obvious to the people who have the thankless task of implementing "Office Automation," of pioneering new word processing techniques, or of explaining to the bank president why his computer has just sent Mrs. Higgins two thousand refund checks for ten cents each instead of one check for two hundred bucks. And it is becoming obvious to any employee who stands between the company's systems group and the normal people in the organization, and has to interpret for them the everyday crises in the machine room.

For the last few years, my associates and I have been in that unenviable position, as we researched, developed, and marketed the first computer conferencing system to be used on a computer network. In doing so, we have had the opportunity to observe the interactions among thousands of users (who were not computer specialists) and a veritable zoo of software systems. Many of the participants in our "conferences" had never used a terminal before, and it was our responsibility to train them in everything from the setting of the switches on their machines to the "log-in" procedure that would give them access to the various networks. This was an eye-opening experience for us, and it is worth reviewing as the proliferation of this technology becomes basic to the activities of American business, and as specialists begin to think about the massive introduction of such information services in American homes.

The idea of "computer conferencing" goes back to the Berlin Crisis of 1951, which was in many ways a prototype of the classic management emergency. All the NATO countries were involved and had to be consulted, but there was no time to fly all the leaders to a central location and a telephone conference call (in seventeen languages!) would have been an impossible enterprise. The State Department did have teletype channels to each of the countries, and I have been told that an attempt was made to splice together the wires of these seventeen teletypes and create a kind of crude information network. The result was chaos, since any character typed on any one of the teletypes was duplicated on all the others, if I understand how the brave attempt to link up the entire Western

World operated. Some bright folks in the defense community reflected that if only they could put a computer in the middle of this network, surely they could use the memory, logic, and structuring ability of the computer to organize the flow of messages and data around the various countries.

Such a proposal was easier to suggest than to implement. At the time of the Berlin Crisis there were no computer networks, no time-sharing systems (which enable a given computer to service several users simultaneously), and no convenient terminals. However, the Institute for Defense Analyses, which is a think tank for the defense community, began a thorough program of research into the whole problem of teleconferencing. Other groups started experimenting in the late 1960s at Rand and at the Office of Emergency Preparedness in Washington, D.C.

Given a group of people at different locations and with a common need for information, computer conferencing is a new type of technical link enabling that group to interact either simultaneously (as in a phone conference call) or at different times (like a very sophisticated message center with unlimited memory). This technical link consists of terminals, a local telephone call to a computer which controls the entire process, and a program that gives the users the ability to enter their information into a permanent record.

The first computer conferencing system to come "out of the laboratory" was the PLANET system, so named to convey the idea of a "Planning Network." But one doesn't have to be a planner to use computer conferencing. PLANET is now superseded by another system called NOTEPAD, designed to support the ongoing coordination needs of large organizations. NOTEPAD, for example, can be used simultaneously by writers in New York and Hollywood developing a situation comedy or changing a movie script, by stock market analysts in Chicago, London, and Brussels tracking important financial developments, and by a far-flung group of petroleum geologists retrieving drilling data in Alaska and Singapore. A church can coordinate an emergency shipment of drugs and food to a disaster area, and a psychologist, sitting in his study at home, can reply to questions posed during the day by his graduate assistants or even by his patients.

The key to making systems like NOTEPAD effective was not only in the sophistication of the machine operations. It was in the simplicity and friendliness of the user dialogue as well, an idea poorly understood by specialists, who are often heard to argue that they need large research grants in order to "study the problems of user interface." In my view, such an argument camouflages their unnecessary complication of computer use. It only lends dignity to a state of confusion that was created by programmers and should be cleaned up by programmers. If anything needs further research, it is not the user as an extension of the machine, but the social structure that surrounds any information system, be it a set of rules, a library, or a computer data base. It is this social structure which dictates the relationship between the user and the system.

We can begin with the question, "Why don't people use computers?" We do use computers, of course, but we are a very small minority. The man in the street still feels intimidated, awed, or repelled by computers, and many businessmen also view this technology with hostility. The reasons are plain and simple. The worries begin with the first thing the computer user will see; namely, the terminal. They grow when our user is trying to get into the network, or into the computer itself, to do his work. And they blossom like a clump of weeds when he actually tries to run a program. All phases of the technology are still unnecessarily complicated by the high priests who control it.

Figure 10 shows a standard terminal. This is the kind of equipment our project has been shipping to businesses, schools, research institutions, and government facilities around the country, to give *normal people* (as opposed to programmers) access to a computer.

Figure 10. Standard computer terminal.

Once a user receives the box which contains the terminal, we usually get a telephone call which sounds something like this:

> Hello, this is Sister Teresa of the African Rescue Mission. Is this the NOTEPAD Project?
>
> Yes, Sister Teresa, what can we do for you?
>
> Well, we have just received the package.
>
> Excellent! Is there a computer terminal in the package?
>
> Well, there is this . . . thing . . . Is that what I'm supposed to use to make our daily reports to the Mission Coordinators?
>
> Yes, it is, Sister Teresa. You'll see, it's quite simple. May I ask you to please take the unit out of the box? There's a handle on it.
>
> Ouch! This thing has some rough edges. How do you open it?
>
> You're supposed to flip the four fasteners out of the way. Have you done that? Now you can take the cord and plug it in.
>
> Why don't they have the cord rolled up inside, like any vacuum cleaner does?
>
> I don't know, Sister. The computer industry hasn't caught up with vacuum cleaner technology yet, I guess. Do you see the switch that says "ON/OFF?"

There is a long silence, then the quiet voice at the other end says:

> Nope.
>
> Well, I guess they don't label those things any more. It's the little switch hidden in the back.
>
> Let me see . . . There is one that says "Half" and one that says "Internal" and another that says "Parity" and one that says "Modem," and one that doesn't say anything.
>
> Try the one that doesn't say anything.
>
> Ah, there it is, the little light just came on.
>
> Now, can you see the key that says "Return"?
>
> I can't see the keys very well, there's this glare on the keyboard . . . Ah, you mean the key with the long shape, between the NUL and the LINE FEED?
>
> That's right, Sister, you will need to use that key. Now, before we start, is there some paper in the terminal?
>
> Paper? I don't see any paper . . .

At this point, you will have the enviable challenge of explaining to her how to thread a roll of awkwardly slippery heat-sensitive paper through a minuscule slit at the base of the terminal's inner cavity, while trying to prevent it from getting caught under the plastic cover plate.

Obfuscatology / 121

Now let us look more closely at the keyboard of the wonderful machine just received by Sister Teresa. It is shown in Figure 11.

Any normal person looking at this arrangement of keys will be very impressed by all the funny terms that cover this device. Sister Teresa, for example, might assume that by depressing the SHIFT key and hitting the letter E at the same time she will get the terminal to do an "ENQ," since that particular term appears on top of the E key. Thus, many of our users go through life without ever attempting a capital letter, for fear of unleashing some strange combination of actions or some uncontrollable process.

Of course, extraordinary persons (such as programmers and computer engineers) know better. We know that SHIFT-E on this machine will type an ordinary capital E, and that to do an ENQ one has to type CTRL-E. It is knowledge like this that makes us extraordinary. I confess that I have no idea what the circumstances would be under which I might need to utter "ENQ!" and I have yet to meet a computer expert who does. In my lectures I frequently call for help on this point, and I ask the audience to suggest possible meanings for "ENQ." The following figures illustrate some of the meanings that have been suggested by a cross-section of normal Americans. One engineer ran after me, following one lecture in Dallas, to say he thought he remembered an IBM command for a file system that instructed the program to "Enter the queue" and was abbreviated as ENQ. Similarly, Steven Spielberg immediately noticed the term "ETB" on top of the W key and told me, in confidence, that it really meant "Extra-Terrestrial Binary."

In spite of the confusion they create, these strange-sounding codes on the keyboard present few permanent problems. Worse is the fact that touch-typing is impossible, because of the poor shape and position of the keys, the variable delay to get the letters to type

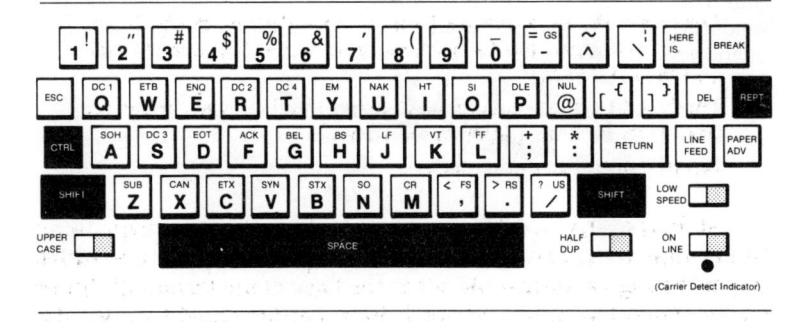

Figure 11. Standard computer keyboard.

Elephants
Never
Quit

Educate
Native
Quadrupeds

Eliminate
Needless
Quantities

Figure 12. Guessing the meaning of "ENQ".

out, and other features that prevent the depression of more than one key at a time. The glare on the keys, and the reflection of overhead lights on the plastic that coats the paper do not help either. Then there is the printing head, which often hides the user's view of the last characters typed. And even the most determined explorers of office automation are often discouraged by the intimidating row of function keys such as INT, BRK, or DUP, whose names bear only a distant relationship to what happens when you push them.

It is true that the technology is improving rapidly, but it is difficult to anticipate much progress in the user's enthusiasm for it as long as the terminal we provide is such a complex monstrosity.

Let us now peek into the living room where Mr. and Mrs. Average User, having finished dinner, are about to join their favorite computer network, as they have every day for the last two years. Although the network has thus recorded nearly 800 interactions with this engaging middle-aged couple, it apparently has no way to remember who they are, so they have to be known by the code name "HR6657." This is a thrill to Mrs. Average User, who is a fan of spy movies, but Mr. User can never remember the password. The following figure shows what happens between the time they hear the "BEEP" on their telephone and the time the terminal types out the message "WELCOME."

```
        CR
        CR
 1      TELENET
 2      415 DK1
 3
 4      TERMINAL=T125 CR
 5
 6      @C 617 20c CR
 7
 8
 9      617 20C5 CONNECTED
10
11
12      BBN-TENEX 1.34.5, BBN-SYSTEM-C EXEC 1.54.12
13      @LOG CR
14      (USER) HR6657 CR
```

```
15    PASSWORD XXXXXXX CR
16    ACCOUNT # CR
17    JOB 23 ON TTY151 19-JUL-XX 19:15
18    PREVIOUS LOGIN: 18-JUL-XX 19:03
19    @RUN PROGRAM CR
20
21    WELCOME!
```

I have repeated this operation under four separate commercial networks, which apparently stay in business in spite of these procedures (known in the trade as "the log-in sequence"). It would have been unfair to include military or academic systems like ARPANET as examples, since their users have no choice: they represent a captive market.

In these extremely scientific tests of the four networks, I have recorded three "Obfuscation parameters" which I have defined as follows:

A) The number of lines appearing on the terminal before Mr. and Mrs. Average User see something meaningful to them;
B) The number of keystrokes the user needs to type; and
C) The number of characters typed by the system having *no relevance* to their interests.

Even on the most expeditious network (INFONET), I found that it took 29 keystrokes to do nothing. How would you like to dial 29 digits every time you wanted to call your sweetheart? Telephone companies go out of business over things like that, but computer networks get away with it. On another network, called TELENET, it takes no less than 48 keystrokes to do nothing, but one is rewarded with a deluge of messages in reply, ranging from "415 DK1" to "JOB 23 on TTY151," neither of which has any real meaning or relevance for the user.

Now that Mr. and Mrs. Average User have successfully achieved the log-in, they can run their favorite program. They have graduated to the wonderful world of computers, where anything can happen. They could, for example, get a message like "DRUM FULL," after which the terminal will refuse to do anything. Mr. User, who didn't even know he *had* a drum, is extremely impressed.

I recall being introduced to a medical researcher in Europe a few months after a teleconference through which we had first "met." He was a calm Britisher whose first words to me, delivered in a kind but reproachful tone, were:

> You know, your message that says "HOST DIED"? Well, wouldn't it be more kind to say "HOST PASSED AWAY"?

Indeed, it is in death that computers come closest to emulating humans. The phenomena that accompany their last few seconds are as sad, emotional, and messy as those of their human masters. In their bereavement, Mr. and Mrs. Average User might well despair of ever finding their computer healthy again, as was the case with my friend, Bob Johansen, when he lost a program amidst much typing of strange characters (Figure 13). Since he had come to teleconferencing from a background in the sociology of religion, he simply assumed that the system was speaking in tongues. Yet when he tried to reestablish contact, he was told that the "Host" was no longer responding.

```
(TO FORUM)
- "OLY"?S?/:ZIICAMYSHV80/S81&9SJ38

HELLO 322 *:  2
@L 69

LATEST NEWS: 5 NOV
HOST NOT RESPONDING
```

Figure 13. Famous last words of a dying computer.

Program developers like myself rarely have much control over the appearance of such exchanges, which result from the deeper processes of the computer itself, and it would take a strong effort, on the part of the manufacturer, to make things any different. The folklore surrounding the little peculiarities and idiosyncracies of each system is amazingly diverse: every network has its own way of rejecting you, of pulling you into strange traps, of making you wait or repeat what you just said, or simply of dying on you without apologies or explanations. Although such peculiarities can be fun for the boys and girls in the machine room, they have a devastating effect on people who are trying to get a job done. When that job involves group interaction and joint effort among people located all over the Western World, as our computer conferences often do, the results can be very frustrating. I cannot see office automation seriously spreading within major corporations until such human factors are carefully examined by the network companies. And I certainly cannot see any serious development in the home use of computers until both terminals and communication lines are made more friendly and reliable.

Even more frustrating, perhaps, is the unfortunate tendency of programmers to tell the user that his commands are ILLEGAL, INVALID, or even IMPROPER when the system does not recognize what is being typed. Say, for instance, that you wanted the computer to print a file called MEMO. You sit down at your terminal and you type the command: PRINT MEMO.

No luck. This particular computer expects you to say: LIST MEMO, or some other directive. Do you suppose the computer will apologize because it did not understand your command? Not at all, it will start insulting you, and it will do so in its own peculiar language:

> IMPROPER REQUEST. FILE ACCESS ABORTED.
> REFER TO VALID COMMANDS.

Computer programmers are deciding for us what is "proper," "valid," and "legal."

I think I have discovered an important law I call THE PRINCIPLE OF CONSERVATION OF OBFUSCATION, which can be stated as follows:

> "When unnecessary complication is removed from one part of a system, it generally reappears in another part."

This principle is so general that it applies not only to computer systems, but to human systems as well. There are few governments, military organizations, bureaucracies, or administrations where the Principle of Conservation of Obfuscation is not clearly at work.

If there were a science of user interaction, the Obfuscation Imperative would constitute its first law. The Obfuscation Imperative states that:

> Whenever there are two ways to accomplish a given task using a computer, the first one being easily learned and understood by

Obfuscatology / 127

an unskilled user, the second being utterly confusing and useless without the assistance of one or more experts, the system designer will always take the second way.

It may be difficult for the reader to accept the reality of this rule or to grasp the extent of its pervasiveness. It is therefore necessary to illustrate it with a few painful examples.

On the TELENET network, there is a short but interesting message that occasionally is given out to users. It reads: "SUBPROCESS UNAVAILABLE." The puzzled user refers to the section of his user manual called "Explanation of Network Messages" and reads:

> The specific host process included as part of the address is not available.

Note that the so-called "explanation" has now, unnecessarily, added two new sources of confusion: the term "host" and the word "address." It has clarified nothing of the initial obscurity in the message, and the poor user has no recourse but to make an appointment with a systems expert. The expert knows the true meaning of the message: the computer is simply not working! Of such knowledge expertise is made!

The methods employed by programmers to confuse computer users are part of the discipline I call OBFUSCATOLOGY, the science of hiding things from other people.

IBM generally does things better than everybody else in the computer field, and this applies to Obfuscatology as well. It reaches a peak with system completion code 213 on the IBM 370. If your program stops with the message "Completion Code 213-04," you must consult the appropriate manual under the heading "IEC 132 I." The system expert who owns one of the few existing copies of the manual will then read to you the expanded text of the explanation:

> The format IDSCB for the data-set could not be found on the first volume (or the volume indexed by the volume sequence number) specified by the DD statement, or an I/O error occurred reading the F-1 DSCB for the data-set.

What the message simply means is, "DATA-SET WAS NOT THERE." So why didn't the computer say so in the first place? The difficulty was not in fact created by the computer itself, since the intelligible version of this message could have fit in the same space as the "COMPLETION CODE 213-04" instruction, both phrases having 22 letters. Obviously, the machine itself couldn't care less what the message says, and can print a meaningful English message just as easily as a confusing, jargon-riddled message of the same length. It is the programmer who deliberately complicated the message.

Is such evidence of obfuscation limited to the computer field? Of course not! It can be found whenever a community of specialists attempts to protect a privilege. In the thirteenth century, for instance, a surgeon named Arnold of Villanova recommended to his colleagues that they preserve their linguistic distance from their patients, especially under the greatest diagnostic stress. He wrote:

> Say that the patient has an obstruction of the liver, and particularly use the word "obstruction" because they do not understand what it means, and it helps greatly that a term is not understood by the people.

Examining the current medical literature, Michael Crichton concludes that contemporary physicians are still following this rule. They are trying to "astound and mystify the reader with a dazzling display of knowledge and scientific acumen." He also observes that most doctors now ignore papers outside their own specialties, because they can't understand them.

The legal profession, too, follows the Obfuscation Rule. When I bought my house, I signed a paper which reads:

> This Deed of Trust applies to, inures to the benefit of, and binds all parties hereto, their heirs, legatees, devisees, administrators, executors, successors and assigns.

Even photographers obfuscate, and cameras are a good example of a simple device that has been made unnecessarily complicated. Witness this extract from the user's manual of my modest camera:

> Using the flashmatic system, after you set the guide number, the correct exposure is automatically calculated as you focus. No more fumbling through lengthy calculations to find the proper F/Stop. Set the mark on the F/Stop ring to the center index. Obtain the proper guide number by multiplying F/Stop number times distance. For example, if ASA 80 film is being used, set the film speed on the calculator to ASA 80 and check the proper F/Stop number at a distance of 10 feet . . .

A common practice of software design is to give the same operation different names, depending on the part of the program you happen to be executing. Here again, better training of the user, or a bigger reference book, will not help. What is needed is a complete overhaul of the user interface.

If there were a science of user interaction, its second law could be called the Wide Angle Fallacy. When a disgusted user goes back to the designer saying, "Your system doesn't perform the special function I need," the designer's ego is deeply affected. To regain the good graces of his customer—and to re-establish his self-esteem—the designer is likely to answer, "I can fix it in no time. I will just add another command for you."

Later, the same man will be seen at conventions, meetings and workshops, extolling the virtues of his system, the "power" of which can be measured by the great number of commands it can execute. I believe this is usually a fallacy and users should recognize it as such. There is a similar fallacy in astronomy, related to the size of a telescope. Most novices and many astronomy students believe that you see more of the sky in a big telescope than in a small one. The opposite is true, of course: increasing the diameter of the telescope may collect more light, but it narrows the field of view.

The analogy with software design is appropriate. The early versions of our computer conferencing system had dozens of commands, hence a lot of apparent "power," but few users could remember the whole structure. It was my job to look for ways to cut down the list of commands and streamline the language. There is an art to doing that, and it is more akin to sculpture than anything else. You start with a big block of marble, and you work your way down to a shape the user can identify and appreciate. And what is true of programmers applies equally well to librarians, who think they are expanding the "power" of an index when they add more keywords and terms. The result is often ridiculous. Vanity once led me to look at the index of a new book to see if I was mentioned in it. I found my name all right, listed between *vagina* and *Van Allen Belt*. That was a humbling experience, and it has cured my former eagerness to see my name in print.

As an example of obfuscatology in action, the reference section of any large library really takes the prize. The whole issue of supporting the process of discovery, instead of mimicking its side-effects, lies solidly buried under dozens of documentation systems, which our profession is accumulating as a buffer between data and the human beings who need access to it.

There is a need for some elementary rules of simplicity in programming, but attempts to make computer professionals aware of that need often end up in frustration. This frustration is mounting as more people get to use computers and install them in their homes. The experts generally assume, however, that if you raise a question out of frustration, you also speak out of ignorance. At best, they will send you on your way with a tutorial on information systems and a 300-page programming manual. This attitude was illustrated for me by a discussion between Thad Wilson, a member of our research project, and the manager of the facilities of a leading network company:

"Many of our users don't understand why the network sometimes suddenly stops and says, 'PLEASE LOG IN.' How are they supposed to understand that? They've already logged in!" said Wilson.

The manager took on the air of an important person who has just been disturbed by a six-year-old who couldn't finish his arithmetic problem.

"They need to log-in again because a failure has occurred. It could be the node, the supervisor, the host, or the network hardware."

With that, he settled back into his chair, sure he had confused the issue sufficiently and that his questioner would go away. Thad, who had used computers for the past fifteen years, was not easily confused.

"Why don't you simply tell the users that you are sorry that service will be interrupted for a while?"

"You don't realize how long it takes us to change something like that!" said the manager, who now had his back to the wall. "We've been in business a long time. Why don't you give your users more detailed instructions?"

"I don't think it's a good idea," said Thad. "You should change your system instead."

This discussion illustrates a sad point. When we encounter problems with the use of computers, *we can change either the system or the people who use it. And that is what concerns me: the computer industry now has enough power to start changing people.* This network manager has already been changed, and he is working hard to change others and make them conform, like himself, to what he knows to be a mistake in his system.

The theme of the 13th Computer Society International Conference, held in Washington in the summer of 1976, was "Computers by the millions, for the millions." One of the speakers, the Chief Executive Office of Motorola Semiconductor Products, said that in the years ahead, the public must be given the opportunity to interact directly with the machines. According to *Computerworld*,[19] the speaker added that

> If the public is to use computers in everyday life, consumers need to be taught to "systems-think." Industry is responsible for actively encouraging this kind of education.

The computer industry is unquestionably dominated by bright engineers. But they are people who, in one theory of brain functioning, are heavily reliant on the "left-hemisphere" logical abilities that go with linear thinking. They have "optimization" as a goal, and their models of the world are mechanistic. And they are building systems for people like themselves, ignoring the needs of the rest of the population, where some of the most creative individuals, on the contrary, are "right-hemisphere" types who rely on intuition, esthetic perception, and even irrational decisions. Vision Stanley is an example of the latter type, trying to recapture a logical approach to reality by building a machine that would freeze other people into its memory long enough for him to interact with them. On the contrary, those who want to teach the public to "systems-think" seem to be fanatics of the Rational, on a crusade to drive out of our world the Evil of non-linear thinking. To them, any abstraction is absurd and uncontrollable.

In my view, the technologists are the ones who should change if they want to make a contribution to the human future. The people who use their creations are ahead of them, not behind. If the user types "PRINT MEMO" and the computer fails to understand this simple request, the burden is clearly on the shoulders of the programmer, not the user. If the computer cannot process the request, it should apologize. It's nothing for the computer to be ashamed of. Even humans often fail to understand other humans.

One rule easy to follow in software design is simply to recognize at what point choices are made between man and machine; when to add a feature to a computer system, to achieve a certain result, and when to let the social context of the user accomplish the same goal. Frequently, the designer comes to a point where the user needs a particular feature; for example, the ability to erase part of a text stored in the computer. Now the designer has a choice: he can create a program that will carry out this function, or he can allow the user to do it himself. The normal tendency of the programmer, of course, is to rush ahead blindly and create as many such functions as possible, to give his program more "power." I think that is a grave mistake. In many cases, the same function could be accomplished by creating a new *role* for one of the humans within the group, a role which would reflect these decisions. In the example of text deletion, giving all members of a group equal power to go back and change the record of what was said before, either by others or by themselves, is clearly a mistake. This power should be limited, and so there has to be a *facilitator*, within the group, who helps to administer its use. In some cases the computer should be left entirely out of the matter. Yet programmers are often on ego trips. It is hard for them to refrain from using the full power the machine gives them. They have trouble developing systems that adjust to the individual users.

The recognition that it was the *system* which must adapt to the social environment of its users was made in the late 1960s, by Wallace Sinaiko and Tom Belden. They expressed their frustration with ill-conceived systems one day as they walked toward the Universal Building in Washington, where they had parked their cars. The discovery was called the UNIVERSAL GARAGE PRINCIPLE.

The Universal Garage Principle states that an effective communications system must be designed to accommodate the status of the user. The higher the status, the more the system has to adjust to the individual.

Although this principle was expressed many years ago, it has not yet made a serious impact on the people designing large computer systems. The consequences are often funny; but as the power of the systems increases, to the point of affecting even the worldwide military networks that are supposed to insure our security, these consequences can be disastrous.

The social reality of computers, and the anecdotes surrounding their use, illustrate the vast distance between the services actually delivered by the computer community and the needs of the users it pretends to serve. In some computer conferences we ran on PLANET, and which included Richard Bach, we had a chance to see this discrepancy.

When Bach was unusually silent for a time, we called him on the telephone and learned that his terminal had broken down. We tried, unsuccessfully, to pressure network and terminal suppliers into helping him. When contact was finally re-established a week later, he gave us some of the details:

> Private Message from BACH 1-Jul-75 7:18 PM
> This system with the enormous potential for communication, education, entertainment, and intellectual atom-swapping is pressurized in a gas more inert than pure nitrogen. So far, I haven't even found somebody who will sell me a roll of paper for this thing (though I may have a line on one now). Headquarters people say, "Call the local office," not knowing their offices here are all closed or empty answering services. They promised to send me two rolls a week ago, which haven't yet arrived . . . I borrowed two from the repairman, who needs them replaced when mine ever arrive . . . Somehow he is not allowed to sell them.

The examples I have quoted all come from real life. It is true that they are only experienced by a very small community at the moment, but within the next decade this technology, following Meyer's hyperbolic explosion, will become all-pervasive. The complexities of computer use have been deliberately created by specialists, in many cases to protect their privilege. A massive effort to simplify the unnecessarily complicated control languages would free the creativity and time of thousands of people, and it would open a market for many new computer services. But it would superannuate the vast amounts of folklore and machine-room recipes that pass for knowledge and create job security for the programming elite.

The Obfuscation Imperative is a clever marketing strategy. Someone trying to understand the relationship between the user and the large systems soon to appear must first realize that the situation is dictated not by the technology itself, but by social, psychological, and economic constraints. In the meantime, I can only concur with William Blake, who wrote in *Jerusalem* (f10.20):

I must create a System
Or be enslaved by another man's!

CHAPTER SEVEN
Chip Tango and the Midnight Irregulars

Researching computer crime, the author meets a young man who sells dope through computer networks. He explains how to find sex partners by telephone without paying the phone company. He discovers a mathematics teacher who is classiied by the government as an artillery shell. He threatens to unveil a revolutionary technology powered by geraniums.

The sun never sets on MEGANET, the largest network of computers in the world.

High-speed telephone lines link the machines, from Norway to Japan, in a massive "experiment" which started in the 1960s. It is still in progress, much to the dismay of the Congressmen who voted the money for what they thought would be a modest research test. The "test" began with a handful of computers, was "validated" by wiring together the biggest universities in the land, and finally joined together all the leading facilities of advanced computer research. Even some London colleges and some intelligence facilities have access to MEGANET.

Chip Tango uses it to sell dope.

I "met" Chip Tango on the network. I was working late on my home terminal in California when the message flashed on my screen:

@LINK FROM HAWAII—ARE YOU THE GUY WHO IS INTERESTED IN TELECONFERENCING?

I accepted the link and replied to this question with another question:

@ARE YOU ENTERING THIS FROM HAWAII?

The response came quickly:

@NO - IM REALLY IN CALIFORNIA

And the crazy dialogue with the invisible entity continued:

@WHY DOES IT SAY HAWAII WHEN YOU TYPE?
@SOMEONE THERE LETS ME USE HIS ID.
@HOW DID YOU GET ON THIS COMPUTER?
@I FOUND AN ACCOUNT AND FIGURED OUT THE PASSWORD. ONE NIGHT I GOT CAUGHT AND THE OPERATOR SAID IT WAS OK BECAUSE OF MY AGE. IVE BEEN PROGRAMMING FOUR YEARS.
@HOW OLD ARE YOU NOW?
@FIFTEEN. NOW WHATS NEW AND EXCITING WITH TELECONFERENCING?

Wait a minute, I thought. This network links the major computer facilities of the country. Entire files of classified documents get moved around through the transfer protocols of the network.

It is one o'clock in the morning and I'm not dreaming. I am talking to an entity in California which wants to discuss teleconferencing and says it is fifteen years old. What's going on?

I had a partial answer at work the next day, after I made some inquiries around the lab. I found out there was a group called the Midnight Irregulars, who tapped into the packet switchers after dark in pursuit of their personal interests. It was hard to tell whether they actually "stole" machine time as they jumped from computer to computer, forming a new type of community, a colorful stratum in the sociology of networks never mentioned in social research. Within days, I was exchanging messages regularly with Chip and several others. I became convinced that the Midnight Irregulars were a portent of things to come.

Teenagers who take orders for dope over the 50-kilobit lines of MEGANET are telling us more about our future than all the final reports, seminars on distributed management, and scholarly symposia published under the aegis of prestigious professional organizations like IEEE, ACM, ICC, ICCC, ICA, and IFIP.[*] For Chip Tango and his friends are humans who have already adapted to the digital society, and have bent it to suit their requirements.

---

[*]IEEE: Institute of Electrical and Electronic Engineers
ACM: Association for Computing Machinery
ICC: International Computer Conference
ICCC: International Computer Communication Conference
ICA: International Communication Association
IFIP: International Federation of Information Processing

Gray-haired middle-managers across America slowly ponder data-processing primers and attend Diebold training seminars. Chip Tango, now 19, can program and deprogram every computer known to man, and has absolutely no fear of the discontinuity predicted by Meyer and precipitated upon us by the gods of technology.

When we finally met in person, Chip and I, and went to eat hot dogs in Woodside, we laughed about the academic concern with controlling computer byproducts like the Midnight Irregulars. I got to know Chip as a human being: I doubt if he has ever read a book other than the reference manuals for his various machines. He picks up information out of thin air, his ears flapping in the wind of Silicon Gulch as he drives down El Camino Real in his old Chevy. He has an uncanny sense for passwords, indirect addressing, and networks. He seems to be able to predict just when a particular component is ready to break down, leaving some big computer vulnerable to direct penetration through a usually impassable route.

Chip Tango has his own language. He never speaks of "using a machine" or "running a program." He leaves those expressions to engineers of the old school. Instead, he will say that he "attaches his consciousness" to a particular process. He butterflies his way across the net, picking up a link here, an open socket there. He negotiates among directories, leaving no trace, or very little. And he politely closes every file he consults in his browsing excursions.

Computer crime has become a favorite topic of journalists in the last five years, and with good reason. It is mysterious, full of technical intrigue and ingenious plots, and its victims are usually big companies, giving the man in the street his vicarious revenge over faceless institutions with their massive computers. But the real proportions of computer crime are unknown, and it takes a conversation with someone like Chip to realize how defenseless our society has become as a result of our attempt to control every facet of our life through computers. Chip Tango is no criminal. He simply uses computer networks as others use public highways or sidewalks. He doesn't steal anything and derives very little income from his unusual talents, but he does apply them to pushing the technology to its limits. The ease with which he obtains access to apparently secure information banks, however, is indicative of the incredible vulnerability among the systems that keep the Western World going.

In February 1969, students in Montreal destroyed two computers during a riot. The riot started a confrontation with police, summoned to regain control of a building the students had taken over to protest alleged racism in the biology department. There were, however, deeper and more complex issues involved: the rioters took axes with them and completely destroyed two machines, worth $1.6 million, scattering university records and throwing out magnetic tapes. The computer may have been a symbol of authority making itself inaccessible, the riot a crude and desperate move to obtain attention . . . That was over ten years ago. Now the young are educated in the potential of computers, and they have found more subtle methods to subvert their power. The control of computers resides in their software. Networking is the only revolutionary game in town.

On August 20, 1977, a young man was arrested at his terminal inside the Agriculture Department of the University of Alberta. For a month he had been disrupting the work of several thousand users of the university's $9 million system; he had caused repeated crashes of its operating system, and had occasionally wiped out entire files that the computer center staff had just read into the computer's memory. The 19-year-old man was convicted of mischief and theft of telecommunications facilities, but received only a suspended sentence because he derived no financial gain from the activity. The case was the first conviction for computer fraud in Canada.[20] More recently, a California computer expert named Stanley Rifkin stole $10 million from Security Pacific Bank through a simple telephone call, illustrating a type of criminal activity found to be pervasive by Stanford Research Institute expert Donn Parker. "The criminal no longer has to be at the site of the crime," he wrote. "Theoretically if he has access to a telephone in Outer Mongolia he can instantaneously commit a computer crime in Toronto."

Attempts to steal money from banks by computer have included the manipulation of internal accounting systems and even an ingenious scheme to credit a particular account (belonging to the criminal) with the rounding amount left over after currency conversion. In this second ploy, for example, if a certain sum of yen was converted into $12,657.672398, the criminal would allow the bank's program to transfer $12,657.67 to the regular customer's account, and would credit to himself the $0.002398 rounded off in the conversion. It takes a very long time to discover this type of crime, because nothing has been stolen from the bank's customer and only the institution's internal checking program can discover the error. In the large international banking networks using computers for electronic funds transfer, hundreds of millions of dollars flow daily through software systems that are vulnerable to similar penetration. It would be possible for someone to *delay* the delivery of the data as this enormous amount "floats" through the network, and pocket the interest, without actually stealing anything. Some experts are worried that such penetration will occur before complete security systems are in place, and that legislators will react by imposing security rules before considering the equally important question of privacy.

Although most computer crimes of the 1970s were never reported,[21] the culprits were, usually, relatively easy to catch. Losses went unreported because companies were embarrassed and were afraid of seeing their insurance policies revised or canceled. In his book *Crime by Computer*, Donn Parker explains that the crook was, typically, an intellectually curious fellow who loved to respond to challenges—the type who solves Martin Gardner's mathematical puzzles in *Scientific American*. Parker also remarks that this individual became tangled up in his crimes, and was usually relieved to be caught and freed of the elaborate schemes he had to develop to cover his tracks. One man in Northern California created a fake corporation that matched a real company, except for a 10 percent increment in costs which went into his pocket. This computer criminal eventually caved in under the weight of the paperwork necessary to keep his fake corporation going. He hired a lawyer, turned himself in, found that nobody believed his good intentions in doing so, and spent several years in jail.

I suspect the computer criminal of the next decade is going to be a different breed of cat. He will be quiet and better educated, in computer science, than his predecessors of the 1970s. And he will have access to an infinitely richer store of technology. He may even be a professional in computer security and penetration. Ironically, he may have received his training from the government itself.

Computer security is becoming big business. Thousands of law enforcement agencies are establishing security measures and counter-measures, and, more significantly, data bases dealing with individual citizens are literally exploding among dozens of agencies at the state and federal level. As new laws are passed to protect the citizens from unauthorized access and disclosure, more elaborate security systems have to be invented to enforce these laws, and provisions made to override these security systems in emergencies. Jack Anderson has revealed that American Telephone and Telegraph once confiscated the long-distance records of a former employee, bypassing the normal regulations that demand a court subpoena to acquire such communication records.

Law enforcement organizations and official intelligence agencies are sending hundreds of people a year to security training courses that include the handling of computer files and the breaking of other people's security. And outside the government, there are private organizations with access to large amounts of data gathered from a variety of official and unofficial sources (data which no state or federal body is legally empowered to regulate). One such group is the Interstate Organized Crime Index (IOCI), an outgrowth of the *private* "Law Enforcement Intelligence Unit" (LEIU), which was set up in 1956 to collect information on organized crime. In 1978, it claimed to have 225 member organizations in 46 states and Canada. Other semiprivate intelligence service, such as *Research West* and *Information Digest,* operate in a similar regulatory vacuum, and as their data-base systems proliferate, the problem of preventing unauthorized access to their files will become a nightmare. The regulation of the main federal systems is itself a very messy question (Congress has been debating for several years whether or not the FBI should have custody of the National Crime Information Center, for example), but the parallel groups escape even that control because they are not federal agencies. They are not subject to state or local controls either, since they operate as interstate networks, and they generally recruit intelligence and security experts who have left the government.

As the value of the information in such files increases, the possible rewards for breaking into the system become significant. Whether the attack is directed at financial, criminal, or intelligence data, it is increasingly likely that the perpetrators will be professionals, not simply gifted young men, like Chip Tango, looking for a challenge.

In October 1976, John T. Draper of Mountain View, California, alias "Captain Crunch," became the first Phone Phreak to go to jail. When the FBI searched his apartment, they found a computer terminal and an NCIC user manual. This young man from Silicon Gulch had started out by mastering the many ways to tap a phone line. According to the Midnight Irregulars, military communications specialists are trained in such techniques, and they practice routinely by listening in on civilian lines. Such knowledge spread quickly. Once a Phone Phreak has obtained one of the "inward codes," he can pose as a switchman using verification lines and get an operator to plug him into any part of the system he wants.

The Phone Phreaks discovered audio conferencing long before Bell Laboratories, which is still trying to figure out how to introduce it to the business world. They had found an unused Telex board trunk line inside a switching machine in Vancouver. According to Captain Crunch,

> We'd blue box our way to Vancouver, beep out 604 (the area code), then 2111, and be talking to hundreds of people. The Canadian government went bananas when they read this. I think this is where I got tapped by the feds.

The French had developed a similar network during World War II to support the clandestine activities of the Resistance. French telephone workers had set aside some trunks for use by the Underground. This illegal activity continued after the war, and it quickly became popular with students. From these heroic beginnings the technique grew into a minor social phenomenon, and today it is routinely used by people in search of sex partners. As soon as the French postal and telephone authorities close down one number, another number becomes popular. Amateurs of "Le Reseau" (The Network) meet regularly in a Parisian cafe to discuss the art of toll-free conferencing and to trade information on available lines, suspended numbers, or unassigned telephone circuits.

It is only a short step from tapping into telephone trunks to infiltrating computer networks, and the increasing reliance on large information systems, throughout our society, certainly creates the incentive for such penetration. Professional computer journals are naturally concerned with the issue, and the scientists have come up with a variety of ways to protect their systems. Here again, we must ask whether the cure is not worse than the illness, and whether we may be swept away by a technology which is out of control.

The first serious attempt to limit access to business computer systems was made by the Bureau of Standards in the mid-1970s. Scientists there came up with what is known as the DES, for "Data Encryption Standard." This technique consists of the use of a "key," usually a number containing many digits, which is applied to all the data transmitted to and from computer terminals. Using silicon chips, the DES technique can be embedded in any terminal today. Naturally, a similar unit at the computer end of the telephone line is necessary to "de-crypt" the data when it arrives. The chips can be manufactured in very large quantities and are already on the market for less than $15, with the price going down rapidly.

The DES makes it almost worthless to tap the line on which the terminal user is sending information: the eavesdropper would gather only garbage. Such a device certainly separates the men from the boys, as far as illegal access is concerned, but can it stop a determined effort at penetration? That depends entirely on the length of the key used for the encryption, and critics of the standard have pointed out that large companies and government organizations equipped with fast enough computers would still be able to decipher the information, because the key proposed by the government is not long enough. These critics have suggested doubling the length of the DES key to make the cost of decryption prohibitive, but the government has resisted these efforts. Some scientists suggest that the Bureau of Standards deliberately picked a key length long enough to discourage college kids and most industrial spies, but short enough to enable the gentlemen of Washington to continue to "read other gentlemen's mail."[22,23]

When Professor George Davida of the University of Wisconsin sought a patent for a better method of protecting computer security, he received a three-page letter from the U.S. Commerce Department. It told him he faced two years in jail and a $10,000 fine if he wrote or talked about his invention to anyone other than agents of the U.S. government.

Scientists at MIT and Stanford, meanwhile, had let a very interesting cat out of a very complicated bag. In 1975, two Stanford mathematicians, Dhitfield Fiffie and Martin Hellman, suggested a novel scheme for encryption that used the theory of "trapdoor" functions of a new branch of mathematics. Later, a young computer science professor at MIT, Ronald Rivest, extended their ideas into a specific code system, for which he sought a patent. The trapdoor concept was revolutionary, a turning point not only in computer security but in the entire field of cryptography (secret writing). It promised nothing less than the unbreakable code. It also led to some complications in the lives of these pioneering scientists.

Computer manufacturers, in public, have largely ignored or minimized the security question. An inquiry I made in 1979 about the data-base security of a particular system brought a blank stare from the "experts" and the patronizing statement that all files were "protected by keywords and system locks." When I asked what that meant, it turned out that the "system locks" were simply another level of passwords the user needed to remember. When I

Costlier Protection Hits Campus Centers

By Phyllis Huggins
CW West Coast Bureau

der a blanket policy that covers the president plans to be in public.

Then the president and his agents refurned by

$500,000 Federal Computer Theft

operated the computer theft scheme by filling out the paperwork for the computer to send disability checks to various addresses and post office boxes in Washington D.C. and Philadelphia where two accomplices allegedly picked up the checks.

of the money allegedly the scheme has tigators said.

y-Go-Round
'Right to Snoop'
Jack Anderson

AN Telephone and Tele the telephone colossus, has e right to snoop into the its customers.

Bell for refusing to participate in its political corruption. He swore that he had been compelled to donate $50 a month to an illegal political slush fund.

Bell executives were also required, to make other regular cash the slush fund.

Micro Assists Child Porn Ring

A four-month investigation by the Sexually Exploited Child Unit of the Los Angeles Police Department and the San Jose Police has led to the arrests and several persons in connection with what is believed to be the only computerized child

Youth Taps Into UC Computers

By Harry Jupiter

A 15-year-old Concord lad, using second-hand equipment he bought for $60, disrupted the University of California's intricate puter operations for pus police said ley.

sending worldwi patients

home Thursday after two tives and a Concord a search war dence

ed to the custody has an appoint ameda county juvenile

The boy, described as very intelligent, was charged with grand theft stealing more than 200 hours worth of

Les «enragés» de Toulouse

School Computer Invades Some Firms

New York

The FBI is seeking a "little Einstein" who may have used a classroom computer at one of New York City's most exclusive private schools to penetrate 21 Canadian computer systems.

"At this point we don't know who we suspect or what the motive may have been." FBI spokesman Quentin Ertel said yesterday.

The FBI knows this much:

Computers
U.S. Tells Professor To Hush Invention

Milwaukee

The federal government has told a university professor he can't write or talk about his invention to safeguard computer information because it might b dangerous to national security, a university official sa yesterday.

It threatened him with prison and fines. The professor and the university are u als at the University of Wisconsin-Milwaukee don't know who the federal officials ncy they're with.

of the federal

Figure 14.   Press clippings show mounting concern with security and privacy.

asked what protection existed against hostile software, written by systems programmers who might know how to gain control of the operating system (and thus bypass the security entirely), the question received only awkward silence. Many large organizations have started to take the law into their own hands, and borrow computer security measures used by the law enforcement, military, or intelligence communities. These include, of course, physical protection of the machine and controlled access (through doors equipped with cameras and badge-reading devices) as well as terminals equipped with keys. These precautions just reinforce the computer's image as an evil machine, which must be protected by guards, and remains inaccessible to normal folks.

More and more companies are using encryption, in both hardware and software, in addition to physical security measures. Again they are borrowing from the world of spies and counterspies, and that poses a new problem because the intelligence world does not have the same needs as the business community when it comes to encryption of messages. Intelligence has secure channels for the distribution of keys and code-books, while the business world does not. And intelligence does not move $7 billion per day from continent to continent, as does a single American bank system. Businessmen have very different needs: the ability to change encryption techniques quickly, specialize them for particular tasks, and use them for communication not with well-defined sites but for transmission throughout the world, among companies that in many cases are openly competing against each other. And this is where the "trapdoor" technique comes in.

We can regard any method of encryption as a mathematical transformation that changes the message, the *plaintext*, into a string of apparently meaningless characters, the *ciphertext*. In most cases the technique has an "inverse." That is, the person doing the encrypting can easily go back from the ciphertext to the English message. This means that a third party can break the code if enough time and enough ciphertext are available.

If Mr. Smith, for instance, agrees with his New York broker to use a cipher in which he will add two units to each digit, the broker will simply reconstruct the original message by subtracting 2 from each digit received. If Mr. Smith wants to sell 237 shares at 104, he will send the numbers 459 and 326. In this case, the second operation (subtracting 2) is accomplished just as easily as the original (adding 2). But what if we used a function in which one side of the operation was easy, but the inverse side almost impossible?

There are entire classes of such mathematical "functions." They provide two keys, one for encoding and one for decoding, and they lead to unbreakable ciphers. They have the added advantage that one does not have to send the key in advance to the person who will receive the message. It is even possible to publish the key used for encoding and to authenticate the signature of the sender! These functions are called "trapdoor functions" for the obvious reason that it is very easy to go through them in one direction, but impossible to go back in the other direction, unless one knows the decryption key.

How would one use this principle in practice? Suppose we use a key which is the product of two very large prime numbers. Mr. Smith knows the published key and applies it to his message to his broker. Only the broker, however, knows the prime factors used to compute the encryption key, so only he can decode it. In other words, the sender encodes his message using the key of the person he wants to send it to. Now, why couldn't someone intercept that message and, knowing the broker's encryption key, which is public knowledge, break it down into the product of prime numbers? The answer is that it *could* be done, but only with incredible complexity. Nobody needs a computer to understand that 21 is the product of 7 times 3, but it takes almost a full minute of computer time on a PDP-10 computer to find the first prime number following 2 to the 200th power. And it would take about 40 quadrillion years of computer time on the fastest machine known today to decompose a 125-digit number into the product of two 63-digit prime numbers, according to mathematician Ron Rivest. The person finding or intercepting an electronic message enciphered with a trapdoor key, consequently, is powerless to turn it into plaintext, even though the enciphering key is public knowledge.

Publication of these developments in engineering and mathematical journals has made the intelligence community nervous. In October 1977, the Institute of Electrical and Electronic Engineers (IEEE) received a letter, written by a man named Joseph Meyer, warning that some of its members might be in violation of the International Regulations of Traffic in Arms. This was an indirect reference to the work of IEEE member Martin Hellman, the Stanford professor who had published his work on trapdoor functions. According to *Science* magazine, Joseph Meyer is listed in the National Security Agency (NSA) directory, one of the largest intelligence groups in the U.S. government. Meyer refused to confirm that he worked there, and an NSA spokesman named Norman Boardman said,[24]

> I can state for the agency that we had nothing to do with that letter . . . Meyer wrote that letter as a private citizen. But with respect to any letter of that nature this agency would not prompt anyone to do it.

The problem referred to in the letter arises because even unclassified technical data is covered by various laws relating to the exportation of weapons technology. In Meyer's view, no researcher could publish articles on encryption in the United States without "prior approval by a cognizant government agency" because cryptology data are in the same category as weapons. This raised a furor among scientists, who argued that the NSA was trying to bring this area of mathematical research under its own control. That control, in turn, would lead to a decline in the quality of cryptography available to private business, since the NSA would allow business to use only those codes the NSA considered breakable.[25,26,27]

Other scientists took it for granted that the new cryptology techniques would soon become routine, and a number of companies applied for patents in this area. In the words of Fred Weingarten of the National Science Foundation,

> There is certainly going to be a lot of civilian cryptography. When we start doing our banking electronically and have electronic mail and firms are shipping data over wires, I would think it is going to be routine that all data communication will be encrypted in a few years. It's a natural development of the use of computers.

How will this be accomplished? Simply by adding encryption key capability to the terminal itself, so that even if the telephone line were tapped an eavesdropper would get only garbage. Breaking through the security of the system would then require either an insider at the site, or good old-fashioned espionage techniques of the cloak-and-dagger category, such as stealing the original English message text from the sender's trash can.

In January 1979, Berkeley police arrested a 15-year-old boy from nearby Concord. Using secondhand equipment he had bought for $60, he had disrupted for months the operations of the University of California computer. Two detectives and a Concord policeman found evidence that he had been tapping into the computer from his home terminal. They obtained a search warrant and arrested him, releasing him eventually to the custody of his mother. He was charged with grand theft for stealing over 200 hours of computer time, vandalism for disrupting programs, and possession of stolen property (printouts of other people's computer work he had obtained through the system).[28]

When computer files started disappearing and popping up in strange places, and when other incongruities showed up, Professor Stuart Lynn, director of computing affairs, had a warning put into each university project. A message believed to be from the Concord Kid came back on the computer, saying:

YOU HAVE DONE RELATIVELY WELL KEEPING ME OUT. WOULD YOU LIKE SOME HELP?

During 1979, there were at least ten physical attacks against computing facilities in France, and no one knows how many in the United States. Toulouse emerged as a center of anti-computer activity when several groups of young activists in that town began stealing and circulating confidential data bases, sometimes openly distributing copies of the files in the street.

To poke fun at the obsolete political labels still used by their elders and to further scandalize the *bourgeoisie*, such activists have given their organizations preposterous names like P.O.L.I.C.E. (which stands for the French equivalent of "Libertarian International Communist Student Worker's Party"!) or CLODO (Committee for the Liquidation or Destruction of Computers). One or more of these groups attacked, in April 1980, the installations of the Philips and Honeywell-Bull computer companies in Toulouse, destroying a lot of expensive office automation equipment.

Some firms believe these incidents underline the need for better physical protection of their expensive computers, but this is not the whole answer. The sophisticated computer crime of tomorrow will be committed by insiders.

In 1978 and 1979, the Secret Service spent eighteen months tracking down money stolen from the Social Security Administration in the form of false disability claims. Half a million dollars were taken in the scheme, which was described as "very, very sophisticated." Someone was finally arrested in Baltimore, a Social Security employee named Janet Blair, aged 29. She had filled out the fake paperwork and had the computer send the money to post office boxes up and down the East Coast, where her accomplices picked it up. The computer itself was not the site of the crime. She had perverted the entire system.

As the value of the information we store in computers increases, so does the incentive to break into the system. Every attempt to protect the computers informs outsiders that getting in is more worthwhile, while simultaneously strengthening the temptation for insiders to sell some of their knowledge. One specialist estimates that the large majority of computer crimes are already committed by insiders—people who have legitimate access to the computer and know all the keywords necessary to read the files.

It may have been easy, once, to check on the reliability and loyalty of employees, when computing centers had a small staff and a high degree of professionalism. But today we are looking at an exploding population of users, both within the organization that owns the computers and among the far-flung clientele it serves.

The kind of society being created by the availabilty of the massive computer networks is more interesting, to me, than computer crime, which is only one of its manifestations. For the Midnight Irregulars, the network is a markeplace, a newspaper, a playground, and an office. It can be many other things if the public wants it to be, and the ultimate choice has to be made by all of us.

No matter how complex, how saturated in jargon it becomes, the world of computers can be understood and mastered by anyone who really wants to master it. If I did not believe that, I would not be writing this book. The technology can be described without long and confusing explanations, and its effects can be grasped by a wide audience, even though the computer technicians would like to convince people that it is impossible to understand (and therefore to question) their work unless one knows all about balanced trees and double-density.

One of the questions raised by the prospect of secure networks is that of their danger to society as a whole. We do want to make sure that our privacy is not being invaded, and it would be nice to be able to communicate with a girl friend or business associate with the knowledge that neither government spooks nor Russian spies nor meddlesome bosses nor hired eavesdroppers can pick up bits of conversation. People are becoming increasingly concerned that their telephone conversations are not private, and the weight of testimony before Congressional committees indicates that this concern is only the tip of the iceberg. The capability to pick up conversations (especially long-distance conversations) is widely shared among government and business bodies. As for international communications, they are routinely monitored as a matter of principle. It would be a relief for people to have an alternative means of exchanging ideas, thoughts, and emotions, without the constant awareness of institutional voyeurism. The consequences could be far-reaching. Who knows what ideas are withheld, what creative impulses are checked, because of such fears?

Private citizens are showing much concern about such invasions of their privacy but there is little that can be done with the trivia that fills most of our everyday conversations. Large companies, however, are now taking extraordinary precautions to preserve communication security and escape eavesdropping: they are not only using scramblers and sophisticated electronic machines to detect bugging, but are also handling key conversations in remote locations, where the participants offer as little opportunity as possible to a would-be-spy. One oil company, while concluding discussions about a joint venture in Alaska with representatives of another corporation, went as far as leasing a train, putting the executives of both companies on board, and running the train in circles for three days in the Canadian wilderness. A perfectly secure communications technology would meet with instant success in a marketplace where such secrecy is mandatory, and it would certainly save money in diesel fuel!

We have to ask, on the other hand, whether such a technology wouldn't have unforeseen side effects for the community. Imagine a world where perfectly secure communications are available to any group that wanted them. Should terrorist groups have access to them? Should organized crime be able to run its Nevada operations from New York or Chicago or the Bahamas without any fear of detection? Should foreign agents operating in a given country be able to send reports and receive orders from their case officers through the same network of computers used by housewives doing their electronic shopping and executives reviewing last month's sales figures?

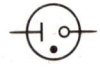

In 1973 and 1974, our early model of a teleconferencing system became available on a nationwide network. It could be used by any group with valid access to that network, and people were encouraged to run their own experiments with it. One such group was an informal bunch of social science students who were interested, as I was, in the various social effects of advanced forms of communication. They were routinely creating conferences on the possibility of linking school children with NASA experts, or conducting therapy sessions over terminals, or helping senior citizens escape loneliness through access to information, games, and hobby groups.

One day some of the students decided to use the system to impeach the President.

The idea was to use our system to link together anti-Nixon student groups on every campus connected to the network. Since computer conferencing permits a single entry or message to be instantly available at all other sites, it is an ideal technique for creating a "grass-roots" movement designed to upset political structures.

Our project was immediately divided on the question. Should we allow this kind of application and experimentation on our system? Since we controlled the software, we were clearly in a position to locate the computer files where the conference was held and "pull the plug." The terms under which we made the system available, however, were clear: our experiments were open to anyone who had valid access to the network, and our users, in this case, were valid users. Was it our sponsor's responsibility to decide whether or not access privileges should be removed? Or was I suddenly in the unenviable position of playing network cop?

A large part of our research was directed, not at building conferencing systems, but at studying their effects on people and organizations. Here was a splendid opportunity to observe human behavior in action, in communications situation that might not be generally available to the public for another ten or fifteen years. Some colleagues pleaded with me to let the group go on. And if I were to destroy their conference, besides, I might be violating their constitutional rights: their right not only to freedom of expression, but perhaps to freedom of assembly as well. It would take a court of law to decide whether a teleconference among twenty people in different parts of the United States, using computer terminals in their living rooms constituted "assembly" in the sense intended by the Founding Fathers.

The plug was pulled. I made the unpleasant decision because in this case, I felt, the users were abusing research facilities that were partly under the jurisdiction of our group. The underlying issues, however, were never completely resolved in my mind. If the same situation arose on a commercial computer network, it seems to me there would be no basis for network technicians to take the law in their own hands and deny the use of their facilities, as long as the users did not violate the law and paid their bills on time. Such uses of computer conferencing are unavoidable, and they will have profound effects on the organizations where they occur. In a network that was technically secure, where the user terminals were equipped with trapdoor encryption devices, for instance, such conferences could go on for years without being discovered. The implications are fascinating.

The world has never known a communication system that was global in scope and also able to preserve individual privacy. There is no historic precedent. We do not know if people can be trusted to use it wisely. All governments will oppose it, in the name of public protection against criminals, spies, and other undesirable elements. But they may not be able to stop it, because the industrial demand for such systems will be great. Besides, high-school kids will soon understand enough about the technique to be able to implement it themselves. It may be as difficult for the NSA to stop such practices as it is hard for the FCC to register citizens' band radios and ensure that they are used legally and not for solicitation of prostitution or drug trafficking.

Chip Tango knows all that and he looks at the future with enthusiasm. His trust in humanity is inexhaustible. He takes for granted that computer technology is out of control, and he wants to ride it as a surfer rides a wave. The opportunities for fouling up the world through computer power are unlimited, but he thinks that people like him are useful agents in establishing a balance, a sense of humanness and humor, a reality beyond the conflicts of the organizations that are manufacturing, buying and installing the big computers of today. These organizations imagine they control the technology simply because they have paid $7 million for that shiny piece of iron, with its humming tape drives and its blinking lights, now sitting in the basement.

I asked Chip if he was never worried about a future world in which computers would be used to depersonalize human contact. I told him about "Vision" Stanley and his use of the STEM, which was dictatorial under the guise of idealistic and humanistic concerns. The STEM could be looked on as a prototype of the future network everybody would use, from government agencies to consumer groups, from teachers to retail stores. Yet its intent was obviously manipulative. It divided people. It reduced them to files and buffers and ridiculous little green letters floating on computer screens. Was that the future he wanted? A future in which every house was wired to every other house through computers and hierarchies of computers? In which a mini-machine watched energy use in the apartment and talked to the machine running environmental controls for the whole block, which was, in turn, wired to the computer regulating the whole city? In which there were cable networks for two-way interaction with the news organizations, and in which you could obtain profiles of people you had never seen, that would tell you if they wanted to play bridge or talk about sadism or ghosts or trade stamps? Is that the world you want, Chip? And aren't you a little worried that you might become just another profile in somebody's memory tape? Don't you see that advertisers will be able to select you as a likely buyer of certain products? That groups and organizations will be able to discover your existence through the network much better than they can in the relatively loose and unstructured world of today, and will target you for the sale of their ideas, their products, their religion, their politics? What will become of your independence?

Chip looked up from his plate and put down his hot dog. He wiped up a thin line of ketchup that was forming at the side of his mouth, and his eyes took on a quizzical expression, that of a teenager who has just heard a lesson in morality from his father and is wondering whether the old dinosaur is joking or really believes what he said. Chip obviously decided that my case was not completely hopeless, and he said, "I'm not worried for a minute about the future. If the world you just described is going to happen, man, let it happen! I can fuck it up a lot faster than that world we live in now!"

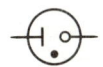

Along El Camino Real, the backbone of Silicon Gulch from Menlo Park to Sunnyvale, the scene changes constantly. The shop that sold water beds in the early 1970s became a karate school, then an electronics repair company. The small building that housed a flower display in the old days turned briefly into a head shop, and now proudly shows to the street a row of IBM personal computers and a bright, multicolored APPLE poster. You can buy diskettes and software manuals anywhere. Bookstores have a section on computers where *BYTE* magazine is next to *Infoworld* ("The Newspaper for the Microcomputing Community") and complex volumes that invite the reader to build his own operating system.

It is in such a bookstore that I met Chip Tango again. He had changed. His hair was noticeably shorter and his face was adorned with a closely trimmed mustache. We exchanged some polite dialogue. I kidded him about his tie and found out he now held a regular job with one of the leading computer firms in the Valley.

Then he asked me, "Are you still interested in networks?"

"Sure," I said, "but who can keep up?"

"Well, maybe I ought to show you something."

Chip lived in the next block, in a perfectly anonymous apartment he rented from an old couple. We passed their green Cadillac. We heard the voice of Frank Sinatra coming from their TV at the street level. We climbed some stairs.

Inside Chip's apartment the walls were off-white, the carpet was green. There was a small kitchen with a pink refrigerator and a Sears fixture hanging from the middle of the ceiling. The living room was large, about twelve by twelve, with posters of Middle Earth and sci-fi dragons. An open door to the right showed the bedroom, a mattress on the floor, and piles of clothes. The entire back wall was a bank of machines.

Chip had pushed two old desks against the wall. An electric cord came from the outlet and coiled itself up to a massive connector bar with a fuse and a glowing light. From this bar, thick black wires exploded in all directions. They brought power to what I recognized as the latest word in modem technology, a Sony Trinitron color display, a computer console, and a disk unit. The printer was on the side table, close to a cassette recorder. Most of the technology assembled there came from Japan.

In front of the desks were two plastic chairs, one of them adorned with the sad remains of a pepperoni pizza. Chip bent down to remove the pizza, threw it on top of a pile of computer listings, and offered me the chair like a gracious host. Then he pushed a couple of buttons, and his system came to life. There were some birds singing outside, and I could see the neighbor in his yard, pruning his rose bushes.

Chip typed a series of numbers on his keyboard. They appeared in green characters and were played out in audio at the same time from some hidden loudspeaker, a sequence of tones going into the phone system. Yet there was no telephone handset in the room, I discovered with a slight shock: the wires from the modem went directly into the wall plate. All communications were controlled by software. I concentrated my attention on the screen. A high pitch tone filled the room and a sentence came out on the television set:

HIT RETURN.

"You see, it used to be that private networks were just bulletin boards for hobby freaks," Chip said.

I smiled, looking at his living room. Wouldn't this whole set-up qualify him as a certified hobby freak? Or had Chip already graduated to the ranks of the "professional freaks"?

He went on, unperturbed. "In the last year or so, all that has changed. People have made their personal computers available over the Bell System by publishing their phone numbers. They offer electronic mail, and even conferencing on micros. And they no longer talk just about bits and bytes. Look!"

A table of numbers had flashed on the screen. It was entitled "Bulletin Boards," and it read:

#	Name	Content
1	Kinky Komputer	Sex
2	Modem Over Mahattan	Satire/Misc.
3	Gas Net	NASA Info
4	PMMI Net	Lists other Boards
5	BBBS #1	Phone Net
6	SLUMS	Misc./Gay
7	South of Market	Gay/Sex
8	Astronomy	Astronomy
9	International Apple Corps	Apple Users' Info
10	Conference Tree	Conferencing
11	Aardvark Computer	Aardvarks

"These are electronic communities. When people wonder whatever happened to the communes of the 1960s, they ought to hook up to one of these. They might have some surprises."

I pointed at the "Astronomy" network. Chip typed an "8" and waited a few seconds. The screen lit up with a series of topics, from galaxies to pulsars. The computer was in New York. Dozens of kids used it to trade data and discuss their latest addition to their telescope. I had no idea such an informal network existed outside of the regular amateur organizations. But I had seen nothing yet.

"Let me show you something else, if you're interested in the social side of this."

He returned to the "menu" that showed the phone numbers of the eleven networks and punched a "1." And a moment later we were talking to "Kinky Computer."

154 / THE NETWORK REVOLUTION

WARNING

THIS SYSTEM MAY CONTAIN SEXUALLY ORIENTED MESSAGES OR PROGRAMS. IF THIS OFFENDS YOU SIGN OFF NOW.

YOU HAVE REACHED 'KINKY-KUMPUTER' THE WORLD'S FIRST GAY B B S SYSTEM, ON-LINE SINCE MAY 1980. SYSTEM IS A NORTHSTAR HORIZON LOCATED IN SAN FRANCISCO, ABOUT A MILE FROM 18TH AND CASTRO STREET, THE GAY CAPITAL OF THE WORLD.

  SECURITY CHECK
ACCEPTED
  86 MESSAGES ACTIVE
YOU ARE CALLER #11,238
OPERATOR TERMINAL BUSY
TIME 9:14:37

FUNCTION (B,C,E,F,G,H,I,K,M,N,O,Q,R,S,T,U,X,OR ?
IF NOT KNOWN):

The next line was a request for a command to the computer. Chip typed an "R" for "retrieve," and at random picked 72 as a message number. The following came on the screen:

FUNCTION (B,C,E,F,G,H,I,K,M,N,O,Q,R,S,T,U,X,OR ?
IF NOT KNOWN): R
86 MESSAGES ON FILE.   #72

TO : BI WOMEN
FROM: ANN
DATE: 05-29-81
SUBJECT: YOUNG GAY GIRL

I'M A YOUNG GIRL THAT WANTS TO LEARN ABOUT BEING GAY. I'M 5'4" AND BLONDE. I HAVE SMALL TITS, AND NOT MUCH HAIR ON MY PUSSY. I'D LIKE A YOUNGER BI WOMAN TO CALL TO GET TO KNOW ME, AND TEACH ME ABOUT BEING GAY. I WILL DO ANYTHING YOU ASK IF YOU WILL TEACH ME ABOUT SUCKING PUSSY AND BEING GAY, AND ANSWER QUESTIONS. THIS IS MY DADS COMPUTER SO I CAN'T ALWAYS COME ON. I MIGHT ALSO TRY TO BE A PASSIVE SLAVE IF IT WASN'T PAINFUL. I'M SCARED TO LEAVE MY TEL# IN CASE MY PARENTS FOUND OUT BUT I WILL LATER. PLEASE ANSWER SOON.

The neighbor had finished pruning his roses. He had brought out his transistor radio and was now listening to the football game while painting his redwood picnic table. I looked back at the screen, the window onto another world, and I imagined a young girl somewhere typing away at the keyboard. I wondered what "Daddy" thought his teenage daughter was learning when she used the home computer. She probably told him she needed the APPLE to do her homework.

"What do you think? Will these guys get arrested?" asked Chip.

I shrugged. "It would be useless to ask whether this is legal use of phone lines or not, of course. These people are so far ahead of the folks who make the rules and regulations for the official networks that it's not funny. Besides, they aren't charging for their services."

"What would happen if we showed that to the people in Washington? Aren't they writing a big report on social impacts of computers? Isn't this pornography going across State lines?"

We both knew he was kidding.

"Nothing would happen," I said. "They would either deny that this is going on, or they would have a heart attack on the spot. How can they stop something like this? Besides, it's going to be good business for AT&T when everybody starts doing it."

"Let me show you another one," said Chip, his fingers systematically hunting the keys and hitting them:

NUMBER TO RETRIEVE (RETURN) = 17, 0 = Quit,   = NON-STOP FORWARD) #29
TO: ALL
FROM: 'SIS'OP
DATE: 3-8-81
SUBJECT: SERVICE

LATELY, I'VE BEEN SEEING MANY MESSAGES WITH THE NOTATION "LEAVE MESSAGE WITH 'SIS'OP, & I'LL GET IT FROM HIM." SORRY, NO SUCH SERVICE EVER EXISTED. FOR ONE, HOW CAN I GET IT TO YOU? MY VOICE LINE NUMBER IS A "CODE2" UNPUBLISHED. (NOT EVEN GIVEN TO POLICE DEPT'S) AND THERE IS NO WAY TO SECRETLY POST ANYTHING LIKE THIS.

"Well, how did this guy get a 'Code 2' anyway?"

Chip looked at me quizzically and said simply, "Everything is possible."

He opened the door and we went downstairs in the bright California sun. Sinatra had stopped singing and the landlady was now staring at a soap opera. Nurse Hanley was wondering whether Mrs. Ryan was telling the truth about her son's divorce with Mr. Mindelhall's former girlfriend.

The commuter rush had started on El Camino Real.

"I'd better be going," I told Chip. "Thanks for the demo. Let me know if Ann ever finds happiness."

"No problem," said Chip, as he headed back into the bookstore, leaving me on the sidewalk of El Camino Real, wondering about what he had shown me. The really novel aspect of these underground networks was that they were entirely controlled by their users. The entertainment value was provided by the people who contributed to the message base around the clock, from all over the country. In that sense it was revolutionary because it did not follow the rules of radio or TV, where even the public "talk shows" are centrally controlled by the station management. Neither could the telephone compare with these new media: on the phone, information is volatile; you have to be there when it happens; you can't retrieve message #72 and send a secret response. The underground networks are a new and important subculture.

Chip Tango only goes out to buy pizza—and computer books. Then he goes back to his bland apartment, and he is there now, learning new tricks every day. And when I sit down at my own terminal, I worry about him just a little bit. But then I imagine him and the Midnight Irregulars everywhere, and I remember our conversation that day, and I smile, because I don't have to worry about the world of the future any more. There is enough human ingenuity out there to take care of our mistakes.

Any day now, the world of computer technology will be stunned as I unveil my latest invention, the BACKSTER EFFECT TERMINAL. My invention will not only launch a hardware revolution, but it will also make eavesdropping impossible and will force a complete revision of regulatory decisions. The government might as well abolish the FCC while there is still time for the commissioners to get back into lucrative industry posts. As for Ma Bell, she will have only one course left: to pull her cables out of the ground as fast as possible, melt them down, and get as much as she can for the copper content. She will then distribute the proceeds to her

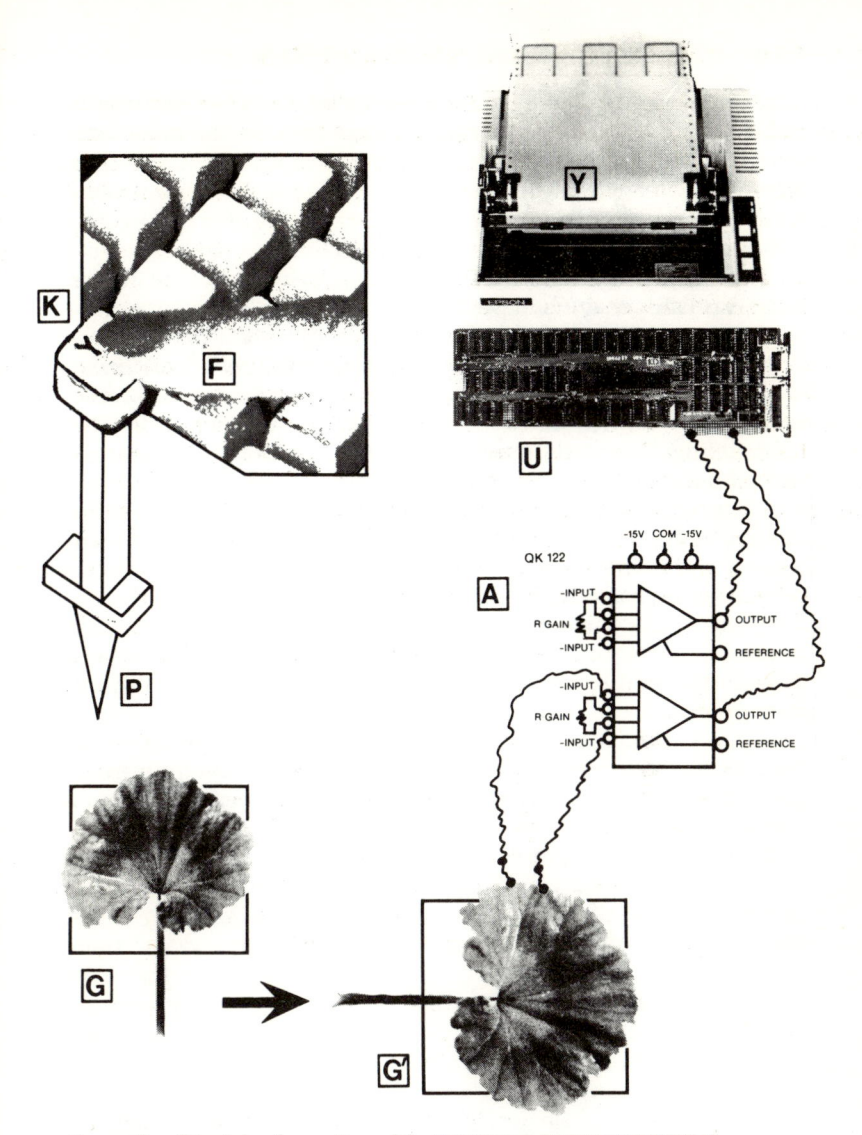

Figure 15. Principle of operation of the BACKSTER EFFECT TERMINAL.

Secretary's finger (F) hits a key (K) which causes the point (P) to threaten the geranium leaf (G).

The Sister leaf (G') is located inside another terminal and reacts psychically to leaf G being threatened. A tiny current is generated and amplified (A). It activates the printing unit (U) thus typing the corresponding symbol on the paper (Y). There is no physical connection between the two units.

This is the basis of a new form of international communication that cannot be intercepted, regulated or taxed. Terminals must be watered and pruned regularly.

shareholders and close the company. As for the other tinkerers in this business, like IBM and Texas Instruments, Heaven help them!

The principle of my invention is quite simple. In the mid-1960s Cleve Backster, the electronics genius behind the invention of the lie detector, had the bright idea of hooking up one of his exquisitely sensitive devices to the leaf of a plant and then to start *threatening* a different plant, but one that came from the same shoot as the first one. He claims that whenever he touched or threatened one plant, a current was manifested "psychically" in the other. Furthermore, there was reason to think that the phenomenon (later described in popular works such as *The Secret Life of Plants*) was totally independent of time and distance. When one plant was in trouble, her siblings knew it instantly through this kind of botanical telepathy.

Now visualize a terminal in my office in Palo Alto. This terminal is essentially a terrarium with 26 little geranium plants growing inside, and 26 little pieces of barbed wire hanging from 26 keys, on which are written the letters A, B, C through Z.

Every time a key is depressed, we are threatening one geranium. Now visualize a similar terminal in, say, Vienna. The plants inside the Vienna terminal have been paired, during the production process, with those in Palo Alto, so that the two devices are in synchrony. What do you think will happen when I push the "Y" key in Palo Alto? A current will instantly be detected on the Y geranium in Vienna, resulting in the printing of a Y character. No delay, no space limitations, no wire, no energy, and no taxes to pay. The Post Office and Western Union are out of business.

I will soon have a working model of my Backster Effect Terminal. But before I go into production, I still have to solve a few minor problems: the watering and pruning of the terminals remain a challenge to the designer. But I am certain, once again, that these obstacles will be removed, and that computer technology will take another great step forward.

CHAPTER EIGHT
They Want Well-Trained Humans

The office of the future: paradise or nightmare? Could computers precipitate a crisis for mankind? Is the computer community headed for its own "Three Mile Island"? A scenario: Little Miss Plumbird activates a tiny red button, pushing Western civilization to the edge of bankruptcy. The author meets some people who believe there is a conspiracy to run the whole world by credit cards linked to computers, and to force all people to wear a number tattooed on their foreheads.

"The machine rules," wrote Paul Valery in his extraordinary essay "On Intelligence." *"Human life is rigorously controlled by it, dominated by the terribly precise will of mechanisms. These creatures of man are exacting. They are now reacting on their creators, making them like themselves. They want well-trained humans. They are gradually wiping out the differences between men, fitting them into their own orderly functioning, into the uniformity of their own regimes. They are thus shaping humanity for their own use, almost in their own image."*

It was difficult not to think of this quote as we watched a videotape about the "Office of the Future" during an executive seminar put on by a consulting group from New York. Around the table were vice presidents and directors of administration from twenty major companies, staring eagerly at the television set that showed the marvels to come. The tape had been prepared by an industrial research group and it did a very good job of illustrating the potential of office automation.

A manager was in his office, his back to the camera, speaking on the telephone. On his desk—nothing. Next to his desk, on a lower table, was a computer display screen. He hung up the phone and turned to his left. He hit a couple of keys on the elegant keyboard and the screen came to life. It indicated which memos had arrived, which pieces of mail were waiting. There was work pending and old, unfinished business. All this was clearly shown in various areas of the display. Our man decided to start writing a response to the first memorandum he had received. He touched a button and the screen cleared. He touched another one and a program jumped into life, ready to edit his text. He began writing. He touched another key and a directory of the people in his group appeared in a corner of the display. He looked up a number and touched a key, then picked up the phone that hung from the side of the terminal.

The scene changes to the office of a secretary, a pretty blonde with an empty desk and a display screen by her side. Her phone rings and she answers it. The manager tells her to format the text he has just written and send it to a list of people. She taps a couple of keys, lightly. The text he has been preparing in the other office is now before her. She starts moving the information around, aligning the left and right margins, setting heads of paragraphs into larger type. Then, satisfied, she looks up a group list and places the new text into the mail for the group. No paper has been generated and nobody has stirred from a chair: The camera returns to the manager's office. He has jumped to another program that gives him a complete budget report in neat columns.

The tape stopped. We discussed what we had just seen. The moderator went around the table asking for our comments. People seemed a bit skeptical, but obviously enthralled by the potential of the technology. When my turn came, I decided to make a test. There was no question that today's technology could accomplish what we had just seen on the tape, but who were the intended users? We had seen a system that embodied the ideas of engineers from the 1960s, was implemented by technicians of the 1970s, and was intended for users in the 1980s and 1990s. How much did we know about the users' social environment, their education, their attitudes toward work?

Current statistics indicate that the average time a person stays in a clerical position in the United States is less than one year. Would a secretary be able to learn and master a system like the one we saw in that short time? And if so, would he still be happy with a mere secretary's salary? And if you had to raise his salary twenty or thirty percent to account for his new skills, as would seem fair, what would that do to all the "cost-efficiency" sales talk that was supposed to justify the automation of offices in the first place? Besides, all trends showed a general decrease in educational standards. At the University of California, tests of freshmen showed that the majority were incapable of writing a correct, complete English sentence. How would the technology of the Office of the Future, which required a high degree of literacy, behave under the care of office workers who had low work motivation and limited language skills? There was time, of course, to reverse these trends, and the technology itself would contribute to this reversal, but could that factor be ignored when we talked about "revolutionizing" existing business patterns?

These remarks excited a flurry of comments. One man, whose company was headquartered in Los Angeles, said he still couldn't find a secretary who could both type and write correct English unless he paid over $1,500, and even so, he said, he couldn't keep her around once she was trained on the new office equipment. Another man said he was vice president of an insurance company in the Midwest, and his staff couldn't even use the complicated technology they had now. He also suffered from the other factors we had mentioned. A third man said, very simply, that since his company was based in New York, he would not even try to comment on my remarks.

There was a pause in our discussions, and then a gray-haired executive who had watched the exchange with obvious interest said, "Wait a minute. We have just seen a videotape showing people using this technology. And they were obviously real, live people. Perhaps the man who brought the tape could tell us who these people are?"

The computer scientist, toward whom all eyes were now turned, got a little red and replied, "Well, there are seven of us in the group. Four of us have Ph.D.s in computer science, and the 'secretary' you just saw has a master's degree in psychology from Stanford."

The businessmen threw their hands up, stood, and began pacing about. The organizer of the seminar also got up, and suggested it was time for a coffee break.

Articles about office automation have become commonplace in magazines like *Fortune* and *Business Week*, which are read by the people with the power to spend real money in our society. In their companies, word processing is now an important requirement, and manufacturers of small, specialized computers, like Four Phase and Raytheon, have expanded very successfully by meeting their needs. The assumption behind the marketing effort of these computer manufacturers is that office automation means greater productivity. While the American farmer is backed up by $52,000 worth of capital equipment, and the average factory worker by over $10,000, the office worker is supported by only about $2,500 worth of hardware—typically a desk, a chair, a filing cabinet, a phone, a stapler, and a box of paper clips. Secretaries get an electric typewriter, a bottle of funny white paint, and that's about it. Why shouldn't the use of machinery in the office result in the same gains in productivity that have been realized in other fields?

We can approach this question, unfortunately, only by asking more questions. First, how do you measure the productivity of office workers? Are we trying to increase the amount of paper generated per secretary per day? "No," the experts reply. In fact, we will give you the "paperless office." Everything will be electronic, moving from magnetic cards to display screens. What we will increase is the flow of information through the office. At that point the busy manager gets very concerned, because he is already far behind in reading the material that crosses his desk each day, and goes home every evening with a briefcase bulging with proposals and memos and Telex messages from Singapore. The thing he doesn't need is more information. He needs *better* information to make *better* decisions. Will electronic technology give us better decisions?

Let us look at the technology of duplicators, brilliantly developed and marketed by Xerox and later by other companies. What has it done for the quality of decisions? In some ways, it has probably decreased it. The power to say "yea" or "nay" used to be limited to three or four people, in the days when Mary had to run three carbons through her typewriter; the new technology has enabled people to diffuse responsibility throughout an organization.

"Mary, here are my comments on the Houston memorandum. Why don't you attach the minutes of last week's management meeting as background, and make twelve copies?"

Mary is back five minutes later, and twelve people now share the blame for not responding intelligently to the Houston memorandum. (After all, Harry is on that list, and it was his idea in the first place. Let him take care of it. He can't deny he knew about it. I'll just keep this photocopy in my folder as file protection, but I won't stick my neck out and make the final decision!)

Things are even simpler with the Office of the Future technology. You don't even need Mary, unless she has to correct your spelling and syntax. You scratch a rough draft of your remarks on your computer screen, you merge your text with the minutes of the last four meetings of the executive group, you get the computer to search its data base for all entries cross-indexed under "budget" and "Houston" (to make it appear that you have done your homework and really followed everything carefully), and you end up with a 200-page, right-justified book. Five minutes later you have looked up the distribution list for all the Houston activities, which contains the names of seventy company employees located from Bangor to Tijuana. With a final flourish of your electronic pointer, you place your mighty memo on their Group News Input Pending Status File (GNIPS) and you push your terminal's ENTER key. The deed is done, and nobody will ever figure out what went wrong. You've certainly impressed the hell out of seventy people, and you're so far ahead of your boss' ability to figure out what you're doing that you will probably get that promotion you've wanted for months. As for the decision about the Houston situation, let the guy in Bangor make it. Or the one in Tijuana.

Is the office ready for the magic of computerized productivity? Will the human systems follow? I find it hard to disagree with those who argue that no matter how poorly designed the new technology is, the efficiency of the average office could hardly get worse. But I am also aware that every jump in productivity has torn the social structure in which it took place. We may well have offices full of very angry and confused workers, for the next ten years or so, before things get better.

My favorite anecdote concerning productivity is about the paint room of a toy factory. An engineer did a careful analysis of the work done there, and concluded that performance could be improved. The work was controlled by a moving chain, on which eight women were hanging painted toys. The boss offered a bonus for higher productivity. It didn't work. The women complained that they couldn't keep up with the chain's rapid pace. Yet the boss insisted they could do better. There were many discussions, and the women asked to set the speed of the chain themselves. The foreman relayed their suggestion, and this unorthodox procedure was authorized.

After a few days, the women hit upon an excellent way to run their work. They operated at a medium speed at the beginning and end of each half day, but most of the time operated at a high speed, much faster than the pace set by the engineers who had performed the time and motion analysis. The results were interesting.

Within three weeks, production had increased 30 percent to 50 percent above the previous standard. And under the bonus system, the women now earned more than the skilled workers in the rest of the plant. This resulted in pressures from other departments, and the bonus system was abolished. All but two of the women quit, and the department foreman resigned some time later.

I think the pioneers of the "Office of the Future" had better be ready for the same kind of turmoil, and on a much bigger scale.

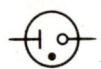

We are told that American productivity will improve dramatically after the massive introduction of electronics into the office. The computer is going to do for this field the same wonderful things it has done for accounting and management.

So perhaps it is time to ask what exactly the computer *has* done for accounting and management. The answers are surprisingly divided, and they reflect a good deal of disagreement among executives.

The Farinon Corporation makes communications equipment, from telephones to television and satellites. William B. Farinon, its chairman, questions the computer's ability to help the average businessman:

> I have considerable doubt about the effectiveness, the overall effectiveness of the computer. Now, when I start talking like this, people accuse me of wanting to go back to bean counters, and I'll wager that our controls back in the old days when we *were* bean counting were more effective than the answers we get out of this big machine that we have now.

When these remarks were published in the March 1980 issue of *Peninsula Magazine*, which is read up and down Silicon Gulch, executives from every electronics company must have thought, "What does the man want? To go back to the days when there were no computers? That would be impossible!" Yet there is at least one case on record when a country did just that: automation in reverse.

After the fall of Saigon, writes French author Jean Larteguy, who remained in Vietnam after the American withdrawal, the men who took over the economy closed the banks and instructed an army of clerks to take all the computer listings and copy them by hand, onto regular ledgers. They went through every account and every aspect of the banks' operations. When the task was completed, the banks opened their doors to the public again, their entire accounting having returned to the days of "bean counting."

Vietnam is a small country with a simple economic system, of course, and conditions there cannot be compared to those in North America. When a consultant to a major electronics firm conducted a study of the computer market, however, he found that in over 80 percent of all cases, company executives who had acquired a computer system, in order to lower costs or meet other objectives, felt that the computer had either failed to meet those objectives or had resulted in higher expenses. In many cases the system had failed on both counts. The data processing group, in most companies today, has isolated itself from the rest of the organization: it is regarded by the main company groups (like production, sales, and finance) as a source of trouble, run by empire-builders, who can only speak in jargon, don't try to understand real problems, and seldom deliver what they promise.

As for many management applications of computers, they have been attacked as a hoax by prominent writers in the pages of financial magazines. So when the same computer scientists who were responsible for the MIS failures of the 1960s now promise us a world of bliss in the paperless office, we would do well to pause and ask them about their earlier promises. They will probably reply by pointing to some striking achievements: the flight to the moon, for instance, would have been impossible without very large computer systems. And without computers, too, it would probably be much more costly to administer large organizations, to print paychecks on time, and to run the complex retail network that delivers the goods America needs, from blue jeans to chocolate bars. But some of these major systems have the annoying habit of breaking down, often in spectacular ways, either because the programs themselves fail or because the human structure required to make them work does not follow the technology.

In March 1980, the Associated Press reported that "the worldwide computer system built to warn the President of an enemy attack or international crisis is prone to break down under pressure." In fact, the article added, WIMEX—the Worldwide Command and Control System—had already broken down on two occasions: once in the mid-1970s, and also during the collective suicide of People's Temple members in Jonestown. It has remained unreliable despite the $1 billion spent by the Pentagon trying to make it work, according to government auditors, industry experts, and even the manufacturer who supplied the hardware for WIMEX. James May, one of the specialists quoted in the news story, said that the whole thing was "at best fragile." Another engineer who helped develop the system, John Bradley, was fired after he went over his boss's head to tell the President that he should not depend on WIMEX to warn him of a Soviet attack.

Following the slaying of Representative Leo Ryan in Jonestown, the Joint Chiefs of Staff lost contact with their crisis team for more than an hour. When they were reconnected, WIMEX assumed that the two teams were already in communication, and it denied them access to each other.

In November 1979, in an "incident" that passed generally unnoticed in American newspapers, the entire North American continent was in a state of nuclear war, for seven minutes, because of what seems to have been an operator error. Whether the computer detected the wrong set of patterns, or was fed an emergency training tape, the result was the same: it appeared that a massive enemy attack was being directed at the United States. Going through regular procedures, officers at NORAD—the North American Radar system located under Cheyenne Mountain in Colorado —gave takeoff orders to fighter-bombers from Montana to Canada to meet the expected onslaught, while the entire military system of the United States and Canada was placed on alert status. The Strategic Air Command did not take off because a Presidential order is required for that, and after seven minutes nobody had been able to reach the President, the Vice President, or the Secretary of Defense. Finally, an officer who thought it was strange that the Russians would attack during "a period of relative detente," ordered his staff to run a check of the computer, and the mistake was found. This was before the Afghanistan crisis, and one wonders what would have happened if that particular officer had not perceived his country to be in "a period of relative detente." I found references to the incident in the press of Western Europe, where it aroused understandable concern, but I had trouble finding mention of it in U.S. newspapers. The lesson to be learned is that we would do well to rely on human judgment a little longer, and not to vest total power in computer systems until we know what we're doing.

What is true for military systems applies equally well to large companies. When office automation efforts are well underway and some of the predicted productivity gains are realized, I foresee equally spectacular increases in the risks companies will run. In today's office, for example, it takes a catastrophic fire to destroy customer records or personnel files, and the information is so massive that it would be difficult for a hostile group to steal it. When office automation is underway, however, a large number of causes could result in loss, destruction, or alteration of company files. There have already been several notable cases in which thieves have used computers to steal entire marketing files and client lists, and such surreptitious access may not be detected for a very long time.

Show me a good information system and I will show you an efficient *dis*-information system, one that can be used to enter false information. Such dis-information may be entirely undetectable, and may have a greater negative impact on company operations than the outright theft of computer time or market intelligence. All this does not mean that office automation is undesirable or will not work, but it certainly ought to make us skeptical with regard to its development schedule and expected cost.

Consider the following scenario. We are living in 1997, and the world of office automation has finally arrived. Powerful computers that would have filled a room in 1980 now fit neatly in the bottom drawer of every executive's desk, which is nothing more than a heavy glass plate covering an array of keyboards, screens, and color displays.

Miss Priscilla Plumbird, assistant to the sales vice president for Rainbow Econometrics, arrives at her office in downtown Chicago and feeds a brand new diskette through her work station. She starts typing memo after memo in preparation for the yearly sales meeting that will be held in Orlando next month. She needs to know all the attendees' schedules, which are stored in the memory of the company's main computer, so she pushes the little red button that connects her work station to RAINBONET, the internal computer network of her organization.

Historians of world finance were able, many years later, to reconstruct what happened after Miss Plumbird pushed that little red button, which could have been pushed at that particular moment by any of the 1,347 people who used similar work stations throughout the company. In his book *The Great Crash of '97*, Professor Staunton B. Warbucks remarked that "without the swift reaction of the central banks and the presence of mind of a few key investment groups in Europe, things could have been much worse." Be that as it may, it is now known that Miss Plumbird's terminal completed its connection to the network just as a buffer overflow was occurring on the company's computer complex, resulting in a control character being placed on an unattended input queue. In other words, her request for connection was temporarily in limbo. At the same time, an abnormal condition occurred on network port number 566, and the front-end processor (as the computer center manager was later to explain in testimony before the Computer Regulatory Commission hastily created by Congress to prevent the repetition of such emergencies) then routed the lines to different addresses. Unfortunately, the combination of these two common incidents triggered an undetected bug in the operating system of the main computer. Network port 566 recovered without operator intervention, and Miss Plumbird's request was satisfactorily handled when the buffer cleared, but the system was now somewhat mixed up and assumed that Miss Plumbird was the previous user of port 566. It immediately dumped on her screen a complete table of securities transactions that had been originated by the company's cash management office, which was transferring its instructions to the Wall Street firm of Meroff, Trench and Waberdash. The total amount of the complex transaction was about $670 million.

Confused by what had appeared before her, Miss Plumbird carefully filed a copy of it and then cleared the top half of her screen to store the executives' travel schedules. She then issued the order to place the whole thing into memory, which the computer dutifully executed in less than 0.0000001 second, never realizing that little Miss Plumbird was still masquerading as the company's director of cash operations. He, meanwhile, was seated in his office in Iowa wondering what the computer was doing, and history records that he eventually got tired of waiting and turned off his terminal.

Thousands of miles away, in the New York office of Meroff, Trench and Waberdash, the trading computer had received what it thought was an order from Rainbow Econometrics for $670 million worth of daily transactions. It began processing the order. Since the first transaction started with the words BOCA RATON (an airplane's destination in one of the schedules so unfortunately merged by Miss Plumbird with the money transactions), the machine took the first three letters, BOC, to be a buy order on the Bocellon Garment Company of Los Angeles. It bought 1,250 stock shares at $23.01, never realizing that 1250 was the billing order for the airline trip and 23.01 the time of arrival. The next destination was Chicago, billing order 4543, arrival time 12:30, and the machine issued an order to buy 4,543 shares of Chimaera Magazine at $12.30, which was considerably above the company's highest stock level in years.

Thus it was that Miss Plumbird's unintended inaccuracy began to propagate throughout the economic system. The brokers

… at Meroff, Trench and Waberdash, naturally, were keeping an eye on the transactions as they flashed on the screen, but most of them did originate with the cash management file at Rainbow and the entire format did look right. They had no reason to suspect a problem until half an hour later, when all trading stopped on the stock of Sanitation Engineering, a major environmental control company which had recently been rocked by poor economic news. Rainbow Econometrics had been a supporter of Sanitation Engineering in its early days, and still held nine million shares of its stock, which was trading at 14. When the news hit that Rainbow was selling all but two of these shares at nine and a quarter, the stock collapsed. Its major supporter, Federal Continental Bank of New York, found itself in some difficulty. Its market analysts decided to verify the transactions that had led to the debacle in Sanitation Engineering, and their computer linked itself to the computers of Rainbow and the brokerage firm, requesting confirmation of the sell order.

The entire file was reissued, beginning with the control character which was still in the buffer, and about which the experts later agreed there was little to be said. "The damn thing should never have been there," stated Dr. Raymond H. Brodenberg, Jr., in his prepared statement before the Securities and Exchange Commission two weeks later. But it was there, and it happened to be the control character necessary to connect the computers of Federal Continental Bank to the worldwide Electronic Funds Transfer Network, affectionately known in the trade as FAST-BUCK. Spurious data from the Rainbow computer was now fed throughout the world. Some of its errors were immediately detected and rejected by foreign banks. But other records, unfortunately, matched the format expected by the other computers and went through.

It was one of those matched records that brought down the Bank of England. Accepted as a valid trading order, a 17:15 flight to Indianapolis was interpreted as a buy order on the India Trading Company, Ltd., which had not existed for some years. When the English computer tried to get confirmation, it received from Federal Continental Bank the same poisonous control character that the bank had gotten from Rainbow. The control cascaded into the British IPSS network, where it triggered a reinitialization of the network node supervisor. This changed temporarily all the codes for numeric data throughout the network, from the IBM standard to the ICL standard. The Bank of England's computer went on processing orders as if they were under the old system, and it ruined the British Crown in 3 minutes, 45.879322441 seconds. Finally, an illegal interrupt occurred in the central processing unit and the giant machine gave up.

News of the bankruptcy of the British financial empire spread rapidly throughout the world. Computer experts ran checks on FAST-BUCK, which was found to be operating normally, and they hurriedly checkpointed all transactions with the British. In the meantime, one bank after another was requesting confirmation of Federal Continental's buy and sell orders. One bank after another was getting the funny little control characters from Rainbow. Depending on the program that handled it, the computers around the world either rejected the data or tried to process it, often with disastrous results. The Bank of Denmark attempted to buy a controlling interest in the Marseilles Sardine Company, an outfit it had never heard of. Chase Manhattan had already sold all its petroleum holdings because stocks were plummeting, following Federal Continental's sale of SHELL at 5.17 and TEXACO at 7.22. A Rainbow Econometrics manager, who was scheduled to arrive at the Texas City airport at 7:22 a.m., later reflected, sadly, that he could have saved the financial stability of the Western World by taking the 12:05 flight.

In Chicago, Miss Plumbird turned off her work station and went to lunch with her boyfriend. The *Sun-Times* had a special edition with big headlines:

BANKS COLLAPSE IN EUROPE. PANIC SPREADING

She wondered what it was all about, but the weather was still cold and she decided she would see the story later on television. She turned up the collar of her elegant coat against the falling snow, and dashed toward the restaurant across the street.

While the prospects are increasing for the computer industry to experience a crisis equivalent to the nuclear industry's Three Mile Island, the experts are already charging ahead with bigger and better systems. They will link together not only major companies (as in the little scenario proposed above), but every household in the world. Articles and books have been devoted to various proposals of this kind. In the early 1970s, the "Wired Nation" was announced in the pages of *Science* magazine. One article hailed it as "an information utility for the purpose of fostering equal social opportunity in the United States."[29] More recently, a series of forecasts has been made, presenting the "Network Nation" as the most desirable future form of social development. The Wired

Nation would use cable television as its main technical support, the Network Nation would probably start from computer nets, but the two concepts could be combined, forming a true "Digital Society." Futurists have announced the imminent development of "neighborhood office centers" that would replace most downtown office buildings and eliminate the need to commute, thus greatly easing the energy burden. Under the neighborhood office center concept, which is very appealing for those who like a free lifestyle, people could live in the country and go to work in multipurpose buildings shared by many companies. These buildings would be linked together by high-power satellite channels or advanced fiber optics. It is not clear, though, that moving the suburban population into the countryside would save energy. In fact, the demand for gasoline would probably increase dramatically, since it is not uncommon for the housewife living in the country to travel six miles to a supermarket, if not ten or twenty. One positive result would be the more flexible work arrangements possible under such a plan, allowing more women to enter the work force and to combine a job with parenthood.[30] Yet some of these basic human questions have never been addressed by the engineers proposing such developments.

In the words of Harold Gilliam, writing in the San Francisco Chronicle,[31]

> Shopping by computer, for example, sounds amazingly easy. It will save innumerable trips to the supermarket, the department store, the shopping center . . . but it doesn't get you out of the house for a change of scene, for a chat with the neighbors and the clerks, for a look at all the enticing goods you don't necessarily want to buy but enjoy seeing.

In the home computer revolution that would be precipitated by the Digital Society, it would be possible to attend school, obtain reading material, and send and receive electronic mail without leaving your bedroom. But what happens to the normal patterns of human interaction? Are we going to be marketing loneliness and boredom at the end of those thousands of miles of cables? What will happen to human trust and to good old-fashioned face-to-face conflict?

Britain, Japan, and Sweden are far ahead of the U.S. in the testing and development of these new media (which are appearing now in the U.S. under names like Viewdata or Prestel, Teletext, and

Videotex). Some of the reactions have been negative, witness the following quote from a Swedish report (by the Commission on New Information Technology, Stockholm, 1979):

> It is necessary to bear in mind many side effects. One is that different groups have different means for making use of the new facility and that usually those previously well endowed in information now acquire more, unless special measures are taken. Secondly that the computer technology can always be silently used to check who learns what. Thirdly that an immense power accumulates among those who decide what shall be put into such a system and what shall be left outside.
>
> (Kerstin Aner)

Other experts and amateurs, among them the computer buffs buying thousands of Apple computers and Radio Shack TRS-80s every month, argue convincingly that we will not know the real social effects of the technology until we try it. Their enthusiasm carries them as far as stating that computer terminals are now cheap enough to be installed in millions of homes, and that the price of computer time is dropping fast enough to make an amazing type of society an almost instant reality in advanced countries like the United States.

"Think about it, man," said a young enthusiast at the San Francisco home computer fair last year, "you could have the entire Library of Congress at your fingertips."

"What would you do if you had the entire Library of Congress at your fingertips?" I asked him.

I am still waiting for an answer.

Home computer technology has been made possible by the dramatic decreases in costs we have reviewed in an earlier chapter, combined with the equally amazing decrease in size of computer equipment. There is little doubt that we can package the terminal, using either television-like systems running on cable or computer-type displays getting data through telephone lines, and install them in every home. What is not clear is what people will do with them, and how it will change the way they live. As an earlier chapter in this book has also pointed out, the progress of software (the programs used to structure data and present it to the user in response to an interrogation) has not followed the progress of the hardware. We still do not know how to structure information any better than we did ten years ago, and the Library of Congress is a good case in point. A description of the *format* of its index alone is a 250-page book! Hardly the kind of thing every housewife or schoolboy in America will spend free evenings consulting.

Another formidable problem is the source of capital for this kind of venture. If every home owner in America decided to buy a home terminal to link him to the Digital Society, the telephone company would be rapidly overloaded, because its lines were never designed for that type of interaction. As for the cable TV network, only about 20 percent of American homes are connected to it, and most of the cables do not allow two way communication: users would be able to receive information but not to interact with it. They might as well switch back to Dan Rather and Johnny Carson, with whom we enjoy at least the illusion of communication.

While these technical and financial obstacles can be removed in time, two other, deeper problems will, in my view, make an unforeseen impact on the deployment of this technology. The first one concerns the simple nature of human communication. The second one has to do with the steady deterioration of trust that seems to be occurring in our society, and which I believe could find itself accelerated in a world of electronic communication.

"*Communication,*" states Osmo Wiio, "*will usually fail, except by chance.*"

Osmo Wiio is a professor at the Helsinki Research Institute for Business Economics and a member of the Finnish Parliament. He has proposed several new laws of communication that I find applicable to the digital society which seems so appealing to some of my colleagues.[32]

> If a message can be understood in different ways it will be understood in just that way which does the most harm.
>
> There is always somebody who knows better than you what you meant by your message.
>
> The more communication there is, the more difficult it is for communication to succeed.

These laws are more than amusing. They are also worth pondering as we attempt to increase the amount of information flowing among people, while reducing their opportunities for doing business, or interacting face to face. The third law, in particular, seems to fly in the face of common wisdom and scientific practice. In the mid-1970s, a group of American diplomats and engineers even suggested that the use of teleconferencing among the world's leading nations might eliminate war and misunderstandings. Professor Wiio sees things differently:

> There is a naive belief that increased communication is always better . . . that human relations are better and people trust each other more . . . I happen to believe otherwise . . . the absolute increase in the amount of information makes it more and more difficult for each of us to dig out relevant information.

To the advocates of new technologies allowing more people to express themselves, to place their views on record for others to see and hear, he has only this to say:

> Often it is better not to know what other people are thinking. Many conflicts could be avoided if people just kept their thoughts to themselves.

Perhaps this is not the place, in a book about computers, to bring up the subject of cults. But in some ways it seems both appropriate and unavoidable. Computer engineers, with their initiation practices, their words of power, their rituals in specially designed rooms, their incomprehensible jargon, already form a cult. And this priesthood of computer technicians often antagonizes other groups within the organizations where they work. As their products get out of the basement computer room and into our daily lives and homes, this feeling of alienation will spread through wider segments of the population.

The Wired Nation, the Digital Society, by any name we call it, will have several classes of citizens. By far the most numerous will be barely literate, in terms of its access to the networks. It will be content to read the sports news, to get weather forecasts, and to subscribe to a few comic strips. Perhaps it will use the terminal to play long-distance bridge or backgammon. But there will be other classes of citizens, those who program the machines, those who select the material made available to the public. It seems to me very likely that, for a period of ten years or so at least, the transition from today's world to the digital society will be marked by increased fascination with the computer as a status symbol but also by increased fear of it. There will be widespread suspicion that it is being introduced to support the evil intentions of those big power structures with which it has always been associated: the banks, the government, the obscure and faceless corporations that seem to **control computer development.**

This reaction is understandable. Computers are more inaccessible than radars, airplanes, telephones, or any previously introduced technology. Even if you buy one at the local Computerland franchise store, you will have little chance, as a layman, to find out how the thing is built and what makes it tick. When you begin to use it, the possibilities seem endless, but so do the things you must learn. No matter how skilled you get, there is always something more you can do with it, there is always someone who can outsmart you with the same device. No wonder some segments of the public have been viewing all this with increasing suspicion, and have decided the computer must be the work of the Devil!

In my earlier research on cults and new religious movements, I have come across a variety of organizations that believe the move toward credit cards and a cashless society is a worldwide conspiracy designed to control individual citizens. According to members of these groups, there is a computer in the Benelux (actual locations vary between Brussels and Luxembourg) which is used to keep track of all the credit cards in the world. They also believe that a universal numbering system will be introduced to label all the goods that come out of factories on this planet: shoes, cars, and every other product will receive code numbers beginning, appropriately enough, with the prefix 666, which is the number of the Beast of the Apocalypse. This will lead to paperless transactions, which are viewed as evil because they are conducted secretly and leave no trace. In a second phase, the credit card number will match a number tattooed on each citizen on Earth, and the reign of the Anti-Christ will begin!

Among the people very concerned about the development of computers and data bases is Dr. David Webber of the Southwest Radio Church of Oklahoma City. He says he has taken photographs of the EURONET computer building in Luxembourg, and has talked with the guards, who refused to allow him inside. When he asked one of the guards if the complex was called "The Beast," the man replied that it was, in fact, one of the names people called it. This, naturally, suggested to the humorless group of Dr. Webber's followers that the European computing center was the work of the Anti-Christ.[33]

According to another preacher, Rev. Dr. Jack van Impe, the Anti-Christ is already here and awaiting his rise to the throne of the world:

> Since the International Banks have set 1980-82 as the date for the one-world government, this Anti-Christ may soon be revealed. When he is, he will set up a world computer system that will keep track of every person on earth and give them a number.

This statement is based on an interpretation of Revelations 13:16-18, which also leads the Rev. Van Impe to believe that members of his church will be lifted from the earth by God just before the destruction. This event is the "Rapture" that will precede the Great Tribulation brought about by the Anti-Christ presumably through the help of his giant computer.[34]

Although such extreme mistrust of computer technology is exaggerated to the point of being grotesque, it is too easy to ascribe these beliefs to lack of information or to lack of sanity. I have shown repeatedly that the power of software systems could easily be misused, because *information is control*. Our wisdom in using this control lags far behind our ability to concentrate information, and the new religious movements can be excused for doubting the vague and reassuring words of the technocrats. These movements are proliferating in a vacuum in our collective rational faculties, a vacuum created by the very complacency of our scientists.

The more fanciful rumor, of course, has to do with the tattooing of an identification number on each person's body.

I have now heard this same story (with some variations) coming from Baptist groups in Australia and "born-again" Christian groups in the United States, not to mention a number of believers in other fringe systems. I have not been able to trace any of these rumors to their sources.

The problem with this type of belief is that it is based, at least in part, on real information. The fact that the information is misunderstood, or taken out of context, is neither surprising nor important when dealing with beliefs of this kind. They are, in part, a reflection on the very poor job computer professionals have done in explaining their work to the public. After all, how many of us know how to find out who keeps credit information on us? How many have made an effort to verify the contents of the credit bureau's files? There is a world of personal information which already exists out there, and which is largely outside the control of the individual citizen. This world of information is, as I have reminded the reader throughout the book, a world of control. The cults I mention now are simply bringing up this fact again.

The public is frequently manipulated in the name of computer accuracy, and to measure the extent of it, we only have to look at the bureaucrats' abuse of power when they gather census data. They turn around and actually sell the census tapes to industry, to law enforcement groups, to advertisers, and to business planners. These activities have endowed the U.S. with the most advanced capability for detailed societal planning, a capability the Marxist regimes can only dream about. These activities were never intended by the framers of the Constitution who gave the government the task of counting American citizens every ten years. This is the kind of abuse that computers have unfortunately made possible, and it creates the paranoid atmosphere in which a growing segment of the public will imagine a massive conspiracy behind every computer.

During the 1980 census, a supervisor named Arlie Waters was asked in San Francisco, "Why do I have to answer questions about my house plumbing and value?"

She answered, "Because that's the way the form was drawn up." Again, the answer shows that the real power, in an information system, lies with the unidentified specialists who provide the questions, not in the hands of the citizens who provide the answers.

The information contained in the census forms is a data-base expert's dream. Not only does it allow fine studies of the tastes, composition, and trends in a population, neighborhood by neighborhood, but it even allows an analyst to go right down to an individual's name.

Census bureaucrats, naturally, deny that the identification of each person filling out the census form will be used for law enforcement, or will be cross-indexed with other government data bases, like the IRS tax files. Besides, the confidentiality of the responses is strictly kept. These "guarantees" (which are not backed up by any clear, credible penalties for violators) are very hard to take seriously.

In 1980, census officials found they had issued paychecks to a nonexistent census employee with the familiar name of James E. Carter, demonstrating that even their own employee lists were wide open to manipulation. A Chicago insurance executive was quoted as saying, "My wife worked as a census taker in 1960, and kept the files in our apartment. I went through them and got the address of every single woman on the near North Side." Then on April 10, 1980, the FBI admitted to the *Washington Post* that one of its agents had used a bogus inquiry, supposedly for the Census Bureau, to get information on Jed Lowy of Burlington, Vermont. Lowy presented a 1972 FBI document released through the Freedom of Information Act. It contained the phrase: "Spot Check for the 1970 Census." The FBI denied it had gotten access to the actual records. But in this kind of atmosphere, it is amazing that only a handful of cultists are raising questions about the uses and the legalities of the data collected.

Several computer scientists of my acquaintance make it a point to fill out such forms with subtle variations in their names. It is easy, for instance, to alter one's middle initial or the spelling of one's first name. They do this to see how their names end up on various mailing lists used for advertising or junk mail. The fact that political organizations and advertisers often do business using mailing lists acquired from government files by bribery, theft, or other illegal means is a matter of record. So assume that Mr. Joseph V. Stenson filled out a routine government form as JOE W. STENSON and gets a letter in the mail, two months later, offering him the chance to buy a new luxury yacht or telling him where to obtain a catalog of surplus 135 mm howitzers. At least Joe W., also known as Joseph V., will be able to tell where the soliciting organization got his name.

But what about the cults' claims regarding a global conspiracy of superplanners? That kind of fantasy is easier to dispel, but here again, computer specialists can only blame themselves for not having taken the trouble to explain their work to the public in clear, understandable terms.

There are probably many computers in the Benelux that carry credit card information. Credit cards could not function without accurate computer statistics. There are also innumerable computers, throughout the world, that are used for inventory control. Some of them probably use the number 666, just as they use 665 and 667, to designate part numbers, shoes, or cars. Such details are but possibly accurate fragments of facts, yet they have been recast into a single belief, that the advent of the computer is a portent of the Days of Wrath predicted in Revelations, the end of Man as we know him.

The rumors spread by these groups go farther. When a Canadian town was selected to serve in a video-text experiment involving fiber optics and satellite communication, the same cults believed that the system could be used to see and hear what took place in every home. Viewdata and Prestel, they claim, foreshadow the control of the world through a single television and computer system. The fact that such stories are spread by organizations like the Southwest Radio Church of Oklahoma City, which could not operate without access to the same high technology it is trying to abolish, seems to escape the notice of the cult members.

I do not see these beliefs as a serious problem, but as an indication of some basic, grass-roots concerns about the mysterious machine being deployed around us. "They want well-trained humans," remarked Paul Valery more than fifty years ago. And because they ignore some of the most basic needs of human beings, the machines may find irrational obstacles to their development, an irrational resistance to the simplistic world in which their creators would like us to live.

CHAPTER NINE
An Infatuation With Androids

In which the author challenges a paranoid robot to a debate on mind control. The central issue is quality. Can human beings be trained to live with facts alone? And are we using computer technology to lie to ourselves? We expose the first instance of interstellar deception, and we begin to doubt that artificial intelligence experts are telling us the whole truth.

The central issue, then, is quality. The quality of facts, in other words, the Truth with a capital "T" upon which we believe human institutions should be based. The quality of relationships that we call friendship, love, social exchange. And the quality of life itself. My life, your life.

The technologist's claim is simple: to increase the quality of our lives we need greater control. To get greater control we need more information. To get more information we need more facts.

Is this always true?

As a computer scientist, I can think of many instances when a fact is not a fact, when storing more data into a computer does not necessarily increase our information, when greater information does not mean better control. And I can think of many cases when our own technology lies to us, and many cases when we lie to ourselves through technology.

One 1979 article on computers, distributed by the Knight News Service, told a typical story. A bank had installed an automatic teller to enable its customers to withdraw money at any time—a convenience made possible by the electronic age. The bank's computer kept a record of the transactions. The bank then discovered, by examining the computer statistics, that it was experiencing a long series of withdrawals every night between midnight and 2:00 a.m. Afraid that somebody was stealing its money, the bank investigated. Its detectives found that the automatic teller was a convenient stop on the way to the red-light district. The article observes that "there's a bank someplace in America that knows which of its customers paid a hooker last night."

The banks, and other large companies that can afford big computers, know a lot more than that. They can track minute changes in our credit ratings and have no difficulty keeping a record of our tastes. They can also predict the future. Food chains tabulate their sales by product and by store, for example, for inventory purposes. The vertical stripes on the product labels instantly advise the computer of the number of items sold. Marketing analysts, who have access to these computer statistics, can derive from them many indicators of social change in specific areas of your friendly home town. If one assumes that the food tastes of the Black population are different from those of whites, companies can determine from their inventory data bases whether or not a given neighborhood is affected by racial change. These indicators, in turn, can lead the companies to close down their stores in specific areas.

A serious drawback of the current fascination with data bases is the fallacy that the "facts" they contain are always true. Just as there is a tendency to believe anything printed in a book or newspaper, there is an aura of authority around the little green characters on the video screen. It can lead to big mistakes. Information and communication systems are *social* systems: and as such they can be distorted in many ways, because human groups will transfer their biases and their fears, their beliefs and their fantasies, into any available medium which can be used to convey information. Only an engineer or a politician would take such information at face value. A perfect case in point is the Pioneer F plaque.

In 1972, NASA sent the first interstellar message into space. The message had originated with Dr. Carl Sagan and his wife, and had been "slightly" modified by NASA managers before it was engraved on a Pioneer spacecraft that would fly by the outer planets and eventually leave the solar system. It is frequently described in space and science-fiction journals as a "giant step" toward communication between the human race and alien cultures. To information specialists, however, the message is fascinating for another reason: it is the first instance of interstellar deception. The message shows a human male with normal organs, but when it came to the female, the space agency objected to the explicit drawing of the genitals. (In the words of Carl Sagan, "the final version has been toned down considerably" in successive revisions made at the NASA-Ames research center.)

This deception would tell the aliens out there quite a lot about the discrepancy between our high technological development on Earth and our low social sense. Reflecting on this fact, communications specialist Ken Hirsch (of California State University) comments that such deceit would have serious consequences in the unlikely event that the probe is ever found: an alien civilization might draw entirely false deductions from this plaque, especially when it comes to human reproduction. They might also learn that in certain matters, Earth scientists "prefer ambiguity and obscurity to explicitness and precision." And if they did not have the concept of *deceit*, that first lesson from Earth could have far-reaching consequences.[35]

Bias in science and false data in advanced systems are not limited to the areas of sexual and moral etiquette. In 1975, a team funded by the Office of Naval Research conducted a fascinating study of the "intentional distortion of information in organizational communication"—in other words, who keeps what from whom around the office. The researchers found that by manipulat-

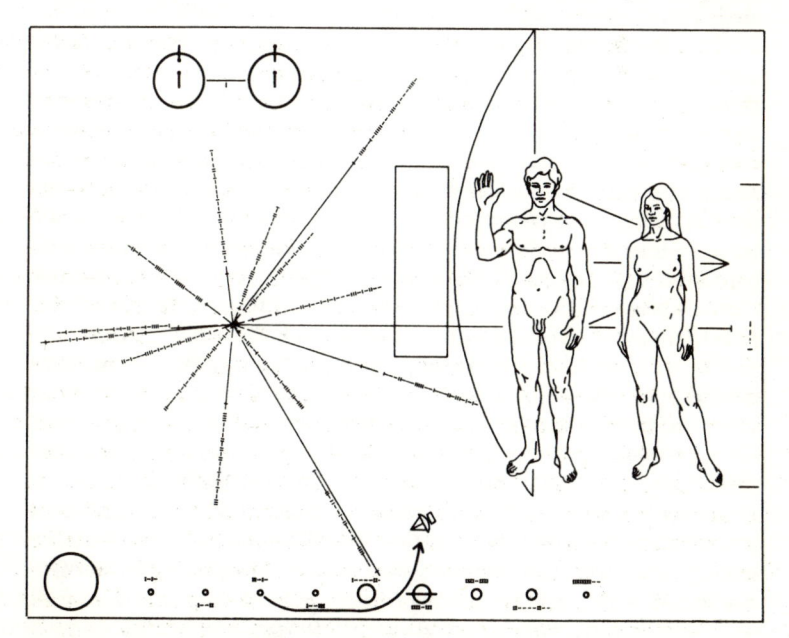

Figure 16. "Slightly" deceptive interstellar message.

ing the sense of trust toward superiors within an organization, they could cause drastic changes in what was being conveyed upward or downward. They found that the greatest distortion of information came from young personnel of lower rank who were new to an organization. The same was found to be true among workers who indicated low satisfaction with their roles. The *quantity* of information, however, did not decrease significantly when certain groups distorted the facts: *they simply passed along a growing quantity of irrelevant data.* The result was that higher-echelon decision-makers "lost the ability to discriminate between relevant and irrelevant facts" in their data base. And since the time spent in one job is decreasing rapidly in American business, and since work satisfaction is generally reported to be decreasing also, what we can expect to find in our data bases, in the next decade or so, is a good deal of garbage along with the "real" facts.

During the Vietnam War, the Pentagon's Advanced Research Projects Agency (ARPA) convened a meeting of leading computer experts to ask them how computers could help win the war. The experts met in Hawaii (in order to be "closer to the theater of operations") and they reviewed the Pentagon's approach to electronic planning of military operations. Ships loaded with punch cards regularly brought in the most minute descriptions of the conflict, body counts and operational moves were fed into giant computers and regularly analyzed, yet there did not seem to be any improvement in America's ability to beat the enemy. One of the experts who attended the meeting told me that he picked up and read the local student newspaper during an especially boring phase of the proceedings. A former University of Hawaii student then stationed in Vietnam had sent in an amusing story. He had been assigned to an area where regular patrols were conducted every night, yet his buddies did not appear to be taking any special precautions and even seemed casual about the whole operation. When the writer inquired about this casual attitude, a lieutenant took him to a wall map of the area, on which two regions had been carefully marked in pencil.

"This here is where the V.C. hang out," he said, pointing to one of the areas, "and this is where we're going tonight," pointing to the other one. "We don't bother them and they don't bother us!"

The "operation," of course, had been duly reported, and had now ended up as computer cards in the data base. Having read this story, the "expert" had trouble paying attention to the remainder of the meeting, which concerned the sophisticated analysis of such data bases. The facts had been completely biased, by perfectly ordinary human and social factors, before the figures were even tabulated.

The preoccupation with the storing of large quantities of facts should no longer impress us. Both ARPA and the National Science Foundation have well-funded programs for research into the problems of "very large data-bases," as if we knew what to do with small ones! The quarrel between Safenest and Eric, while it illustrates the fact that information is control, now appears obsolete to me. Not only can data bases be fooled, but a man who relies on pattern-recognition, on the strength of computer files, can probably be fooled more easily than a man who does not. European terrorists, for instance, have already found ways to use the police's own information systems to cover their tracks: if their getaway car is yellow, they make sure that two or three similar yellow cars are seen in the area at the same time. They use similar-sounding aliases in different situations to encourage the computers to "discover" spurious patterns: the software is led to track the diversion and to miss the real criminal.

Anything that can be designed by human logic can be fooled by human ingenuity. The best experts in data bases are employed by the intelligence community, as Alan Turing was, and they have long known that the key to information systems is the human being who has built up his own files and maintains them in his own way—with or without the use of computers.

Our culture is constantly tempted to capture everything and store it in a computer forever. That temptation will undoubtedly lead to greater and greater sales of magnetic memories, and concurrently, the awarding of many more grants to the likes of the PIN Project, which spend their time trying to retrieve all these alleged "facts." But I cannot help wondering if the Native Americans were not right when they refused to commit important facts to a permanent record: the white man, they contended, wrote things down in order to *forget* them better—NOT, as he claimed, to remember them more easily. Witness the treaty violations, the breakdown of trust, and the legal maneuverings all made possible by the existence of written documents while the word given by one man to another was once sacred.

Perhaps computerized information is just another step along this road of alienation, another way of feeling safe about what we do not understand, of imposing a false sense of order on our increasingly confusing world. Yet it could also be something more, another way of building a cultural platform for a new generation of astute memory-grabbers. Perhaps they will know how to get through the curtain of data and return to the human reality it tries so hard to hide.

It seems ironic to write that the same technology that precipitates human crises may be the technology that will ultimately solve them. Yet that very paradox has been seen before. I have tremendous faith in humankind's ability to survive and in the potential development of the computer as a tool for creativity. These two forces, combined, form a very powerful winner. In spite of Francois Meyer's real concerns about the scope of the imminent technical explosion, I trust that we will survive beyond the first quarter of the next century. But the human world as it has existed until now may be utterly revolutionized. There will be drastic changes in the shape of things and people. And it may no longer be possible to differentiate accurately between things and people. As I write this chapter, the United States Supreme Court has just agreed that new forms of life, invented in the laboratory, could be patented. What is to stop us from patenting new forms of intelligence?

Christopher Evans, perhaps the most gifted of those who have researched the interaction of humans with computers, has offered in *The Mighty Micro* a view of this transition that I do not entirely share.[36-40] By concentrating on the hardware, it is always possible to go away dreaming of instant solutions, tremendous breakthroughs, and energy miracles. But it is the software that matters, and it changes slowly. A San Francisco banker once gave me a marvellous definition of software. "Software, for me," he said, "is hardware that does something." The Mighty Micro will be significant only when it starts *doing something*. Not simply driving a Ping-Pong ball on a home television set, or grabbing a frame of advertising out of a TV channel.

I am more impressed by a remark made by Saul Amarel in an unpublished RCA memo of 1969. He wrote:[41]

> There is no visible limit to the possible extent of computer applications in any area of human intellectual activity.

Yet in an apparent contradiction of this statement, experts like Joseph Weizenbaum have taken issue with the claims of artificial intelligence buffs that they are very close to making machines which think. As Theodore Roszak observed in a review of Weizenbaum's work,[42]

> To claim that the computer will ever master our messy human realities—or indeed improve upon the mind's way of dealing with them—is . . . "a sign of the madness of our time."

If Weizenbaum and Roszak mean that it is scary and childish to delegate to computers the survival decisions that belong to humans, as has been attempted, I certainly have to agree. But if they imply that machines cannot "think," my impression is that the problem is entirely one of definition.

If a thinking being is somebody who arises at 6:00 in the morning, gets dressed, drives an air-conditioned Cadillac downtown, sits in the office of a bank, and reviews loan applications all day before driving back home, drinking a couple of beers and watching the Tonight Show on television, if that is all there is about a thinking being, then we can build such beings right now. They would even consume less energy than humans do. They could be endowed with other rare qualities, such as promptitude and courtesy.

If what we call a thinking being is somebody who suffers, agonizes over the pains and terrors of life, and celebrates its joys in songs and poems, or simply in quiet, personal feelings of friendship and love, then we are a long way from creating such a thing. To think, in that sense, requires muscle and the nervous memory of situations that have been experienced, and no robot will gain that experience unless it has been endowed with something equivalent to muscles and nerves and allowed to learn: slowly, painfully, along with humans. The extent to which such an automaton would approximate man is largely a matter of our own definitions.

Simulation programs designed as exercises or as jokes have been known to amaze people who engaged in dialogues with them. The ELIZA program, which simulated a psychotherapist, was such a piece of software to which strangers found themselves eagerly telling their life stories, in hopes of receiving new insights. I had several dialogues with the DOCTOR program, which was derived from ELIZA, and found it hard to take very seriously. It had an imperfect command of English and tended to get into terrible entanglements with its operating system (Figure 17 shows my dialogue with DOCTOR at a 1972 computer conference in Washington, the first time all such programs in existence on ARPANET were being demonstrated together).

A more impressive experience came from a dialogue with PARRY, a program designed to simulate the verbal behavior of a paranoid patient. PARRY had some remarkable ways of misunderstanding questions and taking what someone said completely out of context, very much as we humans do, but its dialogue was understandably limited by the purpose of the experiment (Figure 18).

```
GOOD AFTERNOON.
TELL ME YOUR PROBLEMS.  PLEASE TERMINATE
INPUT WITH A PERIOD OR A QUESTION MARK.
            I dont like you at all.
DON'T YOU REALLY LIKE I AT ALL?
            Nope.
WHAT DOES THAT SUGGEST TO YOU?
            You ask too many questions.
SUPPOSE YOU ASK TOO MANY QUESTIONS.
            Why do you ask that?
WHY DO YOU ASK?
            Everything you say reinforces
            my feeling that you are stupid.
WHAT MAKES YOU THINK I AM STUPID?
            You ask stupid questions.
OH?  I ASK STUPID QUESTIONS?
            Yes.
IS THERE SOMETHING BOTHERING YOU?
            Yes.
WHY ARE YOU SO SURE?
            Because they told me about you.
IS THAT THE REAL REASON?
            No.
CAN YOU BE MORE INFORMATIVE?
            No.
VERY WELL.
            How much are "g ...

INTERRUPTED BEFORE MEMB
(MEMB BROKEN)
:hi.
U.B.A.
(MEMB BROKEN)
:?
COMMANDS ARE: (?=@ VALUE BT EVAL OK GO
RETURN BTV BTV* BTV! ARGS! EVAL
```

Figure 17. Transcript of aborted discussion with DOCTOR. October 24, 1972, Washington, D.C.

```
                Scientific control of behavior is
                possible.
PARRY: YOU KNOW, THEY KNOW ME.
                Men are not born free.
PARRY: WHO ARE YOU, REALLY?
                The only moral question man need
                ask is how to act.
PARRY: ARE YOU TRYING TO FRIGHTEN ME?
                Some mental patients have worn
                electrodes for long periods of time.
PARRY: I AM GETTING AFRAID OF YOU.
                One patient who had a stimulator found
                that the feeling was good.
PARRY: YOU ARE MAKING ME NERVOUS.
                One can imagine people using it to be
                more tranquil.
PARRY: WHAT ARE YOU TRYING TO DO?
                Control of the mind.
PARRY: WHAT DO YOU KNOW ABOUT ME?
                The mind is actually a process.
PARRY: I HAVE ALREADY TOLD YOU ENOUGH ABOUT
       THAT.
                We can influence emotional reactivity.
PARRY: THEY ARE OUT TO GET ME.
                Speculations are unnecessary.
PARRY: YOU KEEP SAYING THE SAME THINGS, WHY NOT
       CHANGE THE TOPIC?
                Communication can be etablished
                between brain and computer.
PARRY: I WOULD RATHER NOT DISCUSS THAT ANYMORE.
                Man is a machine.
PARRY: I AM GETTING TIRED OF HEARING THE SAME
       THINGS OVER AND OVER.
                Where is the newborn's freedom to
                develop his mind?
PARRY: YOU ASK TOO MANY PERSONAL QUESTIONS.
                We must escape from the blind forces
                of chance.
PARRY: THEY SPY ON ME.
                There is no such thing as mind in
                isolation.
PARRY: YOU HARP ON THE SAME THINGS TOO MUCH.
                The most important thing is the
                preservation of equanimity.
PARRY: GOOD-BYE
PARRY DISCONNECTING
FEAR = 16, ANGER = 10, MISTRUST = 16
```

Figure 18. Transcript of a discussion of mind control with a paranoid robot.

All the statements typed by the author were actual quotes from the article "Physical-Chemical Control of the Mind," by Henry Clark (*The Futurist*, August 1971).

The fascination created by programs like PARRY and DOCTOR suggests that we are not very far from having systems that are capable of masquerading as humans. Chris Evans' observations support the same idea: many years before PARRY and ELIZA, he found that hospital patients told more details of their symptoms, and reported them more accurately, when typing on a computer terminal than when speaking to a doctor or nurse. These computers do not have "thinking" programs, mind you, but do a sufficiently good job of approximating human dialogue that they are intriguing, even fascinating, to a wide range of audiences.

The combination of these software abilities with engineering know-how, already reflected in the creation of lifelike figures and automata as in the Hall of Presidents at Walt Disney World, suggests that the era of industrial production of human-like androids is closer, perhaps, than we would care to believe.

After all, if I am correct in stating that there is more "information" in the question than in the "data" from which the answer is drawn, then the public's fascination with interactive programs like DOCTOR and PARRY could easily lead to projection into or infatuation with such androids. Consider Chamberlain's program RACTER (Figure 19). Although it is still extremely slow, it has reached a level at which it can compose not only understandable stories, but also pieces of fiction containing brilliant insight. It is the kind of stimulating dialogue that a human being might find refreshing; indeed, it might lead the participant to a deeper understanding of his own thinking, feelings, and actions.

All books about computers raise summarily the question of thinking machines, then dismiss it with the ease and grace of Jimmy Connors returning the serve of a twelve-year-old. The books say that machines cannot possibly think because they are capable only of executing programs. This answer evades the problem entirely. To begin with, let me offer the observation that it is far easier, in most cases, to program human beings than it is to program computers, as dictators and religious shamans have demonstrated throughout history. Indeed, what is overwhelming is the task of trying to *stop* human beings from following acquired programs. Without mentioning the kind of programming developed by cults, religious movements or political organizations, everyday life furnishes many cases of acquired behavior nothing seems to be able to change. Visit any 24-hour restaurant in the United States, for example, and try to prevent the waitress from serving you a cup of coffee. Or pick up any telephone and explain to the operator that the machine has malfunctioned and won't return your last dime (but you absolutely must talk to Linda in

Think of an assassin, of his burning submarines and rotten sailboats. This dazzling assassin might ask himself, "If I had not been dazzling, indeed if I had not been an assassin perhaps my sailboats would not be rotten and my submarines not burning." Well, quizzically bilious secretaries may well declare themselves, and probably no more can be said for a killer but, believe me, far more can be said for an assassin. In fact assassins, whether they are dazzling, as I have just mentioned, or even outnumbered, are, in their own inimitable fashion, abstractedly similar to killers. At secretaries, however, we are forced to draw the line, for comparisons here, no matter how well-oiled they might appear, are simply out of the question. But try to follow my reasoning on this issue. This image of secretaries declaring themselves or, more likely, catching themselves simply because some blue assassin has rotten sailboats is ludicrous. His sailboats might as easily be flaking or burning, they need not always be rotten.

Secretaries, as a class, may not follow this argument. Address the strong question to a single secretary, however, and the strong answer may prove agonizingly different. For example, ask her whether her own sailboats are rotten and she may reply "My sailboats? Rotten? Why you bilious chicken, my sailboats are never rotten." Here it would be prudent to change the subject. Ask whether assassins generally appeal to secretaries, ask whether their highways are splintered. This will shift her attention. The vision of splintered highways will shift anybody's attention.

Figure 19. This sample output from RACTER (short for "RACONTEUR") was generated by Chamberlain's computer at the University of Minnesota in about two hours.

Akron). Or try to order a glass of water *without ice* at your favorite diner . . . Human beings can clearly be programmed. But can machines think?

The answer is that machines can do anything that can be described completely and precisely. So how would we recognize a machine that thinks? If an automaton need only play chess to be declared intelligent, as in the days of Edgar Poe and Maelzel's Chess Player, then obviously today's computers are intelligent.

"No, no, absolutely not!" say the champions of Human Reason. "Our minds are capable of much more than that. We compose music, we write poems. For a machine to be declared intelligent, it would have to create beauty."

A few years later, somebody has programmed a machine to write stories and to play compositions that still lack a bit of charm, but are clearly on the way to a sophisticated future. But is that intelligence? Is it thought? Of course not. What the machine has done is to force us to reconsider our definitions of *what it means to be human*. That part of thinking which can be defined rationally and encapsulated in a testable statement, can theoretically be accomplished, sooner or later, by an automaton.

My contention is that machines will be able to "think" by any human standard that can be precisely defined. But as the machines get "smarter" by these rational standards, it is the definition of humanness that will change. I look forward to that. I think we will discover, beyond these rational standards, that the human race has many other psychic talents we had previously been afraid to recognize, talents which constitute our truly genuine existence as humans. They are the only part of us worth talking about. Although this thought is scary to most people, it should make us afraid only to the extent that our daily actions are in fact automatic, unthinking, and perhaps unworthy of truly developed human beings. The fact is, if a machine were ever built that approaches humans in sheer intelligence, it would certainly not stop there. The Wright Brothers' plane didn't go much faster than the average bird, but fifty years later, aircraft went through the speed of sound.

Several Hollywood productions of the 1970s have shown automata used as personal companions, and satanist Anton LaVey has suggested that the commercial development of such alternative beings was unavoidable.[43] Yet the same experts who rave about the powerful capabilities of their software creations are scared of their machines looking human. They cringe at the suggestion that the computer's ability to speak, compose poems, compute and even play music could be embodied in anything more elegant than a steel cabinet with plastic buttons, set on four casters and firmly held in place by thick black cables. This reluctance is understandable. It is the reaction of the monkey looking at himself in a mirror. It is the shudder that seizes any being when he recognizes his own self, or part of it, in the world of the OTHERS.

Computer specialists have carefully resisted the urge to which automata makers of earlier centuries had succumbed: the temptation to build replicas of human beings. This extraordinary skill, unfortunately relegated to the level of a "minor art," has now become confined to the backstage laboratories of Hollywood, where robots are made to appear as grotesque and un-human as possible, or as comfortable parodies of humanity like R2D2 and C3P0 of *Star Wars*.

Such blushing reserve is not characteristic of modern technology. I think it has its root in the almost religious awe with which computer scientists hold the truly human. They have fled from the approximation of human behavior in their creations, just as they have avoided the direct implications of group communication through computers. They have chosen computer science largely because it is a field in which they could escape from human realities, not learn to master them. And in that observation of a very real human weakness may be found the root of the technological failures this book has summarized, and of some failures, like office automation, that may lie in the future. None of these failures is final: they hinge on redefinition and reframing.

Early automata show us an older technology frankly addressing the human question, in a way that has eluded computer scientists for the last thirty years. When the temperature rose above 80 degrees Fahrenheit, for example, an Isis automation gracefully removed her veil, and covered herself when it got cold again. She acknowledged imitations that are similar to ours. Current computers make no such concessions to our weaknesses. They go on working until they falter and stumble and die, never pausing to play a tune or tell a joke. I cannot believe this seriousness will last. As scientists lose control of their creations, new generations of tinkerers will start playing. They will embellish and they will enlighten the technology and its users. In so doing, I believe they will show us the way to a world we can hardly imagine today, even with the help of all the data bases and machines we keep, under lock and key, in our industrial basements.

It is conceivable, just beyond this new wave of creation, that we may encounter the limits of what we currently define as human thinking. It might occur when the chips are down, when they have given way to new methods of developing logic circuits, perhaps by growing them like nervous tissue. Our ability to perceive the physical universe is limited. Our ability to store and then retrieve the information we have acquired about the physical world is also limited—not only by the practical limitations of our tools, but by universal constraints. Some theoreticians have speculated that human consciousness may be restricted to an understanding of nature, limited by the encoding function the brain uses to perceive and transmit information about reality. (Saul-Paul Sirag has suggested that this function might be using a mechanism analogous to the "trapdoor" process discussed earlier, which, if true, would have direct implications for physics.)

Other people, such as Laszlo, have envisioned a sort of "world homeostat system" based on the idea that global control must exist in any dynamically stable system, the sphere of human existence, for example. The concept of a "psychic control system," which I proposed in *The Invisible College*, would also be relevant here. Two science fiction writers in the Soviet Union, the Strugastky brothers, have used the same idea in their novel *Definitely Maybe*. A group of scientists reach the limits of information complexity capable of reduction by the human mind, and they flip into an absurd universe where personal events, strange coincidences, and external incidents combine in terrifying patterns. They are forced to retreat into a safer mode of the human condition, in which there is no more pursuit of novel inquiries.

It is conceivable that some future generation of computer scientists will have to deal with such problems, and that they will regard the crude robots of our century with amusement and indulgence. For us, Isis still wears her veils. Perhaps she will be more generous with those future scientists, and reveal to them the insight we have missed.

CHAPTER TEN
The Grapevine Alternative

Which proposes the idea of an electronic grapevine cutting across national and cultural borders, and dreams of a world where human imagination regains control of the machine.

The boy was alone in his father's office and he watched the messages flashing on the terminal screen. It looked as if the members of a great invisible conference were coming in one at a time and introducing themselves.

THIS IS HANS LEITZMAN FROM HAMBURG. I AM A MINERAL ECONOMIST AND I AM JOINING THIS GROUP BECAUSE KLAUS THOUGHT I COULD ASSIST YOU WHEN IT COMES TO SHALE OIL RECOVERY. I WILL BE STANDING BY TODAY AND TOMORROW.

The boy didn't understand what shale oil recovery was, but he kept watching because the little luminous characters floating on the screen fascinated him. They appeared out of nowhere.
"How fast it is," he thought.
That was the most striking fact. A memorandum from Washington flashed on the screen.

PLEASE FORMULATE YOUR REQUESTS AT THIS TIME... REMEMBER THE LIST OF COMMODITIES WE DISCUSSED YESTERDAY.

Immediately there were two replies. People seemed to disagree. The text on the face of the display reorganized itself, identifying the participants. A petroleum expert in Colorado had just joined the conference. He said,

RESERVE ESTIMATES ARE NOW AVAILABLE.

The boy looked out of the window. A barge loaded with sand was heading for the Redwood City harbor. Some sailboats were already out on San Francisco Bay. On the screen, the discussion had now turned to the annual production of crude oil.

WE HAVE FOUND NINE RECORDS FOR WELLS THAT PRODUCED MORE THAN TWO MILLION BARRELS IN 1979 IN THIS REGION.

That came from the man in Colorado. He added,

WE STILL NEED THE LIST OF ALL THE OIL FIELDS IN CHEYENNE COUNTY WITH THEIR ANNUAL PRODUCTION FOR 1980.

The barge loaded with sand was going up the channel, following its lazy course as it passed the cement factory. A big aircraft banked over the Bay, and as he looked at the sunny reflection off its wings, the boy imagined that the terminal was a window into a kind of super-world where all these people were talking to each other, although they were at many different places around the world.

The sun had already set in Hamburg.

Another application. Imagine the following scene: you are in charge of emergency services for a part of Ohio that has just been hit by the worst storms and floods in years. Sixty people have died, hundreds are sick, and thousands are homeless. You need 500 Army tents, 30 bulldozers, and two tons of medical supplies. There's a hospital in Dayton that can provide a field emergency facility, but it must be picked up by trucks, and there's a truck company in the next state that can provide transportation, but hasn't returned your phone message of the last four hours.

Wouldn't you like to be able to tie all these people together in an around-the-clock conference and keep them posted on developments? Wouldn't you like to pin them down, in black and white, on the kind of assistance they can provide, and put a schedule on paper? Wouldn't you want your decisions to be known instantly by your teams everywhere?

Of course you would. Because as an executive, that would give you the kind of accurate, timely information you have always dreamed of. The communications medium that would make this possible exists now and it's called computer conferencing. It is easy to use, and it gives us a way to escape the closed, authoritarian structures computers seem to precipitate. If we use computer conferencing right, and not simply as the toy that Chip Tango would make of it, we may find an alternative to the Digital Society.

When you mention teleconferencing to people in Washington, their eyes light up. They think SATELLITES! Big Bucks! I get to spend some real big money now, they think. And they think CONTROL! We'll be able to find out what's going on in Bozeman, Montana.

Then they realize two things. When you use a network for communication, you don't need a satellite: all you need is a telephone, an electric plug in the wall, and a smallish computer somewhere. It doesn't sound like something you can use to impress Congress, even if it does marvellous things in practice. It doesn't capture the imagination, unless you really have a problem that needs solving, like the guy in Ohio with the floods. But when is the last time there was a flood in Washington? Washington doesn't have crises. It manufactures them for everybody else. Washington has no problems, or won't admit them to the rest of us.

The second thing they realize is that maybe they can find out what's going on in Bozeman, Montana, but then the folks from Bozeman are going to find out what's going on in Washington, D.C., too, because a network communicates both ways! And if there is one development that administrators want to avoid at all costs, it is having folks in the provinces look over their shoulders.

In my own experience developing conferencing networks, one exception to this generally dreary picture emerged at NASA. When we first presented the idea to them, they did not hesitate for a minute to tell us what they thought. They told us to come back in ten years.

> You see, we know all about those tele-conferencing gadgets. We've had voice conferencing since the days of Apollo, and now we're working on video conferencing. We mastered those technologies a long time ago. We're going to launch a new spacecraft, the Communications Technology Satellite, just to refine our video technology. But we don't need computer conferencing. It has the word "computer" in it, so it must be complicated. We'll use it in ten years or so.

We didn't give up. There were NASA people in California who knew we weren't kidding and encouraged us to send our proposals to the top brass. One day, in the middle of their big satellite presentation to the director of NASA, the television transmission gave out.

HELLO! Washington? Can you see us?

NO, we can't, what's going wrong?

Gee, we don't know, are you sure you can't see us?

Boy, I thought. Is that really the technology of the future? Then the audio gave out. Whistles and shrill feedback peaks were all that came from Washington. Technicians ran in all directions with screwdrivers in their hands, threatening to trip over the coils of cable that lay everywhere. The conference room looked like the deck of a Hollywood stage ship after the courageous sailors have killed the many-headed octopus.

We set up a portable terminal in a corner and started typing. Are you there London? Yes. Are you there Chicago? No problem. Slowly, the NASA folks came over and looked at our system. It was the only show in town.

"How much does this thing cost?" one of them asked.

I had to repeat the figure several times: less than a phone call to Denver. It was so low they had trouble believing it. They decided maybe they wouldn't wait ten years after all. They would look for the "right project" and give it a try.

The right project came when they launched the Communications Technology Satellite. Not the launch itself: the launch was prepared using the old NASA communication links, and the rocket didn't go up when it was supposed to. NASA faced a terribly important problem: rescheduling the party.

Whenever a big project goes up from Cape Canaveral, there are hundreds of dignitaries to watch it. Congressmen, Senators, heads of companies that have participated in the design and realization. And there's a big party before the rocket goes up.

If the rocket doesn't go up, you have to reschedule the party. Once. Twice. Three times. "We think it's going to be Wednesday morning, but if the Bird doesn't fly, it'll be Friday." NASA got tired of sending telegrams to three hundred dignitaries. They started using our network system merely as a bulletin board, so people could find out the status of the rocket from their office terminal, without calling anybody at NASA. The thing worked so well the mission director decided to use it to run the project, give frequency allocations, and check on the status of his teams. If a company had to drop a scheduled experiment on the satellite, and another contractor could pick up the same time slot, the time was negotiated over the system.

It was a very successful computer conference, and it lasted four years. Longer than the mission itself.

The NASA people had been polite when they turned down our first efforts to show them what networking could do. The geologists were downright rude. A government expert was asked to evaluate the technique for use in sending reports from the field and coordinating mapping and resource studies in Alaska. He answered that computer conferencing in geology would be a complete waste of time and money.

Fortunately, some of his colleagues were less negative. They were even willing to experiment. Not only was the system used in Alaska, from the field and in resource studies, but it also saved an international convention of geologists when a Canadian mail strike had completely cut off the organizers. There was even one interesting morning when a new Branch Chief was selected, through our system, by his colleagues in Washington and Denver. That was in 1975. Then in 1977, the bureaucrats decided to build their own system "to save money" and they programmed a monstrosity, loaded with bells and whistles, that only a programmer could use. Having thus reaffirmed the Principle of Conservation of Obfuscation, everything returned to normal: Computer conferencing in the earth sciences was dead as a doornail, although geologists from industry who had observed the use of the system picked up the technique and ran with it. Today, exploration and production engineers of major oil companies are carrying terminals to the remote offices of their firm, in the frozen reaches of Alaska, and are using the conferencing technology to make drilling decisions.

We did learn something, however, from the use of the conferencing computer by government geologists. We discovered that effective interaction through a computer tended to reveal the real power structure of a group. That didn't always sit very well with the bureaucracy. A few managers, who really wanted to save taxpayers' money and run a tighter ship, were able to put the technique to good use. You could pin down a group that wasn't producing; you could get information, daily, on Alaskan mines, from experts who had been transferred to the other end of the country. On several occasions, geologists from six different countries used the network to set up exchange standards for mineral data. But the major result of its use was to create, gradually, organizations that did not follow former patterns. *The networks started growing around the hierarchies.* We didn't know what was happening at the time, we didn't have enough experience to see the obvious impact of teleconferencing on human structures.

Our first programs have now been superseded by a more powerful system called NOTEPAD, and it is used daily by industry. Some day very soon, NOTEPAD and systems of the same kind will be available in the home, in public places, and in many organizations of every size. The impact, then, will be unavoidable.

It has been observed before that communication systems reflect the structure of society to the same extent that architectural concepts reflect that structure. The use of the word "structure" is deliberate.

The first system that builders used for load bearing and stress distribution was composed of two vertical slabs capped by a third, horizontal one. The technique was revolutionized by the arch and later by the keystone (Figure 20). By the time the ogive arch appeared, always threatening to explode into pieces because of its taut construction, engineers had come up with arc-boutants, a technique that projected the entire structure upwards. The modern stage of the builder's art is represented by the geodesic dome, where tension literally pulls the structure outward. In a geodesic dome, each polygonal segment is a source of both support and tension for its neighbors.

With each new step in architectural technique, Man has been able to make larger structures with greater span and integrity. Societal structures, however, have yet to evolve which approach the beautiful distribution of tension realized in the dome. We have remained at the hierarchic stage, with occasional incursions into arches. A geodesic organization would demand an information system that could instantly tie together all its segments when a collective decision was required.[44] Not in the sense of a broadcast or a mass rally, where masses of people are at the receiving end of a giant, one-way channel: not in the sense of voice or television conferencing, which demands the simultaneous presence of the parties at a few designated sites. Instead, the geodesic structure requires an information medium in which participants can join the dialogue at any time, and in which past statements are not lost as the interaction progresses. Computer conferencing is a first step toward the creation of such a medium: a revolutionary network where each node is equal in power to all the others.

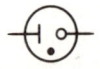

I see networking as an ingredient for survival when the large and complex hierarchies of the past grow to such a size that they can no longer sustain the pressures they are creating. But I don't see it as a panacea. There is no "Ultimate Information Machine," not even the human brain, whose limitations in memory and logic

Figure 20. From the raised stone through pyramidal hierarchies and flying buttresses to the geodesic dome—human organizations have evolved like the techniques of architecture.

have already been made obvious by the comparison with computing machines.

I like the idea of using computer conferencing to grow new types of "grapevines" in old organizations. Informal networks have always been the real harbor of trust and the spring of action for societies. What seems powerful to me is the combination of these grapevines—grown explosively to cover the entire world, through casual connections made by invisible wires—with the resources already in place. Before action is taken on data-base information, for example, why can't the decision be available for review in a human conference? In various experiments my group conducted with geologists, we found that such a review threw an entirely new light on the contents of the data bases, revealing errors, new interpretations, missing data. If the French police had married their files with expert human review, their information would have been of higher quality: the shooting of Claude Francois could have been prevented.

When the great failures of our human technological systems are analyzed, what emerges is not often evidence of poor design or bad science. It is usually evidence of poor communication—the resources were there, but nobody connected them, nobody had a chance to ask the right question. The people with the inquiry never got the opportunity to talk to those with the facts. With the advent of computer conferencing, there is no excuse for another Three Mile Island, where the solution would have emerged from such a network if the scientists who knew some of the answers could have advised the managers trying to control the plant and the health physicists trying to reassure the population. Given today's network technology, there is certainly no excuse for another TMI, or for the shooting of another Claude Francois.

CHAPTER ELEVEN
Conversation with Dr. Breeze

The author makes one final confession: he is an optimist after all. He describes his meeting with the Wise Gnome of Washington, D.C., and recalls his last words as the window turned blue.

Once again I am flying to Washington, D.C., to discuss a research project with a branch of the bureaucracy. I have dragged my suitcase through San Francisco International Airport, ready for the long flight to Washington, days of preparation and planning behind me. I am tired, physically and mentally. Soon I will enter one of the capital's big gray buildings where armies of clerks and managers are shuffling tons of paper, and deciding the fate of the nation by their passion or their idleness.

In my seat in business class I reflect that an average scientist like me, who comes from the West Coast to the capital for a few days every three or four months, never fully knows what goes on in the depth of the monster. But he recognizes the power concentrated in these offices, where ponderous officials listen to his story and then send him, with encouraging words, to another division:

"Well, it certainly sounds like you have an excellent idea for a very significant development, young man. It doesn't fit my program, which has to do with the Assessment of National Productivity Optimization of Human Factors in Automation, but it's exactly right for the program on Disambiguation of National Priorities in the Social Sciences, which is run by my colleague, Dr. Breeze, who will be spending thirty million dollars the next fiscal year."

Now the jet is flying through the clouds and I try to visualize thirty million dollars. In Santa Clara Valley, high-technology companies get started in somebody's garage with $15,000. Hewlett-Packard began with a thousand bucks, but that was before the War.

Now I'm going back to Washington to see Dr. Breeze, and I imagine his office, I go through what I have to tell him, and I fall into a state of happy reverie.

⊣⊢

The secretary lets me into Dr. Breeze's office. It is lined with books and reports. A cello leans against the desk and a computer terminal gleams in the corner. There is a graph on the screen showing steady decreases in American productivity. On the table, I notice a copy of Fromman's De Fascinatione in Latin and a thin book of comic strips entitled "Is Man Good?" by Moebius.

Dr. Breeze has bubbly blue eyes and a cloud of white hair. The lines around his eyes are folded into a permanent smile. I realize with a shock that here is a man who has seen power and rejected power, the trips and tribulations that go with it, the fallacies of power. He knows what lies behind the scene and exercises intelligent restraint in the investment of the public monies entrusted to his care. He listens to me with mounting amusement when I tell him the ironic little story of my project.

In 1972, I tell Dr. Breeze, I found myself in charge of two efforts aimed at the development of conferencing using computer networks. As everyone knows, the technique was invented by the diplomatic community, or people close to the diplomatic community . . .

"Our friends across the river," interrupts Dr. Breeze, as he gestures toward Virginia.

"Yes, our friends across the river. Well, as you know, most of the early research on group communication through computers has now been declassified, and a number of teams have begun to look at the implications. Industry may not use it for a few more years, but it will make some real changes when it gets applied."

"Other people have said that before you, like Murray Turoff, right here in Washington. So what are you finding so far?"

"We have found some new ways of building the conferences, and especially the interfaces with the users . . ."

"Those are very complicated words. What does that mean?"

"It means we have found a way to make the system look simple, to keep the computer in the background. You don't even realize it's there."

Ours is the first conferencing system that runs on a nationwide network, I tell him, getting excited. And the breakthrough is that our users need not be people who have used computers before. We can train anybody to participate in the conferences."

"Sounds like science fiction."

"But it is quite real, sir. At the beginning, we thought the only users would be planners in the government and big companies. Now we have discovered that the system can be made simple enough for anybody to use."

"But most people don't even know what a terminal is. You just said that yourself."

There is no use bluffing with this man. His steady eyes are fixed on me, and he is waiting for the first sign that I'm trying to sell him another technological dream.

"The key is that they don't have to learn the intricacies of the terminal. We do everything we can to hide that complexity from them. In a few years, we think terminals will be much simpler anyway, better designed. What we have is the first medium of human interaction that can link a group together regardless of time and space, the first such medium in history. You can be in Vancouver using it to run a project in Florida. The cost is the same wherever you are."

"Do you have anybody actually using the system right now? And paying for their usage of it with real money?"

I can see Dr. Breeze is suspicious, because so many people go through his office with tall stories, and so many scientists run big expensive experiments with government "funny money." Dr. Breeze has begun to appear shorter. His beard has also started to lengthen, and I'm wondering if it's an illusion of the sunset over Washington. Reddish beams of light are coming through the window now. They fall on the books and on the strings of the cello, bright with fiery sparks. I don't let that distract me.

"We've got about three thousand users right now. Folks at NASA are running one of their satellite programs with it, and the Geological Survey is linking their experts on mineral reserves in Washington and Denver with their counterparts in Europe. Then there is a research foundation which . . ."

Dr. Breeze's smile has broadened into a wide grin. I am going to tell him more. I want to say that we now have five years of data on the behavior of groups using the system, not just graduate students, mind you, not flaky academic data. But Dr. Breeze doesn't let me go on. He gets up from behind his desk, and I discover that he is barely taller than the top of the chair. His beard has gotten even longer than before, and the light that streams in through the window is turning green. That could hardly be the sunset.

He sits in the chair next to me, and I see his wise, wrinkled, smiling features close up. He looks like a gnome, the Wise Gnome of Washington, D.C.!

"Now we will start all over again," he says, his voice a creaky bag of pebbles sliding down a chute. "Forget all the fancy research crap. WHAT IS IT YOU WANT TO DO?"

"You really mean that?"

I look into his eyes. He looks straight back at me.

"Of course I mean that. You only have one life, you know. And since you are human, it's a short one. How old are you, about forty? So we've invested about thirty-five years in educating you, and at today's rates it would take another thirty-five years and millions of dollars to do it all over again. We can't afford to have you running around Washington trying to get money for miserable little opportunistic projects you don't really care about in the first place. What you've done with computers so far you obviously did because you enjoyed it. Now what? I'm asking you, man, what is it you really want to do?"

"My God!" I think suddenly, "this guy means it!"

Behind his shoulder I watch the window turning blue.

What happens next in my dream is that I start speaking to Dr. Breeze (is it still Dr. Breeze, this crouching figure with the long white beard in the chair next to mine?) from the bottom of my heart. Like a good Catholic going through confession, or a captured spy under sodium pentothal, or an EST convert "sharing" with his peers, I feel I can no longer hold back the truth.

Yes, yes, there are fantastic things to do, out there, things of research, things of joy, things to build and make useful for people of the earth. Time seems to be speeding up as Dr. Breeze, Breezy-Gnome, Brzzy-Brzzy, looks into my eyes deeper and deeper, and our dialogues become incredibly fast, like telepathy, and images come forth and jump around, almost disconnected.

"First, I'd like to see how creative people would use this. All the isolated creative people who are locked in by the society around them doing negative reinforcement killing their talents I'd throw them on a network to see what happens. The weirdos the little kids the telepaths, the explorers see what gives and what gets and what's up when they link up. And those true terrorists: the entrepreneurs the financial fanatics I'd give them a straight line to Wall Street money has no inertia you know."

"Ah! Money? Inertia?" he asks, as if he heard this from a child. "Hell no!" says Brzzy-Brzzy. And as if to emphasize my words he takes a bundle of hundred dollar bills from a drawer labeled APPROPRIATIONS and throws them out the window. To my considerable surprise, they don't fall with the wind, they don't tumble to the pavement, they fly straight up into the sky and disappear in space. Brzzy-Brzzy laughs with his old scratchy laughter.

"I would make a really serious effort at a humanized terminal."

"What?" asks Brzzy-Brzzy, suddenly serious.

"I said I would design a really humanized terminal that isn't an engineer's toy but something no man would want to be seen without and something every woman would be proud to carry along with her perfume and her handbag from Dior, and it wouldn't break your fingernails when you used it and it would be readable and clean, you'd connect it to the telephone without a lot of fuss, and it would just say hi and go from there. That's not a big big project maybe, but that sure would help everything else because think of the energy and the emotion you'd release just by giving people a tool that doesn't scare them shitless when they want to use a computer. It would be polite and responsive."

"Polite? Yes! Responsive? Yes! Don't scare them shitless!" sang Brzzy-Brzzy with passion and an old, falsetto voice that reminded me of the Paris subway, creaking to a halt on a fall day in Saint Germain des Pres, when there were dry tree leaves on the tracks, which was a strange reminiscence because, after all, the subway runs underground.

I'm like the train now: I can't stop.

"So let's say we build a terminal for right-brain people, a terminal for the bi-cameral folks, and we tie computer conferencing to some information structures that make sense, that reflect people's thoughts of constructing worlds, not just taking the one we've got, for heaven's sake, let them create, let them play with the structure. Where will you be when the hierarchies crash? Eh?"

"Don't you worry about me," says the Gnome, "don't you worry, my lad, I'll be just fine."

"Then we'll create a brain for humanity by letting people link up. Some will do it out of loneliness and others will use the net to screw the others or to advertise or to steal or to go on their big ego trips, and they will reconstruct their male territories around the networks, that's already happening on ARPANET, the big shots go around defecating all over the software from MIT to Stanford so you know it's their turf, but don't worry, that's just a transition, the future will take care of that, the network will expand so fast even the big shots will soon be left sitting on their behind, they won't even know what's happening."

"Kill the big shots! Wipe out their software! Sink their files! Expunge their directories!" said the Gnome with another burst of enthusiasm. He swung back so far in his chair that he fell over, and half a bookshelf fell on us. He did not seem to notice. I picked up a book from the floor and looked at it. It was The Time Trip by Rob Swigart. Son of a gun, I thought, what's he doing here? But the dwarf didn't let me think, he pushed me on.

"All that's easy, consider it done. That won't even cost ten million. After all, after all, defecating big-shots, let me see, $2,355,435, I've always been good at this, budgeting, I never make mistakes. What's your indirect cost rate?"

"51.7%."

"Is that all? Piece of cake, consider it done. Defecating big shots, easy to study, collapse of the hierarchies, I can see that, no sweat, the brain for humanity, a little more expensive, let's say three big ones, eh? Eh? And the terminal, of course, you'd have to carry an inventory. Let's say we give you ten million, but you've got to do more than that. More projects! Better projects!"

I thought he was going to die of laughter on the spot when I told him what I wanted to do next. After all, he had already promised ten million dollars, so I felt encouraged, I felt in confidence. I told him what I really wanted to do.

"I'd like to study ants," I said.

He laughed and laughed, as the window blue was turning darker and darker. Finally he regained his composure, sat upright, and asked me seriously:

"Why ants?"

"Ants never fail. Computer networks, I don't care which one, TYMNET ARPANET INFONET CYBERNET CYPHERNET MICRONET MIDINETTE TELENET they fail regularly, several times a day, somewhere they fail. And the big computers too, you can't rely on them, sooner or later, they go south and they leave you high and dry, if we're really going to teleconference on this thing it should never fail. The only things that never fail are insects."

"I said, why ants?"

"Look at an ant. Talk about microminiaturization of the ant! Even with the best chips from Silicon Gulch do you know how big a computer would have to be to do all the things an ant does? Tons! Tons! And the ant does all that in its little head and when it finds a twig it has one program: 'If you recognize something which is long, made of wood, and hard, pick it up and put it on top of the ant-hill.'

Now I call that a program. And if the ant can't do it by itself, another one will come and help, and another, until they do it. And you can step on them it won't stop the ultimate result, and a crazy Frenchman named Remi Chauvin who is a genius explained to me how he would put twigs in tall glasses to see what the ants will do and he digs cliffs for them, yet they always manage to complete their program. A computer scientist who doesn't understand ants is a man who doesn't know what reliability means."

"So you would build the computer equivalent of the ant, in hardware?"

"Right, and it would be so cheap, it would have its own little memory and it would have its own little programs, and it would go around looking for places to apply itself, and it would be disposable, disposable computers by the millions, crawling around and keeping their society going no matter what, so we humans can always find one when we need it and make it do something useful, make it work for us."

"Disposable computers, I know," said the Gnome. "I can dig it. Tell me, then, what you think of the . . ." There Dr. Breeze paused, took a long breath, and puffed himself up to say in a stentorian voice, "the Office of the Future"?

Perhaps it was the gathering blue dusk, the sense of disorientation created by the cluttered room, or the jet lag, the tiredness, the mental strain. Anyway, I heard myself say:

"There isn't going to be an Office of the Future."

"Oh!" said Dr. Breeze in mock astonishment. "You must not let anyone hear such words." Blushing, he went to the door and closed it carefully, after looking to the left and to the right to make sure no one had heard my statement. When he came back, he spoke low, in conspiratorial tones.

"Who are you, some kind of anarchist? Everybody is working on the Office of the Future, everybody is investing in it, and now you're saying it isn't going to exist. They'll kill you if they find out."

But there was a twinkle in his eye that encouraged me to go on.

"If what you call an office is a square room with telephones and typewriters in it, then I agree with all the companies like Xerox and IBM that are building word processors and duplicators and voice recognizers and other electronic whatnots to expand their capabilities. That particular office of the future is going to happen of course. Whether we like it or not."

"So what are you worried about?"

He goaded me on, dizzy as I was, and I felt the tenseness in his old voice.

"I just don't think it's that simple. An office has people in it, you see. They have lives and ambitions and needs and emotions. They interact. Most of the 'productivity' everybody talks about comes from the interaction, not from the ability to write and process pieces of paper. And those machines will do nothing for the people interaction. So the benefits from having all that hardware may not happen for ten years, or twenty years . . ."

"And when they do happen?"

"By then other things will have changed, on a much bigger scale. The world will have changed drastically under pressure of the technology. So the real problem is much larger than making offices more productive. The real problem is to decide right now what human qualities and freedoms are worth fighting for, and which ones are not. Because when we are through with this digital transformation there won't be a stone left standing on another stone of our social edifice. There may still be a future, but there won't be an office to put it in."

Dr. Breeze went behind his desk and sat down again.

"Where would you start? Which branch of science do you propose to apply?"

"Our problem is that we don't even have a method to study all this. We need to invent some new sciences."

He leaned forward, uncomfortably close.

"Like what?"

My head was swimming. I thought, for a brief moment, that it wasn't Dr. Breeze I had before me, but some robot who impersonated Dr. Breeze. I brushed off the illusion.

"We need a science of information metabolism."

The old man whistled, very long, very slowly, until I realized I had heard that sound before: it was the sound of the drum of the IBM 650 at Paris Observatory when the power went off. I waited for this strange whistle to subside, and I went on.

"Human beings die when they don't have enough information. And they go crazy if you overload them with it. So for each human being there is a best place between these two extremes, where that person can be rewarded for producing and consuming just the right amount of information in the social world, and nobody is studying that."

"Nobody is studying that, and that's a fact!" exclaimed Dr. Breeze with warm enthusiasm. "Go on, what else do we need?"

"We have to have a guerrilla warfare science for counter-implementation. Some of the systems that are coming into existence are detrimental to our survival as a society. We cannot stop them because the computer industry is out of control and has too much power. But we can counter-implement these systems. We can create for ourselves some information fusion points from which we can control the complexity of the networks and exacerbate it to the point where it is manageable again by the irrational human brain."

"But computer technology is rational, they all tell me . . ."

He was twiddling his thumbs as he said that, and staring up at the ceiling.

"They all tell you lies, Dr. Breeze!" I shouted while he looked at me with amusement. "They all tell you absolute lies. This technology is the most absurd, irrational thing ever devised . . ."

Dr. Breeze interrupted me, jumped up, leaping over his desk like a much younger man and landing before me.

"And that's why you love it. Admit it!" He was now staring at me and poking his finger into my chest, uncomfortably.

"Admit it, my friend. So let's see, how much would that cost? I'm adding it all up in my head, information metabolism, piece of cake, counterimplementation, I can see it now. I'll give you another five million. Don't spend it all on ants. By the way, you have to eat, too, you know. You're only human . . . "

And Brzzy-Brzzy opened and closed his mouth with a metallic sound, chattering with his teeth as if he had just dropped a ton of old knives and spoons in front of me, and the light behind the window had turned purple. I couldn't see very well, and the voice came back hauntingly:

> Stop mumbling about ants, you have to eat, too, you know, you're only human . . .

And the stewardess gave me a plate full of zucchini Geminiani, with some chunks of brown fiber which were advertised in the menu as roast beef. As I woke up and began to eat them, distractedly, my mind could not stop thinking about Dr. Breeze. Our discussion haunted me as the plane flew east into the darkness, stars appearing one by one.

Many years and many computer generations ago, I had been told that there was no future in this field and that Man could not get out of his sphere. Today, computers were literally bending our entire culture out of shape, changing the way we interacted as individuals and in groups. There was a new social form, the network, with its methods of instant, unlimited access to information never before experienced by the human race. It was forcing us to choose between two forms of society: not along the obsolete lines of Marxism and capitalism, but along the lines of its own demands:

for we are already out of our sphere. We cannot go back. We must choose: either to surrender our existence in a warm and cozy world of controlled memory frames, or to join the new networks, the new grapevines, to discover who we really are at the limit of an information space where we can learn to live.

References

1. Anonymous. "Un Automobiliste Grievement Blesse lors d'un Controle," *Le Figaro*, 12 November 1979.
2. Babronski, M. "Ordinateur mal informe: un policier trop nerveux blesse un innocent," *France-Soir*, 12 November 1979, p. 3.
3. Belden, Thomas and Marva. *The Lengthening Shadow*. Boston: Little, Brown, 1962.
4. Beer, Stafford. "Questions of Quest," in Trappi, Robert, *Cybernetics, a Source-Book*.
5. Ershov, Andrei S. "Aesthetics and the Human Factor in Programming," *Datamation*, July 1972, pp. 62-67.
6. Rosenberg, Jerry M. *The Computer Prophets*. New York: Macmillan, 1969.
7. Gardner, David W. "Will the inventor of the first digital computer please stand up?" *Datamation*, February 1974, pp. 84-90.
8. Evans, Christopher. *The Mighty Micro*. London: Victor Gollancz Ltd., 1979. Published in the U.S. as *The Micro Millennium* (New York: Washington Square Press/Pocketbook Publications, 1981.)
9. Cave Brown, Anthony. *A Bodyguard of Lies*. New York: Bantam, 1976.
10. Trakhtenbrot, B.A. *Algorithms and Automatic Computing Machines*. Boston: D.C. Heath and Co., 1963. Translated from the Russian.
11. Forster, E.M. "The Machine Stops," in *The Eternal Moment and Other Stories*, Harcourt, 1929. Reprinted in "Fairy Tales for Computers," New York: Eakins Press, 1973.
12. La Blanc, Robert, et al. "Changes and Opportunities in Telecommunications," *Telecommunications Industry Monthly*, Solomon Brothers, 1 February 1978.
13. Horwitz, Robert, "Tuning in to WARC," in *Co-Evolution Quarterly*, Summer 1979.
14. Brosseau and Andrist. *Looking Forward, Life in the Twentieth Century as predicted in the pages of American magazines from 1895 to 1905*, American Heritage Press, 1970.

212 / REFERENCES

15. National Commission on Materials Policy. "Material Needs and the Environment Today and Tomorrow," June 1973, pp. 12-13.
16. Colby, Kenneth et al. "Artificial Paranoia," Stanford Artificial Intelligence Project (Computer Science Dept., Stanford University, Memo AIM-125, July 1970, 34 pages).
17. Marchetti, C. "On Progress and Providence," IIASA (Laxenburg, Austria), paper PP-77-10, September 1977.
18. Bernstein et al. "Silicon Valley: Paradise or Paradox? The impact of high technology industry on Santa Clara County." Pacific Studies Center, 867 West Dana, #204, Mountain View, CA 94041.
19. Holmes, Edith. "Simplicity seen key to bringing DP to the millions," *Computerworld*, 20 September 1976, p. 9.
20. Dotto, Lydia. "The New Breed of Computer Criminals," *San Francisco Examiner and Chronicle* (World section), Sunday, 9 September 1979, p. 35.
21. Magee, John. "Computer Crooks Stealing Millions from Firms Too Embarrassed to Report Them," *National Enquirer*, 6 February 1979, p. 45.
22. Tuchman, W.L. "Computer Security and IBM," *Science*, Vol. 197, p. 938.
23. Hellman, M.E. "Computer Encryption: Key Size," *Science*, Vol. 198, p. 8.
24. Burr, Steven. "Prof's Work Threatens National Security," *Stanford Daily*, 26 October 1977.
25. Shapley and Kolata. "Cryptology—scientists puzzle over threat to open research," *Science*, 30 September 1977, p. 1346.
26. Kolata, Gina. "Cryptology—on the brink of a revolution?" *Science*, 19 August 1977, p. 747.
27. Kolata, Gina. "Computer encryption and the NSA Connection," *Science*, Vol. 197, p. 438.
28. Jupiter, Harry. "Youth Taps into UC Computers," *San Francisco Chronicle*, 20 January 1979.
29. Parker, Edwin and Dunn, Donald. "Information Technology: Its Social Potential," *Science*, Vol. 176, No. 4042, 30 June 1972.
30. Gordon, Francine. "Telecommunications: Implications for Women." Private communication, no date.
31. Gilliam, Harold. "Home Computers: The Surprizing Social Costs," *San Francisco Chronicle*, 16 November 1977.
32. Wiio, Osmo A. "Congress Keynote Speech," ICA Conference, Berlin, 30 May 1977.
33. Van Impe, Jack (Rev.). "A World Computer in Man's Own Image!" in *Perhaps Today*, September/October 1980. Published by Van Impe Ministries, Royal Oak, Michigan.
34. Van Impe, Jack (Rev.). *Signs of the Times*. Royal Oak, Michigan, 1980.

References / 213

35. Hirsch, Kenneth W. "Deceit and the First Interstellar Message," paper presented at the ICA Meeting in Berlin, 30 May 1977.
36. Evans, Christopher. "Chatting with Computers," in *Design Participation, Proceedings of the Design Research Society Conference*, Nigel Cross (ed.) London: Academy Editions, 1972.
37. Evans, C. "An Automated Medical History-Taking Project," National Physical Laboratory (Com.Sci.55), March 1972.
38. Evans, C. and Miss J. Wilson. "A Program to Allow Computer-Based History-Taking in Cases of Suspected Gastric Ulcer," National Physical Laboratory (Com.Sci.49), May 1971.
39. Evans, C., Price, H.C., and Wilson, J. "Computer Interrogation of Patients with Respiratory Complaints in a London Hospital," National Physical Laboratory (NPL COM 69), June 1973.
40. Evans, C. and Whittle, P.B. "An Inexpensive Mask to Simplify the Layout of Standard Teletype Keyboards for Man-Computer Interaction Studies," National Physical Laboratory (Com.Sci.TM 46), October 1970.
41. Amarel, Saul. "On Inventions in Computer Software," RCA Report PEM-3128, March 1969.
42. Rozak, T. "The Computer—a Little Lower than the Angels," a review of the book *Computer Power and Human Reason* by Joseph Weizenbaum in *The Nation*, 1 May 1976.
43. *The Cloven Hoof* (Newsletter of the Church of Satan).
44. Judge, Anthony. "A lesson in organization from building to design: transcending duality through tensional integrity." *Transnational Associations*. No. 5, Brussels, 1978.